D1499708

Confederate
Visions

A NATION DIVIDED:
STUDIES IN THE CIVIL WAR ERA

Orville Vernon Burton, *Editor*

Confederate Visions

Visions

Nationalism, Symbolism,
and the Imagined South
in the Civil War

IAN BINNINGTON

University of Virginia Press
Charlottesville and London

University of Virginia Press
© 2013 by the Rector and Visitors of the University of Virginia
All rights reserved
Printed in the United States of America on acid-free paper

First published 2013

1 3 5 7 9 8 6 4 2

LIBRARY OF CONGRESS CATALOGING-IN-PUBLICATION DATA
Binnington, Ian, 1972–
Confederate visions : nationalism, symbolism, and the imagined South in the Civil War /
Ian Binnington.
pages   cm. — (A nation divided : studies in the Civil War era)
Includes bibliographical references and index.
ISBN 978-0-8139-3500-3 (cloth : alk. paper) — ISBN 978-0-8139-3501-0 (e-book)
1. Nationalism—Confederate States of America—History. 2. Nationalism—Southern
States—History—19th century. 3. Regionalism—Southern States—History—19th century.
4. Group identity—Southern States—History—19th century. 5. United States—History—
Civil War, 1861–1865—Social aspects. I. Title.
F214.B56 2013
973.7′1—dc23
2013005319

All text illustrations courtesy HA.com

Contents

Acknowledgments

A book is a collective endeavor for which the author takes sole responsibility. Credit goes to the cloud; blame should go to me. This project began, over twenty years ago, as a senior thesis at Lancaster University written under the direction of the late Marcus Merriman. The intellectual genesis of that thesis took place at the University of Illinois at Urbana-Champaign in the undergraduate classes of Vernon Burton and the late Robert W. Johannsen. What became a dissertation was written, rewritten, and refined under the direction of Vernon Burton, my Ph.D. advisor. Vernon's kindness to me as a person, a student, and a friend has been constant since the first day we met. His faith in my ability to complete this project has often exceeded my own, and no one (including myself) has more faith in my virtues as an historian.

At the dissertation stage, Keith Hitchins, David Roediger, Max Edelson, Robert Johannsen, and Kevin Doak all gave good counsel. Bruce C. Levine, then at the University of Cincinnati, provided sharp commentary on the very first piece I wrote on the subject of Confederate nationalism as a graduate student, commentary I have never forgotten nor stopped trying to heed.

In addition to many of the above, Anne Goodwyn Jones, Jeremy Wells, John Mayfield, Don H. Doyle, and Paula Treckel were instrumental in helping me turn a dissertation into a book. More than perhaps anyone, Aaron Sheehan-Dean has read multiple versions and offered substantial, meaningful, and, above all, helpful critiques. A large portion of any credit due on the completion of this project goes to him.

I benefited enormously from the assistance of Linda Jacobson from the Wilson Special Collections Library at the University of North Carolina at Chapel Hill. It was she who suggested Heritage Auctions as a source for images and who specifically suggested that I contact Len Glazer. His generosity in allowing me to use images from HA.com is greatly appreciated. All images appear courtesy of HA.com.

Keeping academics sane is a community endeavor, and I have always benefited from excellent communities. From my time at Illinois, I offer heartfelt thanks to Chad and Tara Beckett, David and Denise Herr, Jon Coit and Sace Elder, John Wedge and Mila Yasko, Jerry and Linda Pelton, Mike Sherfy, Todd and Heidi Larson, and Rob and Amy McLain. At Eastern Illinois University, I was fortunate to make many new friends to add to this circle, not the least of them Michelle LeMaster, Lynnea Magnuson, Michael Shirley, Deb Reid, Anita Shelton, and Martin Hardeman. At Allegheny College, I have too many debts to mention, but foremost among them would be to Paula Treckel, Ron Cole, John E. Guthrie, and Vic Sternby.

My parents, Michael and Janice, have endured throughout this entire process, always asking me how my work was going and never judging when it was not. Their strength, both moral and material, made this project possible as much as anything I did. My sister, Lorna, and my late grandmother Betty Smith similarly provided moral support from the other side of the Atlantic.

Portions of this work were presented at meetings of the Southern Historical Association, the Historical Society, the Social Science History Association, the Nationalism in the New World: The Americas and the Atlantic World conference at Vanderbilt University, and the Douglas Southall Freeman and Southern Intellectual History Conference at the University of Richmond. I would like to thank all participants in those events for their comments and suggestions.

A portion of chapter 4, cowritten with Vernon Burton, appears in *Master Narratives: History, Storytelling, and the Postmodern South*, edited by Jason Phillips, and a portion of chapter 5 appears in *Virginians and the Civil War*, edited by Peter Wallenstein and Bertram Wyatt-Brown. I thank them all for their editorial insights and useful commentary.

Working with Dick Holway and Aaron Sheehan-Dean at the University of Virginia Press has been a delightful experience. Dick's patience and support has been most valued over the years, and he has made this project better in so many ways. I thank the staff of the press, especially Raennah Mitchell, for their patience in answering my questions and their good-natured professionalism. The readers for the press gave me encouraging and substantive critiques, and I hope that I have been able to satisfy most, if not all, of their suggestions and concerns.

Lastly, let me say a word about my immediate family—my wife, Toshia, and my son, Stuart. Without them the dissertation would never have been completed and would certainly never have become a book. They are examples to me in many ways, and I cherish their love and support. It is to them that this book is dedicated.

Confederate
Visions

Introduction

On November 20, 1861, Kentucky became the last state to attempt secession from the Union, the thirteenth to do so since the previous December. Kentucky's secession, like Missouri's before it, was never entirely effective, but as the last of its kind, her Ordinance of Secession is particularly instructive. According to the aggrieved Kentuckians gathered at Russelville in Confederate-occupied territory, the Lincoln government had

> substituted for the highest forms of national liberty and constitutional government a central despotism founded upon the ignorant prejudices of the masses of Northern society, and instead of giving protection with the Constitution to the people of fifteen States of this Union, have turned loose upon them the unrestrained and raging passions of mobs and fanatics, and because we now seek to hold our liberties, our property, our homes, and our families under the protection of the reserved powers of the States, have blockaded our ports, invaded our soil, and waged war upon our people for the purpose of subjugating us to their will.[1]

This statement of defiance set the tone for what was already developing as the narrative thread of Confederate nationalism: Worthy Southrons were innocent of any aggression, only wanting to be left alone to enjoy the exercise of those powers reserved to the states under the Constitution. Southrons were only defending themselves against the unprovoked and merciless depredations of the degraded mob, whose passions had been inflamed by Demon Yankees. Slaves were alluded to ("our property") but otherwise did not speak for themselves. The root of the North's excesses was their usurpation of the Constitution and therefore their rejection of the American tradition of limited government and reserved powers. Northerners were thus un-American, unworthy, and aggressive in their desires to bend others to their capricious will. By implication,

Southerners were American, worthy, and peaceful in the maintenance of their way of life.

In this analysis of wartime Confederate nationalism, the Kentucky Ordinance of Secession stands as representative of the wider notion of a "mythic present." Nationalism exists at a particular moment in time, but that moment, though anchored to the present, also extends backward into the past and forward into the future.[2] Nationalisms are at least partially based on an understanding of past history, whether of a region, a people, a culture, a religion, or so on. They draw strength from that historical past at the same time as they mold it to their own purposes, selectively choosing episodes and interpretations that suit the demands of the present. So, it is fair to say that nationalisms generally speak to an ahistorical past, based on a vision of what should be true, rather than what actually was. Confederate nationalism was no exception.

Nationalisms also look to the future, in that they seek to ensure the perpetuation and growth of the nation in the days to come. The temporality of Confederate nationalism is odd in that it both drew from a shallow well and suffered from excessive compression. While prophets of the future Confederacy did exist in the antebellum era, the majority of ordinary white Southerners did not begin to seriously consider themselves as a potentially separate nation until quite late in the 1850s. In addition, of course, the Confederate nation, and the Civil War it spawned, lasted only four years, a very short period of time in which to construct a new nationality. Nationalisms to that point had generally benefited from a much deeper well of commonality and a far longer span of time in which to construct themselves. In fact, one of the most appropriate examples to which we can compare the formation of Confederate nationalism is the formation of American nationalism in the 1770s and 1780s, a process that would in many ways be replicated by the Confederacy of the 1860s.

Thus, with respect to the peculiar temporality of Confederate nationalism, it makes sense to speak of a mythic present, a place in time in which past and present are compressed, constructed, and reconstructed to meet the immediate needs of the nation. A sober assessment of their reality might have convinced white Southerners that the prospects of their securing independence were limited and that their best course of action would be to acquiesce in the transition of slavery to a more ostensibly benign labor system, akin to the various types of indentures, apprenticeships, and one-sided contracts they eventually adopted under Jim Crow. Yet sober assessments of reality were few and far between in the secession winter. Instead, in the crisis of 1860–1861, the ahistorical past propounded by Southern fire-eaters ran headlong into the harsh realities of a Lincolnian present.[3] In order to justify, explain, and exculpate their actions, Confederates unselfconsciously fell into the narrative of a mythic present, ascribing characteristics and motives to all sides in the bloody conflict that seem unwarranted with the benefit of historical hindsight. As Kentucky hints, Confederates argued forcefully in the early months of the war that the U.S. Constitution, for example, was a pure and good document that had been betrayed and soiled by the rapacious and ungrateful Black Republicans of the North; that if the legacy of the Southern framers had been upheld, slavery would be protected, states' rights would be paramount, and the Southern "way of life" would not be under siege. And if history were a static phenomenon, they might have had something. But of course it is not. The passage of time and the pressure of events, both foreseen and otherwise, had changed peoples' minds, compelled them to adopt new policies, and moved them away from the original intent of documents written seven decades earlier.

This Confederate mythic present bundled together a group of intertwined concepts, specifically tropes of the Worthy Southron, the Demon Yankee, the Silent Slave, and a sense of shared history that we can call "Confederate Americanism." In the first place—underpinning everything else—the Confederacy was intrinsically understood as the *real* American nation, created under the *real* American Constitution, as opposed to the compromise-laden failure enacted in 1789. In this sense, the Confederates cast themselves as the true Americans, the true inheritors of the Revolutionary legacy of ordered liberty and political sovereignty. The Worthy Southron, the constructed Confederate self, was imagined as a champion of liberty, which appeared to mean a champion of the rights of individual and community self-determination, the right to live one's life as one wished, outside of externally imposed controls, and presumably, although this was often left unstated, the right to own, use, and dispense slave property. Counterposed to this self-image was the Demon Yankee other, the antithesis of everything good and Southern—and therefore the opponent of everything American. Yankees were fanatical abolitionists, enemies of liberty, agitators in other people's affairs, debased and inhumane in their actions, and willing to incite race war for their own ends while caring nothing for slaves or the consequences of abolitionist violence.

This constructed South was uncomplicatedly white, but there is a deafening black silence that catches the eye of the historian. We know, as Confederates knew, that their dream of independence and liberty was based on a social and economic foundation of black labor. Yet, while the foundation of a house is largely invisible to the outside observer, the very existence of the house depends utterly on the solidity of that foundation. So too was the black South a necessary, and invisible, foundation for the rhetorically created Confederacy. One simply could not exist without the other; in fact, one could not even be imagined without the other. Thus, the Silent Slave was a companion to the vocal Confederate self, loyal and trusting, reliable and honest within its limited capabilities. This Silent Slave was, however, a product of the Confederate imagination, as it had been a product of the prewar Southern imagination. It was not real. The actual, feared slave was instead a companion to the Yankee other, disloyal and conniving, unreliable and dishonest, seeking to undermine the Confederacy at every turn. This tension in the imaginary construction of the slave—as companion to self and a threatening other at the same time—was palpably felt in the dissonance between Confederate words about the safety of their slaves and Confederate actions designed to contain their danger.

Very little of this imagined nationalism was an historically accurate portrayal of the Southern situation. This picture ignored the eighty-year history of comity, conflict, and compromise between North and South. It ignored the fact that, in spite of the heartfelt desires of white Southerners, almost nothing distinguished in any meaningful religious, linguistic, or ethnic way the inhabitants of the Northern states from those of the South.[4] Yet the absence of historical acuity is beside the point. Nationalisms do not need to be based in historical reality; they are often stronger when they are based in myth. And as Drew Gilpin Faust wryly notes, "Southern historians should be the first to recognize that myths and realities often amount, in practice, to the same thing."[5]

By the time of Kentucky's secession attempt in November 1861, the Confederacy was engaged in a war of national survival. Battles had been won and lost, heroes had already risen and fallen, and it was clear that victory, were it ever to come, would be hard-fought and bloody. The challenge awaiting Confederate nationalism was "and would remain how to create and sustain a firm political and cultural identity in the midst of a bloody civil war while at the same time showing enough flexibility to meet unanticipated demands on resources and will."[6] Four years later, it was clear that victory was not to be. News of the surrender of the Army of Northern Virginia came to Turnwold, Georgia, on May 2, 1865. On that day, Joseph Addison Turner, the editor and proprietor of a plantation journal called *The Countryman*, noted that "the great heart of the nation has been paralyzed. God has touched it, and it is still. . . . The whole southern country is now one gigantic corpse, and a black pall lies listless on its lifeless limbs."[7]

Three weeks later, on May 23, Turner proposed to breathe a little life back into the pallid carcass of the South, with a bold proposal for reconciliation with the Northern victors. He enumerated a five point plan for reconstructing the nation:

1.—A new flag.—Our people have so long fought against the United States flag, and it has waved over the bloody graves of so many of them, and over so many of their ruined homes, and burned towns, and villages, that you cannot expect it to command their hearts and heads, though you do their hands, in its support.

2.—A new constitution should be agreed upon, because the old one is not sufficiently explicit as to our rights.

3.—A full and complete acknowledgement of our state rights, and state sovereignty should be accorded us—together with a complete recognition of our institution of slavery.

4.—An abnegation of the idea that our people became rebels, or were guilty of treason when they seceded, and waged war against the north—they owing allegiance to their respective states alone.

5.—A consolidation of the war debt of the two sections.

Turner conceded that the chances of this plan finding favor in Congress were limited, but he appealed to Northerners to work to conquer their prejudices and "give us good terms."[8]

More than four years after the secession of South Carolina, Turner continued to express the ideas of Confederate Americanism. Even in defeat, Turner wanted to reconstruct the American nation to take account of the South's place within it. He hoped that a new American nation could arise from the ashes of the Civil War, one that included Confederates as full partners rather than vanquished foes. His plan represented a last-ditch effort to accomplish the goals of the Confederate Revolution— to remake the American nation in the Southern Confederate image, to align the mythic present with the actual present. Although the Confederate nation had undoubtedly failed in its intent, Confederate nationalism was still alive and well, at least for Turner.

He hoped that reconstruction could be achieved symbolically, through the creation of a new flag and new constitution, and the recognition that the Southern point of view on slavery and states' rights was legitimate. In the American case in the 1770s and 1780s, and in the Confederate example of the 1860s, American nationalism operated as a collection of symbols, of signifiers into which individuals could invest meaning and understanding of their cause. In short, as historians of American nationalisms in the period through the Civil War, we grapple with the process by which "American" became something other than a geographic descriptor, a mere acknowledgement that one lived in a place called America. Through this period, in ways that historians are working to understand more fully, "American" became a descriptor of intellectual, ideological, and cultural identity. But at the same time that we recognize the existence of this process, we need to understand that the process of forming nation and nationalism in this period was multifaceted, that the road to an American identity that meant something in the conventional sense of national allegiance was not an uncontested journey, that it was one of struggle, political conflict, and ultimately bloody Civil War. We need to take heed of Drew Faust's admonition that we take this concept on its own terms, that "we must begin to explore Confederate nationalism . . . as its effort to represent Southern culture to the world at large, to history, and perhaps most revealingly to its own people."[9]

For Confederates, therefore, the creation of their wartime nationalism was a quest for a symbolic text that would resonate and stay the course of the conflict. That search ultimately resulted in a paradox. The nation failed in that Southern independence was not secured and slavery was not preserved, but a symbolic text of Confederate nationalism was clearly established during the lifetime of the Confederate nation. It was not necessarily fully developed, given the short time span and the pressures of war, but the seeds of a potentially robust Confederate nationalism did emerge. Had the Confederacy won, then, as had been the case in the aftermath of the American Revolution, those seeds might well have taken deeper root. While the symbolism of the Worthy Southron, Silent Slave, and Confederate America remained powerful as the war progressed, the exact form in which those symbols would be expressed never really settled down.

The Confederate Constitutions and their framers represent one early cluster of Confederate icons, but they were too close to symbols used effectively by the Union, too reminiscent of a shared past and so insufficiently distinct. Many Southerners and Confederates thought that slavery would come to serve as the sort of unifying symbol proposed here, but as we shall see, slavery was never suited for that role. It was simply too divisive politically and too unstable an institution. The tension between the Silent Slave of the imagination and the feared slave of the real world came close to tearing the Confederate cause apart, and when, toward the end of the war, Confederates faced the realization that they might have to choose between a last-ditch defense of slavery and the preservation of national independence, many chose the latter.

In the final analysis, after all was said and done, the Confederate military emerged as the preeminent symbol of the wartime nation, the institution that more than anything represented the Worthy Southron and the Confederate American, and which was all that stood between the Confederacy and the horror of a Demon Yankee victory. Yet the military failed to preserve the independence of the nation, and seeds of uncertainty about its role were implanted from the outset. While virtually all white Southerners at the beginning of the war believed in their military's efficacy, they also faced the reality that a military in time of war is a dangerous reed upon which to rest an ideology, as it contains simultaneously the potential prospect of victory *and* defeat. Yet, had the Confederacy been victorious in their war for independence, the military—as had previously been the case for George Washington, for example—might very well have emerged as the centerpiece of a newly solidified nationalism.

While there are many fine studies of Confederate defeat and the effects of Confederate nationalism on the people of that nation, the substance of the nationalist narrative itself remains rather unclear. More than twenty years after Drew Faust asked us to deal with Confederate nationalism on its own terms, rather than as a simple narrative of defeat and failure, we are still waiting for the complete picture to emerge.[10] We have excellent studies of the Lost Cause, but the nature of the cause before it was "lost" has only recently come under the sustained gaze of historians. It is the nature of nationalism studies that we may never see the whole, but this book seeks to add to our understanding of the phenomenon of wartime Confederate nationalism. It builds on a core of works that have emerged in the previous decade or so and started to give coherent shape to the subject.

Several authors have placed wartime Confederate nationalism within a framework of class, arguing that secession and war was the project of the Southern master class. Making this argument most directly, Robert E. Bonner situates the Southern master class at the heart of the narrative of Southern nationalism. In particular, Bonner shows how "slaveholders both before and after . . . 1860 contributed to the American project of 'becoming national.'" This is a story of power: political, social, and cultural. At heart, Bonner's version of proslavery nationalism is a contingent entity, one without conscious purpose or direction until very late in life. Considering the war years, Bonner argues that three "narratives of purpose" sought to explain the Confederacy to itself: the true inheritance of the American Revolution, a sense of reactionary democratic absolutism, and a belief in the perfection of republican paternalism. Added to these narratives of order was a commitment to white liberty, which ultimately proved the most tenuous.[11] Expanding on this argument, Stephanie McCurry posits a master class seeking to make permanent racial and gendered domination: "a modern proslavery and antidemocratic state, dedicated to the proposition that all men were not created equal."[12] For Bonner and McCurry, Confederate nationalism was a classist imposition on the mass of the Southern population, significant sections of which rejected it.

George C. Rable's earlier work on Confederate nationalism concluded that in substance, the phenomenon was "a search for republican purity and an effort to quarantine the Southern world from the plague of Northern radicalism, infidelity, and abolitionism."[13] Confederate nationalism was thus more an active attempt to define a new nation at some philosophical level than it was a simple political tool to effect class discipline. Rable identifies antiparty ideology as the cement that held the polity together, mediating between unitarian and libertarian strains of republicanism. Looking as well at the substance of Confederate nationalism, and more in keeping with the analysis offered in this study, Anne

Sarah Rubin argues that "Confederate identity and nationalism were constructed out of a combination of institutions and symbols," in particular that "these new Confederates created a national culture in large part by drawing on the usable American past." Rubin extends her impressive analysis into Reconstruction and demonstrates how "the shards of the shattered nation" served to shape Southern identity for generations after the end of the Civil War.[14]

Michael T. Bernath brings into admirably sharp focus the "Confederate cultural nationalists" who, he argues, "provided the vision, created the framework, and served as the leaders and driving force of the struggle for Confederate intellectual independence." In particular, Bernath overturns Drew Faust's long-accepted conclusion that material scarcity hampered the development of Confederate nationalism as the war progressed.[15] Bernath's study clearly makes the point that wartime Confederate nationalism was an artifact of an autonomous print culture produced by Confederates, about Confederates, and for Confederates.

Finally, Paul Quigley's work comes closest to the interpretation of this volume while placing Confederate nationalism in a broader national and transnational context. Quigley points to the antebellum antecedents of Confederate nationalism and situates its development in conversation with American nationalism. Quigley argues, as have many recent scholars in this field, that process, rather than success or failure, should be the metric upon which Confederate nationalism is examined. He suggests that this process led Confederates "in three directions: outward, to their understandings of nationalism throughout the nineteenth-century transatlantic world; backward, to their long experience as American nationalists; and inward, connecting nationalism with their everyday lives and identities." He proposes "a new approach to Confederate nationalism. . . . Rather than assuming that because the South lost the Civil War, its nationalism must have been somehow inadequate, attention can instead be paid to how white southerners drew on their long-standing engagement with . . . [nationalism and citizenship] to manage the stresses—practical, intellectual, and cultural—of modern war."[16]

This study complements the emerging scholarship in various ways. It seems clear that wartime Confederate nationalism was a classist project, one that sought to bind common, nonslaveholding white Southerners to the political and cultural designs of the master class. The exigencies of war made that goal hard to achieve, but even so, the symbols of that nationalism *were* those shared between the various white class elements of the wartime South. Also, wartime Confederate nationalism lived in print culture, with artistic, musical, and other forms as adjuncts. It is therefore appropriate to concentrate our gaze on newspapers, periodicals, novels, and other forms of literature. And it is apparent, as this work discusses, that viewing nationalism as process rather than as product is the most fruitful way to proceed. It is in terms of the substance, the symbolic text, of Confederate nationalism that this study finds its place. The notion of the mythic present and its attendant tropes of the Worthy Southron, Demon Yankee, Silent Slave, and Confederate Americanism offer a depth to the symbolism of Confederate nationalism that is yet to be found in the literature on the subject.

The influence of the peculiar institution has been central to any discussion of Confederate nationalism, because, regardless of whether contemporaries were willing to concede it, the future of slavery was the main issue at stake in the Civil War. Scholars have held slavery responsible for the emergence of a particular Southern political culture based on honor and a variant of republicanism.[17] More pertinently for our purposes, scholars have attributed to slavery the origins of a particular brand of antebellum Southern nationalism, as well as calling it one factor behind the secessionist impulse. According to John McCardell, the institution of slavery "came to represent for Southerners a whole ideological configuration—plantation economy, a style of life, and a pattern of race relations—which made Southerners believe that they constituted a separate nation. . . . But some Southerners believed that distinctiveness had little value so long as the South remained commercially dependent on Northern industry and commerce."[18] Admittedly, the antebellum prophets of this movement—men like George Fitzhugh, Josiah Nott, James D. B. De Bow, and Edmund Ruffin—constituted a distinct fringe minority that in the end did not emerge as the ruling group of the Confederacy. But their voices were loud and carried a long way in the secession winter.

While this overt preoccupation with slavery may serve in the antebellum era, what this study finds is that slavery was very much a silent partner in the wartime exegesis of Confederate nationalism. There is no doubt that the Southern states seceded to protect their peculiar institution; even when they were trumpeting their states' rights, they were conscious of the fact that the paramount right was the one to own, use, and dispense slave property as they saw fit. Furthermore, Charles B. Dew's work on the commissioners sent from the already seceded Confederate states to their reluctant, Upper South brethren in the winter of 1860–1861 clearly shows that concerns over slavery were uppermost in their minds. For example, Stephen Hale wrote that Lincoln's victory in the election of 1860 was "nothing less than an open declaration of war, for the triumph of this new theory of government destroys the property of the South, lays waste her fields, and inaugurates all the horrors of a San Domingo servile insurrection, consigning her citizens to assassinations and her wives and daughters to pollution and violation to gratify the lust of half-civilized Africans."[19] Here, Hale deploys the feared slave (often associated with Haiti) as a blunt instrument of terror to scare recalcitrant white Southerners in the border states into joining their already seceded cousins so as to forestall the race war that was presented as the inevitable consequence of Abraham Lincoln's election. Secession, therefore, was necessary to maintain the illusion of the Silent Slave, domesticated in the cause of the South, from the specter of the feared slave, unleashed in the service of the North.

During the war, however, the central place of slavery became more problematic for the nationalist narrative Confederates were creating for themselves. Slavery was a divisive institution, between the classes as well as between the races, and as the arc of Confederate nationalism developed, slavery became a relatively quiescent partner. The furor raised over the so-called Twenty Negro Law provides one manifestation of this class hostility. Passed in October 1862 to combat the very real fears of slave insurrection in the aftermath of the first Emancipation Proclamation, this act permitted the exemption from military service of one white man for every twenty slaves. Although it only affected a small number of Southerners, it quickly became a powerful symbol for the common people that the war was being fought by them on behalf of the planters. Similarly, the actions of slaves themselves, in running away to join the Union Army for example, powerfully conveyed to attentive Southerners that their casual attitudes with respect to the loyalty of slaves were built on a foundation of sand.[20]

Recent studies of Confederate nationalism, including this one, have drawn sustenance from the wider historiography of nationalism. In thinking about nationalism as a concept, it would be helpful if we could simply borrow Justice Potter Stewart's famous concurring opinion in *Jac-*

obellis v. Ohio that he knew obscenity when he saw it but that he could not otherwise define it.[21] Similarly, historians and other scholars seem to know nationalism when they see it, but they discover that it is an elusive target when they try to define or create typologies for it. Nationalism encompasses the universal and the particular, it encompasses the state and it lives outside the state, it resides in the local community as much as at the regional or national level.[22] Nationalism is complex almost beyond belief. As Philip D. Curtin noted of imperialism, so too has the concept of nationalism "long since expanded into a cloud of loose implications and emotional overtones."[23]

Nation and nationalism, then, are analytical terms that continue to resist precise and universally accepted definition. Summarizing the state of the field in nationalism studies in 1997, Craig Calhoun suggested a set of ten "features of the rhetoric of nation" from which most particular nationalisms draw in part or whole. They are "boundaries," "indivisibility," "sovereignty," "an 'ascending' notion of legitimacy," "popular participation in collective affairs," "direct membership," "culture," "temporal depth," "common descent," and "special or even sacred relations to a certain territory."[24] In terms of nationalism's ability to satisfy human needs, and therefore to take root in the core of people's identities, Joshua Searle-White has argued that "nationalism provides a way for us to join together with others, to be convinced that we are good, and to live in the service of a just nation."[25]

The problem is that while each definition works perfectly for the particular circumstances for which it was devised, once you pick one, you are left wondering how to incorporate the insights of all the others. It is possible to offer some general propositions about the nature of nationalism but only at such a general level that they are unhelpful in analyzing the particulars of each nation. First, nationalism either seeks to legitimate a particular form of political or cultural rule in a preexisting, defined *territorial space* (a nation-state or country) or else it seeks to establish such a regime in territory currently ruled by others. Nationalism and territorial borders are fundamentally intertwined, either in actual or desired fact. Second, nationalism seeks to achieve its goals through the *assumed commonality* of the people living under its aegis. This commonality can be ethnic, linguistic, religious, historical, purposive, or any other form of identity that binds humankind together. This commonality is sought in contradistinction to the particular other (or others) of the nation in question. So, nationalism is both a claim to internal unity and legitimacy, and a claim to solidarity in the face of the alien and hostile world. Third, nationalism is a *self-conscious process of creation*. Spatially, nationalism can descend from the top of society—from the political, cultural, religious, and media elites—or it can ascend from the bottom of society—from the popular consciousness, from the village and town. Or more likely, if a specific nationalism is to be successful, it will be created from both directions at once, meeting in the middle to contextualize the interior meaning of the nation. But someone, somewhere is consciously creating a nationalist story. Fourth, all of this is a social, political, cultural, or other form of *construction*. None of the above has to be "real" in any historically demonstrable sense. It can be the sheerest fantasy bound together by the power of belief that it is true or that it ought to be true. The human mind is a powerful tool of self- and collective deception, and nationalism makes full use of that faculty.

Advancing a theoretical framework for studying nationalism in 2010, Umut Õzkirimli defines nationalism as a Foucaultian discourse, "a particular way of seeing and interpreting the world, a frame of reference that helps us make sense of and structure the reality that surrounds us." That discourse then makes "three sets of interrelated claims": identity, temporal, and spatial. In terms of identity, the nationalist discourse "divides the world into 'us' and 'them', 'friends' and 'foes', positing a homogeneous and fixed identity on either side and stressing the characteristics that differentiate 'us' from 'them.'" In terms of time, the nationalist discourse "always looks back in time, seeking to demonstrate the 'linear time of the nation.'. . . The particular past the nationalist elites opt for reflect present concerns and is usually deployed to legitimize the decisions they took regarding the eventual shape of their nations." In terms of space, "the nationalist discourse is also haunted by a fixation on territory. . . . This involves the reconstruction of social space as national territory, often with a force and intensity that erases alternatives and grafts the nation on to the physical environment and everyday social practices." Finally, and of most significance for this project, is the "mode of operation of the nationalist discourse—or the different ways in which human beings are made 'national.'" The successful nationalist discourse is the one that "*consolidates its hegemony* by *reproducing* and *naturalizing* itself. . . . [T]he national . . . is . . . constituted in the volatile settings of everyday life."[26] Õzkirimli's last proposition is key to explaining the process of nationalism: it is a regularly replicated discourse that provides meaning in people's lives related to the nation. Following this formula, subdiscourses on issues that animate people to ponder, discuss, write, argue, and possibly fight are likely to reinforce the nationalist discourse more than those that are less inspiring.

Scholars of nationalism have noted that this focus on process is fruitful. Writing on late nineteenth-century German nationalism, Alon Confino emphasized the need for scholars of nationalism "to encompass the malleability of nationhood" and to embrace "its ambiguous and often contradictory meanings." Õzkirimli's work echoes Confino's desire for an exploration of "nationhood as a process by which people from all walks of life redefine concepts of space, time, and kin."[27] Furthermore, in one of the last things he wrote, the late Robert W. Wiebe called for scholars of nationalism to start to think "laterally" and to recognize that, "where nationalism succeeds, it arises out of a cluster of shared beliefs that are always contested, always labile, always in the process of re-creation." Wiebe argued,

> Nationalism is the desire among people who believe they share a common ancestry and a common destiny to live under their own government on land sacred to their history. Nationalism expresses an aspiration with a political objective. Behind that aspiration lies a sense of kinship that is simultaneously fictional and real—that is, culturally created, as all kin systems are, yet based in some measure on an overlapping of customs, histories, and genealogies.[28]

This definition has particular relevance for the South, as questions of kinship are critical in understanding notions of community.

The most ubiquitous academic definition of nationalism, Benedict Anderson's notion of the "imagined community," prefigures Õzkirimli's emphasis on process. It also directs our attention, however, to the substance of the nationalist discourse, which is the methodological focus of this study. The process by which the discourse exists and is replicated is, of course, central, but so too is the content of the discourse. That aspect of the discourse speaks to Anderson's notion of the imagination. Anderson defines the nation as "an imagined political community. . . . [I]t is *imagined* because the members of even the smallest nation will never know most of their fellow-members . . . yet in the minds of each lives the image of their communion. . . . [I]t is imagined as a *community*, because, regardless of the actual inequality and exploitation that may prevail in each, the nation is always conceived as a deep, horizontal comradeship." Anderson's formulation is so ubiquitous precisely because it connects process and content through the creation and dissemination of the imagined community. For Anderson, the rise of "print-capitalism" in the seventeenth and eighteenth centuries is the cultural root from which nationalism emerges. In his view, the development of the printing press and the desanctification of language were important factors that contributed to the formation of a vernacular culture with a common language, a common perception of time, and the means to transmit itself to future generations. Before this facilitation of communication there could be no popular national consciousness.[29]

So, while recognizing that all definitions of nationalism are likely to be incomplete, it is worth repeating the insight distilled from the work of Umut Õzkirimli, which itself borrowed from the earlier theorizing of Benedict Anderson: nationalism is a regularly replicated discourse that provides meaning in people's lives related to the nation. This discourse has both form and function. The form—which, in the case of Confederate nationalism, is the topic of this work—is the symbolic text of the discourse itself. The function—which, in the case of Confederate nationalism, has fruitfully been the topic of scholars like Michael Bernath—is the process by which the discourse is constructed, replicated, and disseminated. In practice the two are of course closely intertwined, but for the purposes of study, we can seek to separate and analyze them discretely.

Methodologically, this book is not intended to be the total history of wartime Confederate nationalism. Instead, it approaches that topic from a particular vantage point, one that uses case-studies of certain important elements of the symbolic text of the ideology of the Confederate nation. It therefore borrows from the model of writing history espoused by Jim Cullen in *The Civil War in Popular Culture*. In his introduction, Cullen stated that he wanted to "reveal juxtapositions and suggestive observations that can enrich our sense of past and present," as much as he wanted to construct what he referred to as a "traditional," tightly argued unitary narrative.[30] Following Cullen, this project sets out to achieve a similar goal: to reveal and to suggest.

In successive chapters, then, we deal with the debates seeking to legitimize the Confederate Constitutions, antebellum literary imaginings of the future Confederate nation, the symbolic text of nation presented on Confederate Treasury notes, the wartime fictional literature of nationalism, and the depiction of the military in Confederate print culture. What we seek to reveal is that Confederates shared certain assumptions about the ways they constructed and depicted their burgeoning nationhood. What we seek to suggest is that this shared understanding represents a manifestation of the Confederate mythic present.

As this is, at heart, a study of various aspects of Confederate print culture, questions of literacy and media access in the South are important in shaping its understanding. Contemporary print media were a primary means of transmission for a nationalist ethos in the making. Readings reinforced a sense of nation linked to community and helped to bridge the gap between the experienced reality of everyday life and the emotive abstraction of a national life. In the America of the 1860s, most classes of white people had the opportunity to participate to some extent in the "taking of the news," which often included novels, broadsides, and poems, many of which were first printed (for the novels, as serials) in the leading newspapers or journals of the day. Thomas C. Leonard notes that reading the news was often a public and participatory affair. For example, newspapers were readily available in taverns, where they were often read aloud to attentive and sometimes fractious crowds.[31] Community members read aloud in accompaniment to such patriotic activities as preparing comfort packages for the troops. Shortages of paper during the war also meant that people read to each other and shared most print media. Within the home, families read aloud as a form of entertainment, a way to relieve boredom. The entire family shared newspapers, and though there was a commonly held notion that politics were a male preserve, by the middle of the nineteenth century, women's interest was becoming more overt. Women's magazines were extremely active, and women were increasingly targets of subscription drives.

The eloquence of Confederate letters testifies to soldiers' literacy. According to James M. McPherson, "Civil War armies were the most literate in all history to that time." He found more than 80 percent of Confederate soldiers and more than 90 percent of white Union soldiers could read. Elisabeth Muhlenfeld notes that Southern soldiers devoured all forms of print media, and that "novels were usually read literally to pieces."[32] Moreover, given the centrality of evangelical Protestant religion in Southern culture, with its premium on reading the Bible, Civil

War–era white Southerners were a literate people. Even enslaved African Americans, under threat of severe penalty, wanted to learn to read, and some did so.[33]

James L. Machor, though writing specifically on questions of gender, notes that reading is "defined by specific historical conditions and interpretive strategies in force for particular reading communities at particular times." This assessment of Civil War Confederate print culture corresponds with Machor's attention to "the way current interpretations of response can intersect with past codes to give a historical account of reading characterized by the convergence among past conventions, the textual engagement of audience, and cultural ideology."[34] Therefore, while specific reader responses to a particular text are largely unrecoverable by historians, possible readings of the same text may be open to historical reconstruction. In an environment beset by war and privation, some individuals chose to write about the war, and others chose to read about it. In particular, literary expression sought to validate sacrifice and bind the community together, indeed to awaken a sense of a wider community than the local area. Alice Fahs, writing on "The Civil War as a Popular Literary Event," makes the point that authoring, publishing, and reading became vitally important acts of nationalism in the context of the Civil War, for both Northerners and Southerners. For Confederates, "the act of reading itself now took on a strongly ideological cast. . . . Suffused with nationalistic aims, reading was less a private than a public, patriotic act."[35]

In 1860 and 1861, white Southerners set out to change their world. They convinced themselves that secession was the proper response to the political, economic, and cultural changes they saw reshaping their nation, and in so doing, they recast themselves as Confederates, partisans of a new nation. They primarily seceded to protect the institution of slavery—and so ultimately doomed it—but they also seceded to protect their idea of Confederate America from the encircling Demon Yankees. Worthy Southrons, Silent Slaves at their side, idealized themselves and their struggle. They did not succeed in their quest for independence, and perhaps it was quixotic to make the attempt. The reasons they gave for seceding are anathema to all but the most deluded minority in the present day, and so we do not mourn their failure. Yet we must take seriously the symbolic text of their nationalism, their attempt to explain their world to themselves. In some ways, Confederate nationalism represented the road not taken in mid-nineteenth-century America, but in other ways, the effects of the failed Confederate Revolution were long-lasting and profound. Scholars interested in the reconstruction of American nationalism in the aftermath of the war have looked to gender, ethnicity, religion, and of course race, but in every case, the South had to reintegrate into the Union on some reasonably equal basis, or, at least, on a basis that would become equal over the course of time.[36] Perhaps the ultimate test of the strength of wartime Confederate nationalism was that it took over a century after the fall of the Confederate nation for the overturn of the invidious racial order at its heart, and that into the twenty-first century, the battle flag of the Army of Northern Virginia still flies on the grounds of the South Carolina capitol and as part of the state flag of Mississippi.

1

"At Last, We Are a Nation among Nations"

The Constitutional Confederate Nation

At last, we are a nation among
nations; and the world shall
soon behold in many a distant
port another flag unfurled!

HENRY TIMROD,
Ethnogenesis (1861)

In an impromptu speech given in Newcastle, England, on October 7, 1862, William Gladstone, then British chancellor of the exchequer in the government of Lord Palmerston, remarked, "We may have our own opinions about slavery; we may be for or against the South; but there is no doubt that Jefferson Davis and other leaders of the South have made an army; they are making, it appears, a navy; and they have made what is more than either; they have made a nation."[1] Gladstone's certainty on this issue may have followed from his belief, as he remarked later in the speech, that the success of the South in defending secession was "as certain as any event yet future and contingent can be."[2] Not surprisingly, many Confederates agreed with Gladstone's assessment, but they did so for one reason quite American in nature: the existence of a written, ratified constitution. Gladstone was likely not thinking about the word "constitution" as he spoke, but many white Southerners understood that before Jefferson Davis and the other leaders of the South made either an army or a navy, they had made a constitution, and thus, in their eyes, they had made a nation. Moreover, those same white Southerners saw the Provisional and Permanent Constitutions of the Confederate States as part of the constitutional tradition inherited from the American Revolution. Many of them believed that their actions represented "a restoration of the original federal order."[3] In short, the Confederate adherence to a particular vision of American constitutionalism was one of the first acts the new state took of Confederate Americanism.

In this telling of the story of the Confederate nation, in the early months of 1861, the Confederate founders laid claim to the constitutional heritage of 1787, modified it in light of the nation's experiences, and, to safeguard their particular way of life, then set about defending it. This reality provides the context for the Southern congressman who remarked in January 1865, as the war was all but lost, "'This is a war for the *constitution*, it is a *constitutional war*.'"[4] Asserting this version of the American constitutional tradition would thus secure the purpose for which they had seceded: the defense of slavery. This was the understanding of Confederate Americanism with which the South began the Civil War. Due to the usurpations of the Demon Yankee, the Worthy Southron—in the Jeffersonian tradition inherited from John Locke—was honor bound to secede in order to protect himself and his loyal Silent Slaves from the depredations of fanatical abolitionists. Given that the Worthy Southron was, in his own mind, the true American, it is not surprising that he set out to demonstrate his adherence to Confederate Americanism by replicating the actions of the revered Founders, taking pains at the same time to undo the errors unwittingly made in an earlier time.

Not understanding this interpretation of Confederate Americanism, historians tend to concentrate on the speed with which the Confederacy created itself and miss the significance of that haste. For example, Donald Nieman notes, "The priority that the Confederates gave to constitution making—especially when faced with the prospect of war with the United States—must have struck foreigners as quintessentially American."[5] Similarly, in another interpretation of the causes of the Civil War, Brian Holden Reid comments that "it says a lot for the legalistic bias of American political culture in the nineteenth century that immediate priority was allotted to perfecting this provisional document instead of taking practical measures to secure Southern independence, working out a viable policy towards the Upper South, and establishing a satisfactory foreign policy and the means to implement it." Reid later argues that "drafting a constitution, no matter how delicate the legal refinements, does not make a nation."[6]

At some level, this is undoubtedly true. This narrative, however, deals with the foundation of an *American* nation, and the existing tradition of such nations, from the 1777 Articles of Confederation to the 1787 United States Constitution to the 1861 Confederate Constitution, says otherwise. In this context, we need to understand the force of the constitutional imperative in the United States. We need to take seriously, for example, the opinion of a Louisianan author for *De Bow's Review*, who declared in March 1861 that "every nation and every sovereign State exists only by virtue of a constitution."[7] After all, this was a central way in which the United States distinguished itself from European monarchies, and in the first eighty years of the Union's existence, the Constitution of 1787 came to occupy a very important place in the national self-image. That this was the case in the South as well seems quite certain from the tone of the editorial debates surrounding the Confederate Constitution. The Confederate nation was, in that respect, an American nation. Indeed, for Confederates it was *the* American nation.

John M. Murrin persuasively argues that "the Constitution [of 1787] became a substitute for any deeper kind of national identity," because the "Americans had erected their constitutional roof before they put up the national walls."[8] In like fashion, the Confederacy's Permanent Constitution of 1861 was an attempt to repeat the experiment, getting it right this time, at least in the eyes of a section of political and editorial opinion in the South. Had the Confederacy won independence during the Civil War, its Constitution might have acted in the same way, providing a roof under which the new nation could grow and coalesce. We will never know the outcome of this process, but it does demonstrate that in the American experience, nation-building has had two distinct parts: first creation out of whole cloth, and second, sustenance, if necessary in the face of hostile enemies. The Confederacy failed miserably in the latter aim but had the war ended differently, the groundwork was laid for a future, less contested nationhood in the American tradition. So to suggest that failed Confederate nationalism was a root cause of the Civil War's result is to put the cart before the horse; rather, we should say that the Confederacy, and particularly its military, ultimately failed Confederate nationalism. The latter could not and would not survive without the nourishment of military victory and political success.

Nation, nationalism, and national identity are deceptively simple concepts, as the wealth of literature attempting to explain them demonstrates, and we must come to terms with them if we are to understand what the Confederate Constitutions were really about.[9] In one sense, nation is conflated with state when taken to mean simply a politically organized entity ruling a specific geographic area. In the American context, however, this association is complicated by the peculiar development of the governmental system of the United States.[10] The term "nation," when associated with government, tends to assume a relatively unitary form of government, perhaps because the word developed in the eighteenth and nineteenth centuries with special reference to the monarchies of Europe. In the United States, by contrast, the national "roof" of which Murrin writes was a *federal* one, that is, a form of government that shares power among a central authority and a number of constituent territorial units that retain some degree of individual sovereignty. Thus, the state over which the umbrella of American nationalism developed under the Constitution of 1787 assumed a distinctly federal tone. By 1860, the South feared that the federal government, in practical terms, was coming closer and closer to the unitary system the colonies had rejected during the Revolution. Yet we can still best understand the intentions of the Confederate framers concerning nationhood if we bear this idea of a relationship between federated states and nationalism in mind. These Southerners were experienced politicians, and we should take their efforts seriously.[11] What they sought, however, was a return to their understanding of the original American idea of nationalism, as remembered from previous generations.

From this viewpoint, the Confederate Constitution and the debate surrounding it form part of an attempt to turn the imagined community of the Antebellum South into a freestanding nation, from the fictive past of an imagined South to the mythic present of an imagined Confederacy.[12] That community desired a return to an earlier form of national government and was white in color, quite local in nature, and connected to the wider world by kinship ties as much as anything else. The project of the Confederacy in 1861 was to turn this foundation into a wider political and cultural affiliation.[13] We should therefore be clear about something else peculiar to the American national tradition. As Murrin's idea of a national roof implies, in the case of the United States after 1787 and the Confederacy after 1861, we are discussing *state nationalism*, produced from the upper echelons of politics and directed downward toward the masses of citizens from whom it requires loyalty and service. As a concept, we must distinguish it from *popular nationalism*, produced from the lower echelons of society and directed upward toward political elites. The two, of course, are not mutually exclusive: to be successful, they must be symbiotic, and the effort to sell the Confederate Constitution was precisely an attempt to legitimize the actions of state nationalists in the popular mind.

That the Confederacy began as the nationalist project of a central state authority does not, and should not, make it any less valid as a species of national feeling. This chapter demonstrates that a certain sector of white Southern opinion was generally receptive to this effort, but an attempt to sell the Constitution occurred regardless.[14] This was an effort to sell not the provisions themselves but rather the idea of a Confederate nation to the Upper South, North, and the world. Such an action was necessary as nations have to be validated both internally and externally. It is insufficient that a people regard themselves as a nation; they must be recognized as such by others. The Confederacy sought such recognition long and hard, most notably from the British, but in spite of Gladstone's opinions, they never really came close to obtaining that much sought-after external validation.[15]

The window through which we can begin to see this effort is the Southern print media. The sources used here are periodicals and newspapers primarily from the states that participated in the Montgomery Convention.[16] It is difficult to exaggerate the importance of print media in the political life of the Confederate nation at this time. There were no other regular, alternative sources of news, and newspapers especially assumed an importance they have lost in the multimedia environment of the twenty-first century. In this case, Southern print media provided a vehicle through which the producers of Confederate nationalism tried to reach their intended constituency and in which the latter replied. First, before the Montgomery Convention, a spirited discussion took place in the periodicals over a purportedly organic idea of nationhood that militated against the establishment of any federal nation. For some of these observers, though they did not say so directly, a government with the powers of the Articles of Confederation appears to have been the ideal. Their opponents, meanwhile, perhaps recognizing more acutely the coming need to defend their new nation against Northern tyranny, rejected this 1777 notion in favor of the 1787 concept of a more centralized government. This was the anticipation phase.

Second, after the publication of the Provisional Constitution and through the promulgation of its successor, the Permanent Constitution, commentary on the new documents filled the pages of Confederate newspapers and periodicals, mostly approving but not exclusively so. Almost every newspaper considered these constitutional developments important enough to print both Constitutions in full, taking up a considerable portion of their pages.[17] This is the reaction phase.

Third, leading Confederate politicians recommended the documents to their constituents using language that associated nation with a people and an American political system. Among these speeches and letters are contributions from President Jefferson Davis of Mississippi, Vice President Alexander H. Stephens, and Benjamin H. Hill of Georgia, Robert H. Smith and Thomas Fearn of Alabama, and Louis T. Wigfall of South Carolina and Texas.[18] This is the legitimation phase. After this time, by late April 1861, attention in the Southern print media had turned to the unfolding war, and discussions of nationhood and nationalism moved away from the Constitution. These three phases were not discrete, separate, or neatly consecutive periods of time; in many cases, they overlapped. They do, however, allow us to organize the constitutional debates into a coherent process.

Two caveats are necessary at this point. First, while this approach tends to flatten out political differences among the debate's participants, it would be an error to ignore their existence altogether. Discussions over the provisions of the Constitution, although they occurred in secret, were not without argument and controversy. The South Carolina delegation, perhaps more than any other, failed to get its way, even though South Carolinians chaired both drafting committees.[19] Notably, then, sources from South Carolina were the least likely to fit the mold described here. In addition, very real political differences soon split the participants in the constitutional debates over the prosecution of the war, of which the schism between president and vice president was only the most visible. This chapter highlights strands of political and editorial opinion that, while not necessarily identical on every issue, were pointing in the same direction in early 1861: toward the Confederate American nationalism outlined above.

Second and more important, considering the impact of the debate on the wider public, we should be careful not to suggest that editors or politicians could shape public debate at will. As one commentator observes, the public nature of the news meant that "editors could preach, but, unlike in a church, heretics sat in the congregation and some were passing out their own versions of the truth."[20] People had their own beliefs, prejudices, and preferences, and they saw the vitally important issues of the day through those lenses.

Confederates, therefore, had ample opportunity to notice the importance their leaders attached to creating a frame of government, and to follow the debate that accompanied their actions. Constitution-making was one of the first collective actions the seceding Southern states took, well before the creation of an army or navy. Very soon after South Carolina seceded on December 20, 1860, plans went forward to call a convention of the South in Montgomery, Alabama, for February 4, 1861. At that convention, after presenting their credentials and establishing procedures, the delegates resolved to draft a Provisional Constitution.[21] Only once that document was in place, on February 8, 1861, four days after the convention opened, did formal considerations of leadership and policy begin to take place. Although its framers allowed for the Provisional Constitution "to continue for one year from the inauguration of the President," the convention appointed a committee to draft a Permanent Constitution on February 9, immediately after the election of Jefferson Davis as provisional president.[22] The speed with which the wheels of Southern government turned attest both to the urgency of the situation they faced and the great weight they accorded the formal structures of government.

The limited scholarship that does exist on the Confederate Constitutions occasionally gives weight to the idea of a Southern nationalism based in the doctrine of states' rights. On the one hand, several works give prominence to the Southern attachment to states' rights as a key motivating factor behind the constitutional developments of 1861. Charles R. Lee Jr., for example, argues that the Confederate Constitutions "represent the ultimate constitutional expression of the states' rights philosophy and the state sovereignty concept in nineteenth century America."[23] On the other hand, some recent works tend to point as well to the more nationalist aspects of Confederate constitution-making. Many of them locate the Confederate Constitutions centrally in American constitutional development.[24] Scholars often employ the essential similarity of the documents of 1787 and 1861 to point out the fragile foundations of Confederate nationalism. After all, the "other" the South sought to identify itself against was not that different. That, however, was precisely the point, insofar as the Confederacy sought to right the unwitting errors of the original framers in permitting the creation of what one commentator referred to as the "new [Republican] Constitution" of 1861, a document that had as its goal the "'ultimate extinction' of Southern civilization."[25]

Most pertinently, Don E. Fehrenbacher argues that "the truly striking feature of this constitution . . . is not the extent to which it incorporated states'-rights doctrines, but rather the extent to which it transcended those principles in order to build a nation." He also suggests that "the quality of southern nationalism at the beginning of the Civil War compares not unfavorably with the quality of American nationalism in the early days of the Revolution."[26] Marshall L. DeRosa maintains that "the Confederate States of America was premised upon principles dating back to the American Antifederalists of the constitutional convention" and suggests that the Confederate "Constitution intentionally reinvigorated the states with the spirit of the Tenth Amendment's reserved-powers provision as interpreted by its Antifederalist sponsors."[27] These scholars base their interpretations on the constitutional documents themselves, while this chapter places them in their nationalist context through an analysis of the debates that surrounded them in the Southern press.

This study of Confederate nationalism, in the context of its Constitutions, begins in the anticipation phase, before the Montgomery Convention. Two strands of opinion dominated this phase. First, a few intellectuals contested the desire of the Confederate leadership to capture the established American model of constitutionalism and put it to the service of a revitalized Confederate American nationalism. The roots of the principal alternative lay both in the most extreme form of Southern states' rights tradition, and in an organic conception of nationhood that romanticized the origins of the original colonies and their development before the Revolution. Second, a considerable body of opinion, contrary to the intellectuals, advocated the adoption of the Constitution of 1787 with varying degrees of amendment to take account of experience and the Southern situation. For the most part, the Constitutions of 1861 eventually embodied the desires of this latter strand of opinion.

George Fitzhugh, often a maverick in Southern intellectualism, was at the head of the first movement. Writing in *De Bow's Review* in November 1860, he simultaneously struck two blows when he argued that the several states were the natural repositories of nationhood, and that constitutions were "for the most part, mere idle figments of the brain."[28] Further articles by Fitzhugh, and by J. Quitman Moore of Mississippi in subsequent editions, reiterated the basic points.[29] Simply put, the position of these organic nationalists was that "nations . . . are not made but born; born of identity, of race, language, interest; born of similarity of climate, production, pursuit; born of congeniality of thought, feeling, habit, taste, religion; born not of treaties, leagues, constitutions, born not of man; but of nature and God."[30] The immediate corollary of this position was that "the States . . . are anatomically nations; and that is the only real nationality."[31] Nationalism in the American tradition of federated states was thus an oxymoron, as nothing above the level of the unitary state was truly a nation, a term Fitzhugh invested with a certain degree of reverence.

For these commentators the whole idea of "creating" a nation was a non sequitur because God, not man, planted a nation. This meant, of course, that the effort of the U.S. Constitution of 1787 to create a nation out of thirteen separate states was something approaching an abomination and deserved the death it would receive at the hands of the secessionists in the South. As Fitzhugh noted, "Our ancestors were guilty of the absurd attempt to make a nation on paper—the nation of the United States. There never was such a nation, for it was not planted, did not come up, and grow into a nation. . . . A nation without a people or a territory! Was there ever such an absurdity?" For him, the founding of the original colonies in North America was an act of divine intervention, and each of them was indisputably a "separate nation" before the Revolution and clearly "nations in fact" after.[32] Constitutions, insofar as they had any substance at all, were merely reflections, or codifications, of the social reality lived by the citizens of the nation. The "constitution of society," far from being embodied in a written document, "is its 'life' . . . its principle of growth, development, and existence; its coherence, subordination, and adaptation of parts, and its co-operative faculty."[33] A constitution was the lived totality of a nation, rather than any literary attempt to capture the polity on paper. A problem with the analysis that Fitzhugh and his peers never confronted was the accretion of new states to the nation since 1787. Had God planted Illinois and Iowa, Mississippi and Arkansas, or had men created them?

These authors did not abandon their principles in the face of a federal Constitution for the Confederate nation; instead, they spent their time warning their peers of the folly they were perpetuating. Writing in *De Bow's Review* just before the formation of the Confederacy but presumably aware of the upcoming convention, Fitzhugh suggested that, "when we go about forming a Southern Confederacy, let us learn from the fate of the Union that man cannot make a government at all, much less make a sovereignty above a sovereignty, a national government above a national government." He continued with the advice that the South should not be "fused," either by politics or economics, into a "large nation" because such edifices had always been "weak, ignorant, and contemptible."[34] Writing in the same issue, Moore suggested that the Constitution of 1787 had already failed in its original goals, and that it would fail again if re-adopted by the Confederacy.[35] Finally, the unnamed author who contributed a piece to the September 1861 issue gave a grave warning to those who would repeat the errors of the United States: "The very moment any administration mistakes the Southern Confederacy for a government proper, and attempts to exercise all the powers of government, that moment will be its last, or at least the beginning of its downfall."[36] For these commentators, the project of the Montgomery Convention was as absurd as it was dangerous. Exactly how these intellectual purists would see the separate and independent Southern nations defend themselves against the unified North was not given apparent consideration.

It is the practical effects of this strand of political opinion—states' rights–induced obstructionism—that many scholars see at the heart of the Confederacy's downfall. It is certainly true that such ideas did not remain confined to the pages of periodicals.[37] For example, the *Augusta Daily Chronicle and Sentinel* remarked on January 31, 1861, "our Constitution [of 1787] . . . has proved a failure," and then asked, quite pertinently, "what assurance have we that another formed on the same basis will be stronger or more permanent?"[38] Similarly, the *Huntsville Southern Advocate* wondered on February 13 at the folly of the fact that "the Seceding States will organize *the very kind of Government* they sought to get rid of by seceding!"[39] Finally, the reaction of the *Charleston Tri-Weekly Mercury* to the Provisional Constitution was to "regret" that it had ever been formed at all.[40]

This was not, however, the dominant theme of the reaction phase of the Constitutional debates, nor did it have the unqualified support even of the journals in which it appeared. Others realized that the South required some form of federal system for its future prosperity. In unity they saw strength. For example, the February 1861 edition of *De Bow's Review* that contained articles by Fitzhugh and Moore also carried a sermon by

Reverend B. M. Palmer of New Orleans that looked forward to the creation of "a new and homogeneous confederacy," not something the others would have endorsed. In the March 1861 edition, the unattributed article "What Is a Constitution?" forcefully stated the organicists' position and warned the Confederacy not to overstep its bounds, following on from the argument of A. Featherman of Louisiana that constitutions were the bedrock of all nations. Later in the edition, an editorial strongly endorsed the Provisional Constitution.[41] Even the *Mercury* conceded that the Provisional Constitution was only temporary and therefore "excusable." Several days later, an editorial pointed to the opportunity, promised by the Permanent Constitution, "to rectify all the equivocal passages and deficiencies in the United States Constitution."[42]

The *Mercury* was in line with a large body of editorial opinion that saw the Montgomery Convention as an opportunity to correct the errors, intentional and otherwise, perpetuated by the original framers in 1787. Most of these opinions sought to reassert the original federalism of the United States. On January 17, 1861, the *Augusta Daily Chronicle and Sentinel* argued, "We most earnestly desire that the attempt be made to put new guaranties and provisions in the Constitution, to provide for the present, even if the near future holds out no shadow of evil."[43] Specifically, the *Chronicle and Sentinel* required that the right of secession be written into the document, that the ban on the slave trade be reiterated, and that direct taxation be outlawed. Later in the month, the *Charleston Daily Courier* pointed out the experimental nature of the Constitution of 1787 and suggested that the prevention of public corruption be the overriding goal of the framers of 1861. In the opinion of that newspaper, "the first great object and value of a definitive written Constitution is not to leave much to the discretion or honesty of its administrators, but to guard securely against all temptations, aberrations, or perversions that can be foreseen."[44]

Several commentators laid out detailed plans for constitutional reconstruction. Among them was the *Charleston Daily Courier*'s "Rutledge," whose summary of the people's wants neatly characterized the desires for government of many Confederates: "Our object should be to establish a government which should be efficient for all the functions which fall properly within its jurisdiction—impotent in every other respect. We desire a Federal Government which should represent us in our dealings with foreign States; we wish it to ignore it absolutely as the administrator of our domestic affairs."[45] While this desire to secure efficient and limited government was widely shared, Rutledge also wanted to roll back democracy, something less widely popular. He desired a government that represented the states, not the people, thus endorsing a narrow, elitist, republican vision of government, outdated even before he proposed it.

In general, the desires of constitutional reformers in the South, proceeding from the American constitutional tradition as well as from an appreciation of the Southern situation, found fulfillment in the Permanent Constitution of the Confederacy. It is fitting, as this was the intended roof for the new nation, to outline the changes the 1861 framers thought appropriate. Starting in the Preamble itself, the Constitution recognized the "sovereign and independent character" of the states and invoked "the favor and guidance of Almighty God," neither of which appeared in the 1787 Constitution.[46] Key provisions, repeatedly pointed to during the reaction phase of the debate, included the citizenship clause, the trade and appropriations clauses, the slave property clauses, and the political reforms. The Constitution banned voting by noncitizens as well as protective tariffs and appropriations for internal improvements. It repeated the existing ban on the slave trade, and a new provision gave the Confederate government the power to prevent slave imports from states outside the nation. Not surprisingly, one new provision forbade any legislation "denying or impa[i]ring the right of property in negro slaves," and another gave slave owners right of passage throughout the Confederacy with their slave property, including such territories as the government may have acquired.[47] In the future, following on from concern over corruption in the antebellum period, the Constitution limited the president to one, nonrenewable six-year term; placed restrictions on his ability to dispense patronage by circumscribing the causes for dismissal of most government officials; and made executive officers directly answerable to Congress.[48]

As constitutional scholars note, there is a distinct flavor of both states' rights and republican traditions in the amendments made by the framers of 1861.[49] What is remarkable, therefore, is the extent to which the reaction phase of the debate demonstrates that producers of political and editorial opinion in the Confederacy in March and April 1861 understood the new Constitutions as close copies of the original Constitution of 1787. The reaction to the documents was by no means unanimously approving, but most commentators pronounced the founding of the Confederacy as "a striking improvement upon the old Constitution."[50] In addition, many of the articles in praise of the new Constitution clearly showed their understanding of what had transpired: the framers had laid the basis of a Confederate American nation.

What this debate indicates is that, while the Confederacy established a new nation, it was one enfolded within the preexisting national and constitutional tradition of the United States—it was Confederate Americanism writ large. The terms of the debate suggest that white Southerners believed they had written the Constitution the original framers would liked to have written, had the need to appease the Northern colonies not hobbled them. This may be bad history, but that is beside the point. The manner in which Southern editors asserted that the Confederacy had adopted the U.S. Constitution while at the same time informing their readers of its differences, suggests that they saw a document that was as familiar as it was an improvement over the original. In 1861, the Confederacy laid claim to the original intent of the framers, modified by the experience of eighty years fighting off centralizing tendencies. In the final analysis, this reliance on inheritance rather than differentiation is what makes the Confederate nationalist story so ironic. In creating an insurgent nationalism that sought to sunder the United States in the service of slavery and states' rights, Confederates instead created a nationalism that served to reinforce the similarities between the sections. Digging out from this conundrum would become the project of wartime Confederate nationalists.

Some contemporaries went so far as to argue that the Confederate framers should not change a word of the Constitution of 1787. For example, a letter to the *Huntsville Southern Advocate* in mid-December 1860 argued that "the Constitution of the United States makes the best government in the world . . . as near perfection as human frailty can ever approach Divine wisdom."[51] The *Milledgeville Southern Union* argued for the readoption of the old Constitution "without dotting an i or crossing a t," at the same time as it announced that it was changing its name from *Federal Union* in honor of the events then transpiring.[52] After the publication of the Confederate Constitutions, a number of newspapers actually reported that the Federal Constitution of 1787 *had* been readopted, and others remarked approvingly on the likeness between the two documents. The *Southern Union,* for example, reported that "the Southern Congress have adopted the Constitution of the United States," though on the same page another article outlined the substantive differences between the two documents.[53] The paper's cross-town rival, the *Milledgeville Southern Recorder*, did exactly the same thing on exactly the same day.[54] These seeming contradictions are in fact nothing of the sort. They are a visible manifestation of the expression of Confederate Americanism.

Many commentators who did immediately see the differences between the Constitutions of 1787 and 1861 still praised the framers for using the original as a template. The *New Orleans Daily Picayune*, otherwise critical of the whole process, remarked that the "main and gratifying fact . . . is that the constitution of the United States is the model for the new frame of government. It was the work of wise men and patriots."[55] The *Huntsville Southern Advocate* approvingly reprinted an appeal to the border states from Georgia's *Savannah Republican* that called for dissenters to compare the two constitutions, with the obvious implication that the new version was the one that "assimilates the more to the principles of justice and truth, to the spirit and intentions of the early patriots, who conceived and built up the great institutions under which, until recently, we have long lived and prospered."[56] The *Milledgeville Southern Union* argued in early March that the convention's "adoption of the Old Constitution with only such alterations as experience and the change of our conditions required, has given general, if not universal satisfaction among the people."[57]

Even the fire-eating *Charleston Tri-Weekly Mercury* wrote rather wishfully in early April that the new Constitution would, "with a little repression of [their] fanaticism on the slavery question . . . be sufficiently acceptable to the Northwest to constitute no permanent difficulty in the way of their consenting to adopt it."[58] Another Charleston newspaper, the *Charleston Daily Courier*, only slightly less intransigent than its cousin, praised both what remained of the 1787 Constitution and what the new framers had added, concluding that "A great work has been done, and done well . . . considering the grave problems and difficulties presented to the Montgomery Congress, and the important duties apart from the Permanent Constitution, which they have discharged—and considering also the time they have occupied, and the circumstances that have surrounded them they have done not merely well, but far beyond sanguine expectations."[59] The author drew special attention to the introduction of God into the Constitution, and particularly the provisions dealing with restricting the power of the executive and providing protection for slavery. At the end, the author looked forward to South Carolina's being the "second or third" state to adopt the Permanent Constitution, although it was the sole state where the ratification process even seemed in doubt, and was the sixth of the original seven states to ratify.[60]

This should not suggest, of course, that the work of the Montgomery Convention satisfied everyone. Some negative opinions flowed out of the earlier, anticipation phase of the debate, with commentators questioning why the new nation should adopt a failed basic law. Commentators in the reaction phase, however, were far more likely to wonder at the haste of the whole process. At one end of the political spectrum, the *Charleston Tri-Weekly Mercury* initially regretted any constitution-making.[61] At the other end, and perhaps more thoughtfully, the *New Orleans Daily Picayune* remarked on March 19 that "the policy of forming permanent government in the midst of revolution is, at least, a doubtful one. Unless the framers of the constitution enjoyed more than mortal exception from the weaknesses of human nature, it might be expected that a constitution so formed would bear more traces of the passions which produced the revolution than might prove consistent with the future well-being of the State."[62] The *Picayune* perhaps remembered that the cessation of Revolutionary hostilities long predated the writing of the Constitution of 1787, and that abject failure marked its predecessor, the Articles of Confederation. Given the circumstances in which the Confederate delegates worked, and the political strictures they could not escape, it is perhaps surprising that the Constitution of 1861 they created was so national in outlook.

Given that America's tradition of governance rested, at least in theory, on consent of the governed, it is not remarkable that one of the most vociferous strands of reaction to the Constitutions should be the issue of placing the document before the people, or at least a convention of delegates elected for such a purpose. Only the state conventions in Louisiana, Texas, and Mississippi put the idea of popular ratification to a vote among themselves, and each motion failed miserably. State conventions deliberated on the cornerstone of their new nation from one to five days, at most nine days in South Carolina, and then delivered large majorities in favor.[63] Overall, the state delegates voted 861 to 42 in favor of ratification, and half of that opposition came from one state, South Carolina, where the margin of victory was still almost 75 percent. This should not disguise the fact, however, that a certain section of Southern editorial opinion, much of it almost pro-Union in origin, thought popular ratification indispensable.

In the *Augusta Daily Chronicle and Sentinel,* the *Huntsville Southern Advocate,* the *Milledgeville Southern Recorder,* and the *New Orleans Daily Picayune,* editorials or prominently placed articles argued that the people had the right to ratify the Constitution themselves. None of these journals thought that ratification was in doubt, though they may have been stalling in the hope of a political compromise between North and South. Before the convention even met for the first time, the *Augusta Daily Chronicle and Sentinel* argued that "it will clearly be an assembly without legality, and its action can only be binding on the people by their own consent." The next day, the newspaper published an article pointing out the folly of readopting the failed Constitution of 1787. After the promulgation of the Provisional Constitution, the paper printed a heavily underscored reminder that "*at no time* can this be binding *on any State, except by consent,* the Government manifestly having no authority to enforce itself, as any State can, by either a real or factitious majority, *secede from the Confederation.*"[64]

Reflecting ambivalent loyalism, the paper also admitted that "the Congress has done perhaps the best that was attainable under the circumstances," an opinion it followed up over the succeeding weeks with a series of approving articles on the provisions of the new document. The *Chronicle and Sentinel* repeated its call for popular ratification as the convention debated the Permanent Constitution in early March, and again after its promulgation. The paper advanced two reasons for ratification: the traditional American right of the consent of the governed and to allay the fears of malcontents within the Confederacy at the reimposition of a federal form of government. Finally, on March 19, three days after the ratification vote in the Georgia Convention, the paper's correspondent at Savannah argued that "a heavy, overwhelming sanction of the Constitution by a popular vote would have given it a moral power and grandeur, which ratification by the convention may not do." The paper, however, later wavered a little on that harsh stance toward the nationalism of the Constitutions. On March 28, in what sounds like a reversal of their earlier disapprobation, the paper noted that it looked forward to the reconstruction of the Union *on the basis* of the Confederate Constitution. Four days earlier, the newspaper had strongly endorsed Alexander

Stephens's Savannah speech, which, as we shall see, contained a strong thread of Confederate American nationalism.[65]

The *Chronicle and Sentinel* was not alone in its reluctance to rubber-stamp the Constitutions. In North Alabama, later a troublesomely disloyal area of the Confederacy, a letter to the *Huntsville Southern Advocate* warned that "the people are not satisfied with the distrust that has been manifested toward them, and the indecent haste by which power has passed from their hands into the hands of those who were not only not chosen by the people, but about whose position they were not even consulted."[66] This was after the Alabama State Convention, sitting in Montgomery, had ratified the Permanent Constitution within one day. Three weeks later, however, the paper fully endorsed the sentiments of Robert Smith that the Confederacy was now a nation. Similarly, in New Orleans, which would labor under Union occupation for the vast majority of the war, the *New Orleans Daily Picayune* endorsed the call of an unnamed Mississippi "secessionist" journal that the Constitution be submitted to a convention of delegates elected for that purpose. That same day, the Louisiana State Convention voted 26 to 74 against popular ratification, three days before it even saw the Permanent Constitution.[67]

Thus far the framers were attempting to enfold their efforts within the American constitutional tradition, but that endeavor was not without opponents. Given that in most cases the states never even considered submitting the Permanent Constitution to the people, it was technically accurate for Charles Lee to suggest that, "although newspapers played an important role in the ratification of the United States Constitution, such was not the case in the Confederacy."[68] Ratification per se did not involve securing popular approbation, and the delegates to the Montgomery Convention who returned home to address their state conventions were far more effective advocates than ill-informed newspaper editors could be.

Still, there was some effort to sell the Constitution to the people. In one sense, Confederate leaders sought to head off complaints about the haste of ratification, especially in those areas where cooperationist sentiment was strong such as North Alabama. More important, the delegates sought to explain their actions in Montgomery and therefore to justify them to their constituents, who would have an opportunity to voice their disapproval of the framers' actions in the elections for the presidency and Congress in the fall of 1861. As some scholars note, judicial and extra-legal repression on the Confederate homefront early in the war assured a favorable result, but at the national level, Confederate leaders sought to reassure their prospective citizens that their accomplishments were within the American tradition, and at the same time, that they had truly created a nation.[69]

The most widely disseminated speeches were of course those of the president and vice president of the Confederacy. Many of the newspapers surveyed here reprinted Jefferson Davis's Inaugural Address from February 19. Some published Alexander Stephens's response to a serenade in Montgomery on February 9, and most reprinted his Savannah speech from March 21.[70] Apart from these national-level commentators, there were a number of local politicians who made similar speeches and echoed the same themes. Among this latter group were Robert H. Smith in Mobile, Alabama, on March 30; Louis T. Wigfall in Charleston on April 3; Benjamin H. Hill in Atlanta on April 4; and an open letter by Thomas Fearn at Huntsville on April 13.[71]

A number of themes stand out. First, these speeches stressed the internal unity of the South under the umbrella of the Confederacy. Second, they pointed to the ways in which the Confederate and American constitutional traditions were the same. Third, they defended their decision to make changes to the Constitution of 1787. Fourth, they appealed for unity in the face of external enemies. Finally, they directed an appeal to be left alone to the outside world. Of course, not every theme appeared in every speech, and some stressed certain themes more than others, as you would expect of politicians who tailored their remarks to specific audiences. Taken together, however, these speeches provide a powerful insight into the intentions of the Confederate framers.

First, many of these speeches stressed the unity of the South within a Confederate nation. Stephens noted, soon after the publication of the Provisional Constitution, that "this day a new republic has been formed. The Confederate States of America have been ushered into existence, to take their place amongst the nations of the earth."[72] Then, speaking after the publication of the Permanent Constitution, he took particular care to address those who would argue that the Confederacy was "too small and too weak to maintain a separate nationality." On the contrary, he remarked, the seceded South had 200,000 square miles of territory, more than the original thirteen colonies, and was actually larger than "all of France, Spain, Portugal and Great Britain . . . together." Similarly, it had over a million more inhabitants than the United States at its formation, and five times the amount of taxable property, not to mention an aggregate debt level only a tenth of that of the United States. Quite simply, Stephens concluded, "with such an area of territory—with such an amount of population—with a climate and soil unsurpassed by any on the face of the earth—with such resources already at our command—with productions which control the commerce of the world—who can entertain any apprehensions as to our success, whether others join us or not"?[73] Of course, had the South faced the original thirteen colonies of 1787, instead of the United States of 1861, these figures would have been as impressive in fact as they sounded in rhetoric.

Few of his peers went to such lengths, but on a similar note, Davis's Inaugural began with the hope that the convention would soon form a permanent government, "which by its greater moral and physical power will be better able to combat with the many difficulties which arise from the conflicting interests of separate nations."[74] Benjamin Hill expounded on the theme of culturally appropriate government when he argued, "National characteristics must be considered in making a Government and laws for any people."[75] Robert Smith made the point most simply when he closed his Mobile address with the bald assertion that "we are now a *nation*."[76] Finally, Thomas Fearn went even further when he declared in his letter to the *Huntsville Southern Advocate* that "a new Empire has been founded in the South."[77]

Any tendency to read these protestations of impending nationhood merely as recognition of the fact of the creation of a Confederate *state* ignores the cultural baggage that the republican tradition associated with republics and governments. Ideally, as Hill noted, republics should reflect the national characteristics of the area they govern, and as such the Confederate government needed to reflect the special genius of white Southerners. The remainder of his speech revolved around the theme that the new Confederate government fulfilled this end. The other speeches also highlighted this desire that the new national government reflect and be supported by the people. Stephens, for example, argued strongly that "our republic, and republics, to be permanently prosperous, must be supported by the virtue, intelligence, integrity and patriotism of the people. These are the corner stones upon which the temple of liberty must be constructed to stand securely and permanently."[78] His assertion neatly reflects the federal nature of Confederate nationalism, with Stephens's image of republics within a republic.

Other politicians expressed similar themes in their addresses. Davis pointed to the power of the people as he closed his Inaugural Address, noting that, "obstacles may retard, but they cannot prevent the progress of a movement sanctified by its justice, and sustained by a virtuous people."[79] Robert Smith went further still, arguing that "the great object of the Convention was to bind together the broken fragments of a separated, but homogeneous people." He illuminated his understanding of the multifaceted nature of nationhood by following the assertion that the South was "now a nation" by saying, "with nationality will come development of commerce, of manufacture, of arts."[80]

Second, and apart from these assertions of nationhood, many of the speeches noted the ways in which the nascent Confederate constitutional tradition was enfolded within the American tradition. This is significant because the opposition to constitution-making, from the likes of Fitzhugh and Moore in *De Bow's Review,* required the belief that statesmen could not capture the national character, or the national culture, in a basic law. American constitutional tradition suggested otherwise. Davis made this point explicit when he proposed in his Inaugural Address that the Provisional Constitution of 1861 differed "from that of our fathers in so far as it is explanatory of their well-known intent, freed from the sectional conflicts which have interfered with the pursuit of the general welfare." He repeated his point toward the end of the address, remarking that "the Constitution formed by our fathers is that of these Confederate States."[81]

Stephens, too, speaking in Savannah, made much the same point when he argued that, fundamentally, "all of the essentials of the old Constitution, which have endeared it to the hearts of the American people, have been preserved and perpetuated."[82] Smith reminded his listeners at the outset of his speech that the mandate of the Montgomery Convention was to form a temporary government on the principles laid down in the Constitution of 1787, and Hill noted that, "in all its essential features, its original character, and instinctive purposes, it is the same as that under which we were born and brought up."[83] Fearn, too, asked his recalcitrant constituents whether they could deny that the original Constitution of the United States "is so perfect in all its provisions, that little or no alteration could have been required, but for the wilful perversions of unscrupulous and wicked men?"[84] He made the point that the signal success of the Confederate framers lay simply in the fact that they had the original in front of them as they worked. This strand of opinion met with an already receptive audience, as the reaction phase of the constitutional debate illustrates.

The third theme these politicians dealt with, after assertions of nascent nationhood and their fidelity to the preexisting constitutional tradition, was why they felt compelled to make changes to an almost perfect document. Charges of sectional perfidy featured prominently, but some of these commentators echoed the more radical aspects of the anticipation phase of the debate when they argued that the Constitution of 1787 was a failed experiment that time and experience had shown to be flawed in execution, if not intent. Hill made this point clearly, saying that the "Old Government was an experiment, and was made by human hands. . . . The evil of the Old Constitution was, that it had not been able to maintain itself and keep the country together."[85] In an explanation that Fearn would later echo, Hill argued that the original government had failed in its purpose, but the fault lay with those who sought to selfishly grasp at power for themselves, and who used the issue of slavery to divide the nation and create a situation where they might profit. Smith and Stephens also looked to long and persistent abuses against the Constitution as the root cause of the South's need for reform.[86]

Each of these men attempted to explain the differences in the original and improved Constitutions, concentrating on such matters as the tariff, citizenship, executive privilege, and the protection of slavery. Stephens's Savannah address of March 21 and Smith's Mobile address of March 30 provide perhaps the most comprehensive coverage of the provisions of the new Constitution. Slavery featured prominently in the Savannah address as well as in Hill's Atlanta address from April 4. Wigfall's Charleston speech on April 3 started with the issue of citizenship, before stressing issues of taxation and executive privilege. Fearn's Huntsville letter from April 13 covered most of these issues as well, but he, more than his fellow delegates, faced an audience hostile to the idea of the Confederate Constitution, or more precisely, hostile to the speed of its adoption and the failure of the framers to pay more than lip service to the idea of the consent of the governed.

Consequently, Fearn's letter most clearly articulates the fourth theme of unity and solidarity in the face of a supposedly hostile enemy. He had to admit, he wrote, that "it would have been more in accordance with my wishes, to have submitted it to a Convention elected for that express purpose," but that he found considerable justification for haste. First, of course, there was the matter of a "bitter and vindictive enemy" to the North. Second, he argued that the South was virtually unanimously behind the new frame of government, and that to submit it to the people would merely delay the inevitable approval. Third, he noted that amendment after ratification was possible, as in the case of the original Bill of Rights, but that a united front was necessary immediately, if for no other reason than to stand behind the soldiers of the South, and to "sustain" the benighted citizens of the Union-occupied border states.[87] This theme of necessary haste echoed the earlier speech of Fearn's Alabama colleague, Robert Smith, who reminded his listeners that "we had much to do in a short time and the matter was of the gravest importance; for we had a nation to form, and peace and war hung trembling in the balance."[88]

The urgency of war was probably not so great in early February as it was in early April, but the framers were certainly aware of the threat as their earnest pleas to be left alone suggest. The North, more so than with the others, was the intended recipient of this fifth theme. Stephens, for example, argued in Montgomery on February 9, "We ask of others simply to let us alone," a cry Davis reiterated on April 29, after the outbreak of hostilities, in an address to Congress. There was, however, a point beyond which the South thought sacrifice for peace too costly, and that, Davis said, was the point beyond which they would relinquish "honor and independence."[89] This then was the raison d'être of the constitutional debate: to secure Southern independence by creating a nation and presenting it as an accomplished fact to the Union.

Some, at least, eagerly received the message of Confederate American nationalism and set about employing it. There appeared around this time in the print media of the South a certain belligerence based on the newfound nationhood of the Confederacy. Perhaps the strongest expression of this viewpoint, published after the outbreak of war, appeared in the July 1861 edition of *De Bow's Review*. The author pointed to the glorious achievements of the framers when he declaimed, "Thrice, thrice welcome is this hour! From this moment a Nation is born, that will stand first among the Nations, and perpetuate on this continent the ideas and institutions of free, civil Government." That he directed his attention northward, toward the Union, became clear a few pages later when he insisted that "the present conflict in America is not a *civil* strife, but a war of *Nationalities*."[90]

Here, then, the themes of the constitutional debate come together. This unnamed author understood that at the same time as the Confederacy was a nation, it was a nation in the American tradition, a Confederate American nation. It was thus a nation that would "perpetuate" a republican form of government and protect the intentions of the founders, which in the South of 1861 had coalesced into one overriding goal: the protection of the institution of slavery from those who would seek either to slander it and besmirch Southern dignity or who would attempt to interfere with the sovereignty of the individual states. In the constitutional debate of 1861, the American constitutional tradition focused on that one point to the exclusion of all others, giving peculiar force to Alexander Stephens's contention in Savannah on March 21 that "the new Constitution has put to rest *forever* all the agitating question relating to our peculiar institutions—African slavery as it exists among us—the proper *status* of the negro in our form of civilization."[91] The war was about differing interpretations of the Constitution, but in context, those different interpretations pointed in one direction: the defense of slavery. As we shall see in subsequent chapters, another irony of Confederate nationalism was that while slaves were present as subjects from the outset, they were often rendered mute, a silent partner, understood to be standing in the background but rarely seen in the foreground.

So what had the framers of the Confederacy wrought in Montgomery? The *New York Herald* thought it knew. In an article published on February 11, 1861, the *Herald* flatly stated, "There it is: The systematic initiative government of an independent Southern confederacy, organized, located and in practical operation within fifty days from what was considered the ridiculous secession ordinance of South Carolina."[92] Within another thirty days, the Montgomery Convention accomplished much more. They elected a president, swore him in, and began to erect the detailed substance of a national government. They drafted a Permanent Constitution, debated its provisions, amended them where necessary, voted to adopt it, and sent it out to the state conventions for their approval. Before fifteen more days passed, the state conventions, in turn, ratified the Constitution with a swiftness that attests to its significance.

Writing in *De Bow's Review* in the summer of 1862, Rev. J. H. Thornwell laid out what was at stake for the Southern Confederacy: "We are struggling for constitutional freedom. . . . We are not revolutionists— we are resisting revolution. We are upholding the true doctrines of the

Federal Constitution. We are conservative. Our success is the triumph of all that has been considered established in the past." In this statement, Thornwell encapsulated many of the themes of the Confederate nationalist project, asserting that it was a quintessentially American movement, a movement to turn back the clock of Lincolnian Republicanism and abolitionism, of radical change inspired by Northern demagogues who cared nothing for the sanctity of contracts or property rights nor for the hallowed words of the U.S. Constitution. Confederates were the true Americans, fighting tyranny and usurpation of right. As Thornwell continued, "We are . . . fighting not for ourselves alone, but, when the struggle is rightly understood, for the salvation of this whole continent. . . . It cannot fail; it must not fail. Our people must not brook the infamy of betraying their sublime trust."[93] Constitutions were important, as freedoms were important, as nation was important. All was at stake, and if we ignore the urgency and magnitude with which Confederates regarded their nationalist project, then we ignore something fundamental to their struggle.

Three weeks after Mississippi became the fifth state to ratify the Permanent Constitution on March 26, the Confederacy was at war. The fact that a Confederate Supreme Court never existed, and that thus issues of constitutional interpretation or disputation in the Confederacy went unmediated, means that the attention of historians has fallen lightly on the Confederate Constitution after it was enacted. But to return to John Murrin's metaphor about the role of the 1787 Constitution in the development of postrevolutionary American nationalism—that "Americans had erected their constitutional roof before they put up the national walls"— once a roof has been erected, it does not need much thought so long as it functions as intended, in this case, providing shelter under which the walls of Confederate nationalism could develop. In the American tradition, constitutions legitimize nations. For white Southerners, they created a constitutional nation squarely within the American tradition, which was all they needed to think of themselves as Confederate Americans. In acting as they did, the framers of the Confederate government had a national plan in mind. It was not a unitary nation they desired, for that was outside the American constitutional tradition as they understood it, but a federal nation, somewhere between a unitary state and a pure confederation. That circumstances made such a goal ultimately un-

realistic should not blind us to its power as a symbol in Confederate political and editorial thought. The Constitution remained the roof under
which any further attempts at nation-building would have to occur. To
neglect the constitutional debates is to neglect the vital period in which
Confederate leaders sought to transmit their national idea to their prospective citizens.

2

"In That Cold Eye There Is No Relenting"

The Confederate Nation in the Antebellum Literary Imagination

The palace of a tyrant is a prison. There is no mercy here. . . .
Our friends *may* rescue us. They WILL avenge us. But in that
cold eye there is no relenting.

BEVERLEY TUCKER, writing as Edward William Sidney,
The Partisan Leader (1836)

The year 1861 was not the first time that white Southerners had imagined a Confederate America. Before the Civil War began, some Southern writers were imagining a national future for their region. So the strain of Confederate Americanism at work in the debates surrounding the ratification of the Confederate Constitutions was an extension and amplification of earlier acts of the imagined Confederacy. The starting point for consideration of this antebellum envisioning of Confederate Americanism is Beverley Tucker's 1836 novel *The Partisan Leader.* A quarter-century after its initial publication, this book was joined by two other novel-length narratives of an imagined Confederate future—John Beauchamp Jones's *Wild Southern Scenes* and Edmund Ruffin's *Anticipations of the Future to Serve as Lessons for the Present Time*—and was itself re-published in both the North and South. As they imagined their nation into being in 1860 and 1861, Confederates had an embryonic nationalist text upon which to draw, a literature that prefigured the symbolic text of wartime Confederate nationalism.

The centerpiece of these antebellum visions of the imagined Confederacy was the conviction that secession and the Southern nation were not revolutionary at all, that they were acts of American nationalism, made necessary by the depredations and abuses of Northern abolitionist demagogues and the too-easily swayed mobs of the Northern cityscapes. This vein of Confederate Americanism is an integral component of the imagined Confederacy and of the mythic present it represented. While this trope is rarely expressed outright, the literature of Tucker, Jones, and Ruffin make clear what their nations and nationalists are, and what they are not. In short, the actions of self and other, read from above, delineate for us the sinews of Confederate Americanism.

In 1836, Edward William Sidney published a novel called *The Partisan Leader: A Tale of the Future*. In this novel, set in 1849 and purporting to be written in 1856, Sidney set out his account of secession, the creation of a Southern Confederacy in opposition to the pseudo-monarchical tyranny of Martin Van Buren—embarking in 1849 upon his fourth consecutive term as president—and the travails of an occupied Virginia as she seeks to free herself from the yoke of tyranny and join her Southern brethren. Sidney, who was in fact Beverley Tucker, a former judge, professor of law at the College of William and Mary, and confirmed opponent of Jacksonian economic policies and the tariff in particular, intended the novel as an anti–Van Buren campaign tract to influence the 1836 presidential election. It was published too late for that goal to be achieved, and was perhaps too far-fetched an account for the contemporary audience. It was also poorly written and unfinished, as Tucker leaves the audience hanging with the fate of his principal character undetermined and the tyrant still in power.

Beverley Tucker died in 1851 and so did not live to see his novel achieve its greatest success, which came during the fulfillment of his prophecy: secession and civil war at the hands of an ostensible tyrant. In its initial— and, for a quarter-century, only—print run, *The Partisan Leader* enjoyed rather modest success. The publisher could account for the distribution of only 1,303 copies.[1] A quarter-century after its initial appearance, it was reissued in Richmond as *The Partisan Leader: A Novel, and an Apocalypse of the Origin and Struggles of the Southern Confederacy* (1862). The year previous saw the publication of a New York edition, *A Key to the Disunion Conspiracy: The Partisan Leader*, which apparently sold 7,000 copies in just about three weeks.[2]

As the possibility of secession and perhaps even civil war loomed larger in the late 1850s and early 1860s, Beverley Tucker's novel gained company. In 1859, John Beauchamp Jones, then a Philadelphia newspaper publisher, issued *Wild Southern Scenes,* hoping to re-create the success of his 1841 novel, *Wild Western Scenes,* which was in the process of selling some 100,000 copies.[3] The next year, in June 1860, South Carolinian Edmund Ruffin published *Anticipations of the Future to Serve as Lessons for the Present Time,* just as the Democratic Party was splintering in Charleston in an act of slavery-induced self-destruction that would ultimately throw the 1860 presidential election to Abraham Lincoln and precipitate the start of the Civil War.[4]

Three basic elements connected these novelists in their articulation of the imagined Confederacy. First, each positioned their Southern protagonists as noble and worthy opponents of a demented, tyrannical, and overweening Northern power that sought subjugation rather than comity and compromise. In all three cases, the Worthy Southron faced the Demon Yankee. Second, each positioned Southern slaves as opponents of abolitionist radicalism and unsure of their desire for freedom from their masters. In each work, slaves served in some military capacity to oppose the Northern foe, and in so doing, the Silent Slave fulfilled the political purposes of its master.[5] Third, and most important, each positioned its respective Southern confederacy as an American nation, in stalwart opposition to the tacitly un-American actions of the North, which principally coded as New England. These three novels, therefore, are expressions of Confederate Americanism.

Although Beverley Tucker was in many ways an exponent of "Virginianism," his overall vision encompassed the broader idea of a unified South in opposition to Northern tyranny, and the future of a Southern league or confederacy.[6] In Tucker's alternate 1849, Virginia struggles in the grip of an "army of observation" sent by Martin Van Buren to prevent the state from joining the newly seceded Southern Confederacy.[7] The narrative centers on the Trevor family, principally brothers Owen, Douglas, and Arthur. The younger brothers are partisans of a free Virginia, the eldest a Federal soldier and tool of the president. Owen Trevor, the villain of the piece, commits all sorts of crimes against honor, ending with his delivering his brother Douglas, the "partisan leader" of the title, to the clutches of Owen's master. Owen is slain without fanfare in the final battle. Douglas's fate is left uncertain. Although Tucker lived for another fifteen years, he never completed the manuscript, so far as we know. Given its original purpose of influencing the 1836 presidential election against

Van Buren, a purpose in which it failed, it is perhaps not surprising that Tucker did not return to complete it. However his work was received on the eve of the Civil War, it is clear that he had no direct purpose in 1836 to write a future history of an imagined Confederacy. He did so as a corollary to his main intent, attempting to prevent the election of Martin Van Buren. Tucker's political descendants, the secessionists of the early 1860s, recognized no such nuance. For them, Tucker was a prophet and a seer.

Jones's *Wild Southern Scenes* is also a family tragedy, centering on three fictional families, the Northern Langdons, the Southern Blounts, and the (Southern) Federalist Randolphs. As the book begins, thirteen Southern states have seceded from the Union by virtue of their delegations' having withdrawn from Congress. They are followed, in pique no doubt, by an "equal number of Republicans." President Randolph, though a Southerner and a Democrat, is determined to maintain the integrity of the Constitution, and does so admirably as the novel unfolds, playing North, South, and Great Britain off against one another while leading glorious cavalry charges at propitious moments. As order breaks down in the Northern cities, and abolitionists are shipped off to Liberia or humiliated and executed for their agitations, a strongman emerges, General Ruffleton, who ultimately connives and murders his way to becoming Lord Protector of the United States, a position he maintains through fear and the guillotine. Although initially allied to the North to ensure that neither side attains a clear advantage, President Randolph eventually throws the full weight of his government and military genius behind the South. After an army of slaves turns coat on the North to fight for the South, Ruffleton is forced to flee and is heard from no more. The Constitution is restored, and the "Reign of Terror" is ended.[8]

Edmund Ruffin chose a different literary path for his novel, which he wrote as a series of letters to the *London Times* from their correspondent in the United States. *Anticipations of the Future* commences in the immediate aftermath of William Seward's election to the presidency in 1864. Seward succeeds Abraham Lincoln, whom Ruffin added as the first Republican president after Lincoln unexpectedly secured the 1860 nomination. In Ruffin's alternate future, during the 1860s, first under Lincoln and then Seward, the abolitionist Congress continues to attack the South and its institutions, as they had since 1846. This theme is common to all three works—legislative indifference, executive tyranny, electoral manipulation, and so forth. In December 1867, unable to take any more, the states of the Deep South secede, followed shortly thereafter by the Upper South after Seward's army crosses into Virginia.

To this point, Ruffin's imagined political machinations of the next decade do not seem far-fetched, but after the war commences, his fevered hatred of the North takes hold and the novel degenerates into an orgy of bloodshed, perpetrated in the first instance by an interracial army under the command of one of John Brown's sons, Owen. Ultimately, this force is betrayed by the loyal slaves of Kentucky they sought to free, Owen Brown is hung along with every one of his surviving officers, and not a single white member of the expedition survives. In Maryland, a similar attempt to incite slave revolt ends the same way, with loyal slaves hewing to their masters. Instead of the corpse of John Brown being hoisted to another gallows, as is symbolically the case with his son, this time the centerpiece of the mass hangings that follow is William Lloyd Garrison himself. The end of the war comes in October 1868, as the newly seceded West joins with the South to vanquish the Northern foe. The defeated North regresses to a state of chaos, with prophetic riots in the streets of New York, along with Philadelphia and Boston, all three cities destroyed in flames. The South, although bruised and bloodied, emerges victorious.

Of the three, we know the most about the last, *Anticipations of the Future,* because of Edmund Ruffin's voluminous diary and the scholarship associated with it. According to one of Ruffin's earliest modern biographers, Avery Craven, *Anticipations* was "a glorious picture of ruin turned to prosperity; of a people suffering because they had delayed taking steps which in the end proved to be necessary; of a majority, drunk with power, blundering forward to ruin and forcing a minority to defend its superior social-economic system; and in the end, of urban-industrial things bowing before the superior merits of agriculture."[9] Yet this is in fact not what the modern historian takes away from *Anticipations* or, indeed, *The Partisan Leader* and *Wild Southern Scenes.* If we may steal Craven's formulation here, the real Confederacy, of which the visions of Tucker, Jones, and Ruffin were imaginary forebears, was an inglorious picture of white planter prosperity turned to ruin; of a people suffering because they had delayed taking steps that in the end proved to be necessary—the abolition of slavery, for example; of a white majority in the South, drunk with power, blundering forward to military, political, and economic ruin; and, in the end, of agricultural things bowing down before the superior merits of the urban-industrial system.

Fred Hobson, writing in the *Southern Literary Journal* in 1977, and then expanding his analysis in the 1983 book, *Tell about the South,* places Ruffin's solitary fictional adventure at the intersection of his antebellum Southern nationalism and his experience of personal tragedy in the decades before the Civil War. As *Anticipations* clearly demonstrates in its myriad scenes of Northern death, devastation, and ruin, Ruffin nursed hatred toward the Damn Yankees that Judge Tucker and James B. Jones could not come close to matching. As Hobson puts it, "The tension between North and South began to grow most heated just as Ruffin came to experience a void in his own life that he could fill from nothing within himself."[10] He had lost his mother when he was young, three of his children died in infancy, his wife died in her prime in 1846, and in 1855, three of Ruffin's surviving daughters died unexpectedly. As he wrote in his diary in October 1859, "If I had died five years ago, how much of unhappiness would have been escaped!"[11] By 1865, when he died, Ruffin had lost two more daughters, a son and grandson dead in Confederate gray, and both of his plantations ransacked and burned by Union forces, with the 1862 burning of his home, Beechwood, memorialized on the cover of *Harper's Weekly.*[12]

For Hobson, while Ruffin was already "a committed Southern nationalist" before the mid-1850s, "it is undeniable that his need to write voluminously . . . was greatly motivated by the emptiness and misery which he found in his own life." Accordingly, *Anticipations* is where Ruffin— for the one time in his literary career—achieved a "freedom" from the restraints of "an editor and . . . the essay form," which allowed him to express "his dream, his hopes, and his total identification with the Southern cause" to a greater extent than "anything else he ever published."[13] The most famous statement of Ruffin's creed, of course, comes in the final entry in his extensive diary, written on the day he committed suicide, Saturday, June 17, 1865, and repeated in the concurrent letter of instruction he wrote to his son Edmund Jr. concerning the disposition of his effects. In his final sentences, incongruously just after he broke off another screed against Northerners to bequeath a watch to his grandson, Ruffin wrote, "And now, with my last writing & utterance, & with what will be near to my last breath, I here repeat, & would willingly proclaim, my unmitigated hatred to Yankee rule—to all political, social, & business connection with Yankees, & to the perfidious, malignant, & vile Yankee race."[14] For Ruffin the specter of the Demon Yankee was very real and the coming of his victory unbearable.

Edmund Ruffin is the prototypical personification of the Southern fire-eater and Confederate loyalist, stoking his hatred of the opposing race and nation until quite literally the moment at which he pulled the trigger to end his life. He is therefore at one end of the spectrum of the imagined Confederacy. Tucker and Jones, in contrast, are much further toward the middle. Jones, while a committed pro-Southern activist and editor, who fled Philadelphia in April 1861 and served honorably as a clerk in the Confederate War Department, was also a somewhat detached observer of the war around him. In distinct contrast to Ruffin, the last words of Jones's diary condemn the assassination of President Lincoln as "a dastardly act—surely the act of a madman."[15] One does not hear echoes of Ruffin in that reasonable statement. Jones is also the only one of the three who maintains the power of the federal government in his narrative, albeit allied to the seceded South. Where for Tucker and Ruffin the Union (as usurper of constitutional rights) is the problem, for Jones, the Union (as guarantor of constitutional rights) turns out to be part of the solution.

In *Tell about the South*, Fred Hobson explicitly compares Tucker and Ruffin: "Tucker's novel . . . lacks the intensity, the repeated scenes of death and destruction, and the unrestrained glee at Yankee misfortune which characterize *Anticipations of the Future*. Sir Walter Scott, rather than some private demon, was the force behind *The Partisan Leader*."[16] Ruffin himself, rereading *The Partisan Leader* in October 1864 for the first time in almost thirty years, noted in his diary: "I have been much more of a true prophet than the author of the 'Partisan Leader.' Yet he has, at last, received great praise on this score, & my book & its predictions, & the lessons designed to be taught through these hazarded & unreliable anticipated incidents, have met with notice from very few readers, & total disregard & neglect from the reading public. Possibly, some thirty years hence, my turn to be noticed may arrive."[17]

Ruffin was uniquely placed as an observer here because he wrote in his diary in minimal detail about both *Wild Southern Scenes* (February 1860) and *The Partisan Leader* (October 1864). In fact, it was his derision toward the former that encouraged him to write *Anticipations* in the first place. Writing on February 26, 1860, Ruffin reported, "Finished reading 'Wild Scenes of the South,' a very foolish book, which I regret having bought, or spent time in reading. But the subject promised something, & the idea might be carried out to good purpose. It is a *prospective* narrative of the supposed incidents & results of a separation of the Union. But the writer, I think, shows little sagacity in his conceptions of future political consequences & events, or of genius to contrive a natural & interesting narrative of fiction."[18] Ruffin, the South Carolina radical fire-eater, had little time for the predictions of Jones, the border state middling secessionist, or indeed those of Tucker, the Virginian nullifier. For Ruffin, who has come down to posterity as the archetypal, tragic figure of secession, blood and fire was in the future. In many ways he welcomed that development, at the same time that he feared its consequences.

It would be an oversimplification to assume that there were no differences among *The Partisan Leader, Wild Southern Scenes,* and *Anticipations of the Future.* Each was a product of its time and place, and each the result of the literary and political sensibilities and purposes of its respective author. Each bears the hallmarks of being written in haste, as all three authors hoped to influence imminent elections. Each is relatively formulaic and uninspiring, indeed often tending toward being overwrought and melodramatic. But a modern reader, when placing them next to one another, can discern the skeletal structure of an antebellum imagined Confederacy. Most compellingly, perhaps, this structure offers significant similarities with the vision of the imagined Confederacy that politicians, journalists, and authors would lay out in the midst of the struggle for Southern self-determination.

The first element of the imagined Confederacy was the trope of the Worthy Southron in counterpoint to the Demon Yankee. The former was attached to place, character, and family; the latter to alien rootlessness and selfish ambition. The South itself appears almost as a character in this portrayal. *The Partisan Leader* displays this tendency most acutely. As the novel opens, we find Arthur Trevor, the younger brother of the hero, Douglas, riding through the foothills of the Blue Ridge Mountains in search of the partisans led by his brother. Instead of signs and countersigns to identify allies, the partisans subscribe to what we might call the mysticism of "Old Virginia." The younger Trevor tells Christian Witt that he did not need a sign, because he knew they were for Virginia: "'I knew it by the place where I find you. I heard it in *your voice;* I saw it in *their eyes;* and I felt it in *my heart.*'" In fact, we come to find out that one difference between Douglas Trevor and his Van Burenite elder brother, Owen, is that Douglas had been "infected" with Virginianism during a winter spent at home.[19] In Tucker's conception, Virginia was a place that got under the skin, that infected the very soul of the individual. In essence, place sets the table for everything else: place (the soil and terrain) gives Virginia her particular economic institutions and practices, notably slave-based agrarianism. Therefore, white Virginians could not help but be opposed to the manufacturing-led, tariff-based tyranny of the Van Burenites.

We can see a similar notion of place as destiny at work in *Wild Southern Scenes*. General Crook of Alabama, although at that point opposed to President Randolph, acknowledges of him that "he is Southern by birth, and cannot be Northern by inclination or interest." Randolph is a proper Southern gentleman of honor and integrity, a counterpoint perhaps to Tucker's Owen Trevor, who is weak and easily swayed by the tyrant Van Buren. Place must work in concert with character in order to achieve the desired result. Interestingly, Jones, though in every other aspect geographically accurate to the real United States, refers to the capital city of the Union from the very first page as "the Federal City." Perhaps the name of that "Worthy Southron" George Washington should not be sullied in association with federal power, especially as a key episode in the narrative is the burning of Monticello by the Royal Navy, then allied to the tyrant Ruffleton.[20]

Ruffin, the last of the three to write, and the one most determined to produce a particular, real-world outcome, spends a good portion of his epistolary narrative bemoaning the reluctance of the Worthy Southron to act; or, to put it another way, the reluctance of the Southron to be Worthy in the first place. In this story, the minor trespasses of the one-term Lincoln administration give way to the much more significant abuses of the Seward administration. All the while, Southerners were appeased enough with words and monies so as to keep them quiescent in their own subjugation. No "overt act"—a phrase very much in the currency of the day—was precipitated and so no casus belli presented itself.[21] In Ruffin's opinion, the South's "trusted leaders were . . . corrupted by their own ambition and greediness for the presidential power—and so were induced to work secretly to thwart the . . . objects of their followers, and to palliate northern wrongs to their section and to their principles."

By 1866, repeated Southern bluster and inaction has convinced the rapacious Northerners that the South is all words and has no stomach for action. For Ruffin, this was the danger of compromise: "For nothing that they [the South] can plan, or threaten, will be believed . . . until actual and important deeds shall take the place of violent and boastful words."[22] This, then, is Ruffin's call to action for the Worthy Southron: to eschew fine words and deliberation, and to take action against the insidious tides of Northern usurpation. The character of the Worthy Southron is being tested, and Ruffin is its self-appointed guardian.

The trajectory of these three works in real time is interesting. For Tucker in the 1830s, the Worthy Southron was something mutable that could be influenced by external stimuli and was protected by the temporary inoculation of Southern soil and character. For the relatively moderate Jones in the immediate prewar period, Southernism had hardened, become immutable, no longer susceptible to the blandishments of Northern corruption. But for the radical Ruffin, on the cusp of the secession crisis, the Worthy Southron was under assault from within and needed to have his backbone stiffened so that the inevitable conflict could be recognized and embraced. Time and political vantage points, therefore, had a considerable effect on the portrayal of the Worthy Southron. For Tucker, the path of the Worthy Southron was but one of several, while for Jones and Ruffin it was the only one for the Southerner but not necessarily one with an inevitable result, as Ruffin's chiding demonstrates.

In addition to the destiny of place and character, family is vital to these authors' conceptions of the Southern self and Northern other but expressed in more variegated ways than place.[23] Again, this trope is most acutely displayed in *The Partisan Leader*. In the first instance, the Trevor family itself is split, with Hugh and Bernard Trevor, brothers and parents of the main protagonists of the novel, divided on the question of Union. Hugh, the elder brother and father of Douglas, has an honest disagreement with Bernard, father of Delia, the principal female character and love interest of Douglas, about the fidelity owed to the national government. This is not a debate about Van Buren, whom they both abhor, but about the value of loyalty—in short, does duty to the forms of government outweigh duty to the principles of government? Not only a debate within one family, this is a debate writ large within the United States as a kin community, both in 1836, when the novel was written, and in 1860, when some of its predictions came to pass. Bernard Trevor, speaking to his nephew Douglas, sets this dichotomy precisely: "What if your views of the constitution had shown you that the acts of the Government were violations of the constitution, and that the men denounced . . . as traitors were its most steady supporters. What duty would your oath have prescribed in that case? Would you support the constitution by taking part with those who trampled it under foot, against those who upheld it as long as there was hope?'" Earlier in their discussions, Bernard had urged Douglas to consider a situation where his duty to his father would conflict with his duty as a soldier, if his father were in rebellion against the central government, thus subtly leading Douglas to the eventual conclusion that Virginia, acting in this sense as a meta-father-figure, trumped Van Buren and the United States.[24] Here, the Worthy Southron has to debate the choice he must make between Constitution and Union, if loyalty to both is impossible.

In Jones's work, President Randolph exemplifies the progression of this dichotomy. A Southerner by birth and inclination, he is also the sworn defender of the U.S. Constitution and the federal order, and as a Worthy Southron, his oath and duty are a tangible and indivisible part of his existence. In his speech to the remaining members of Congress after that body's dissolution, Randolph clearly states his position:

> I still regard the Federal Constitution as the paramount authority. I have sworn to defend it—*and I do not doubt my ability to do so.* I could not prevent a dissolution of Congress. . . . But what then? Cannot government exist in the absence of Congress? Has it not done so, at least one half of the time, since its creation? . . . Therefore, I beg that it may be made known to the Quixotic Disunionists, North and South, that the Federal Government does not intend to succumb until its abandonment is decreed by the people.[25]

Here, instead of the president's betraying the Constitution, as was the case with Tucker's Van Buren, elements within the states had betrayed it instead, and it was the responsibility of the loyal Southern president to restore order in the face of fanaticism and ambition. Jones never really deals with the fact that it was Southern congressmen who precipitated the schism, as the South is redeemed through the military heroics of their soldiers, ably led by Generals Crook and Blount. In this telling, it is loyal sons of the South who hew to the Federal Union and—most important—the Constitution. As we have seen, an image of that document occupied a venerated place in Southern political life.[26] For Tucker and Ruffin, the Union—in this case coded as Northern usurper of constitutional rights—had to be defeated in order to preserve the Constitution; but for Jones, the Union—coded as Southern defender of constitutional rights—had to be sustained in order to achieve the same end. It is important, however, to recognize that the Union Jones was preserving was led by a Worthy Southron who sought to protect the Constitution, and was firmly opposed to the Demon Yankees who sought to usurp it.

If the Confederate Constitution was the roof under which a new nationalism would be erected, then it is clear that some of the building blocks of those nationalist walls already existed when South Carolina seceded in December 1861. As demonstrated here, several white Southern authors were already in the process of imagining a future in which the South would be independent and would have to defend that independence from a North that simply would not let them go in peace and friendship. This latter point is key because, to the extent that white Southerners were American nationalists before the coming of the Civil War—and it seems clear that many of them were—they understood the nation as they understood their more local communities, as part of an extended kinship group. Thus, at a visceral level, Southerners and Northerners were family. And when family betrays you, as Southerners believed of the North, the hurt cuts all the deeper. Confederates saw themselves as Americans, as part of an American family predicated on freedom, liberty, and republicanism. As Confederate Americans, they believed that they were protecting those virtues from Northern depredations.

We see this phenomenon clearly in *The Partisan Leader*, for the honest debate between Hugh and Bernard Trevor on the value of principle is constantly distorted by the interference of the North—embodied in President Van Buren. Owen Trevor, the eldest son of Hugh, has been flattered and seduced into Van Burenism and away from filial and hereditary loyalty, and Douglas's attempts to wrestle with the intellectual dilemmas just posed are greatly complicated by the president's attempts—at the behest of the villainous Judge Baker and his son—to have Douglas court-martialed for some convoluted offense he gave to the latter. In fact, Douglas's offense was in protecting the public reputation of his cousin Delia, a goal for which he was willing to sacrifice his career and perhaps even his life. In stark contrast, Owen Trevor is so debased from the ideal of a Worthy Southron that at the climactic moment of the book, he breaks his parole, kidnaps his brother, delivers him to the certain injustice of the tyrant, and then reneges on an agreement to surrender the Lynchburg garrison to the partisans.[27] He is killed in the ensuing battle, and Tucker spends not a word mourning his passing.

For Jones, character appears much more static and immutable. President Randolph is the Worthy Southron and cannot be anything else, while General Ruffleton is the Demon Yankee and only pretends to be other in order to grease his eventual bloody ascension to power. Jones's first description of Randolph is effusive in its praise:

> Of middle stature, and erect frame—an eye that seemed to penetrate the thoughts of all—a commanding mien, and features indicating firmness of purpose and decision of character, no one living, perhaps, was better qualified to inspire the respect and win the confidence of mankind. Vigilant and indefatigable in incessant labors—endowed by his Creator with the highest gifts of genius, and his mind improved by the attainment of every species of knowledge imparted by books, or derived from association with the best intellects of his country.

This is the model of a man who should be president—distinguished, respected, learned, purposeful, and commanding, and so worthy in every respect. General Ruffleton, by contrast, is known not by his noble appearance but by his ignoble deeds. In his first appearance in the novel, we see him accosting Edith Langdon in an effort to gain leverage over her father, the senator.[28] Yet this is the smallest of Ruffleton's myriad crimes, including scheming with the British, using foreign assassins to further his cause, erecting guillotines in the streets of Northern cities to execute his opponents, overthrowing the ostensibly legitimate government of the Northern Confederacy, installing himself as a Cromwellian Lord Protector, and ultimately conspiring to return North America to the British Crown with himself installed as a Prince of the Realm. Fanciful though these crimes may be, or even "foolish" or "wretchedly carried out" by the author, as Ruffin would have it, they are nonetheless indicative of the lack of character of the Demon Yankee.[29]

For Ruffin, the "overt act" previously mentioned finally comes to pass in December 1867, when six Northern states—New York, Ohio, Minnesota, Kansas, California, and Michigan—all agree to split themselves in two, so that six new abolitionist states may be formed. Thought to be the brainchild of President Seward, this "constitutional coup d'état" is

the impetus for South Carolina to convene a Southern convention to discuss the issues, which results in the secession of the Deep South states
in January 1868. Again, echoing Tucker and Jones, Ruffin's Yankees are
known by their secretive and undemocratic machinations, in short by
their usurpations of the constitutional order. This trope of usurpation, of
an un-American indifference to republican principles, is a key theme in
all three of these works. As Ruffin's book continues, the states dither for
some months, but in the aftermath of the start of armed conflict on the
soil of Virginia, the remainder of the South secedes in June. The key to all
of this unrest, as is made clear as the novel progresses, is the radical and
unyielding fanaticism of New England, which is considered a parasitic
and malignant growth on the American body politic. As the novel ends,
with New England isolated, Ruffin predicts that, "should New England
be left alone, thenceforward its influence for evil on the southern states
will be of as little effect, and its political and economical position scarcely
superior, to those conditions of the present republic of Hayti."[30] In this
telling, the defects of character inherent to the Demon Yankee are such
that the only recourse for honest men is to isolate the source as though it
were carrying a contagion.

Ruffin's flights of rhetorical fancy are a product of his times, just as *The
Partisan Leader* is a product of its times—the mid–1830s In the aftermath of the Nullification Crisis, and given his own personal proclivities
as "a States Rights Man," Tucker was far more interested in the relationship between the states as family than are his literary descendants.[31]
The whole narrative thrust of *The Partisan Leader* revolves around the
question of whether Virginia will secede—and in fact whether she will
be able to secede—to join her Southern brethren. Yet, they do not necessarily want her. After Bernard and Douglas flee to North Carolina, they
are party to a tavern conversation among a shopkeeper, a planter, and
a wagoner. Mr. Hobson, the planter, is particularly leery of "them high-
headed Roanoke planters," whom he blamed for handing the election to
Van Buren in 1848, and who now want to enjoy the benefits of the trade
agreement worked out between the Southern Confederacy and Great
Britain. In particular, he is concerned that Norfolk merchants will si-
phon off much of the trade advantage North Carolina was then enjoying
in tobacco. Douglas Trevor, overhearing this byplay, is disgusted at this
"sordid desire to monopolize" trade, but as so often happens in this novel,
Tucker moves on quickly, having introduced a point he is either unable or

unwilling to follow through to its conclusion.[32] Here, Tucker's Virginian-ism shines through clearly. It is, however, an open question as to whether Tucker was merely being elitist, or whether he truly saw the sort of nar-rowly conceived, crudely economic self-interest of Hobson to be against the best interests of Virginia and her position within a future Southern Confederacy.[33] In the real 1836 in which Tucker wrote, secession was a possibility of the vague future. In the real 1859 and 1860 in which Jones and Ruffin wrote, secession was a concrete likelihood assuming the elec-tion of 1860 went to the Republicans. Long dissertations about the value of states' rights versus confederation were therefore something of a lux-ury that Jones and Ruffin did not permit themselves.

Certainly, though, in the conceptions of all three authors, Northerners represented a clear and present danger to white Southern liberties. The Demon Yankee is heavily caricatured in these pages, but from the South-ern point of view, the pattern of Northern hypocrisy, sanctimony, and interference in Southern domestic institutions was quite real. Whether those same phenomena were historical and empirical is another matter altogether. Ideologies—of which nationalism is one—are at least partly creatures of the mind, and the mind requires neither historical nor em-pirical accuracy. Late antebellum Southerners, of which Jones and Ruffin are prime examples, were starting to conceive of a future in which they would need to resist by force the Demon Yankee and in which they would need to articulate and stand behind the rights of the Worthy Southron.

Although the Worthy Southron was more often than not implicitly male, nations are not genderless. There are enough counterexamples in these novels to imply that the distinctions of the Worthy Southron were not gender-exclusive. Both *The Partisan Leader* and *Wild Southern Scenes* have strong female characters who play central roles in the narra-tive, as adjuncts to men and in their own right. In *The Partisan Leader*, Delia Trevor is represented as in many respects the emblem of Southern womanhood, albeit a woman who is politically aware and astute enough to be an advisor to her father. She earns the romantic attention not only of the loyal Virginian Douglas Trevor, her cousin, but also the son of Van Buren's principal henchman, Judge Baker. Delia recognizes instantly the loathsome qualities of the son, Philip, as the supplicant of the lead-ing Demon Yankee himself, the president. As Tucker puts it, "When the manifest audacity of his pretensions led her to think of him as the supple slave of power, as one who had prostituted himself to the service of his

master, with an eagerness which condemned his zeal to be its own reward, her disgust increased to loathing, and her pride was kindled into
resentment."[34] Douglas is an independent man, possessed of his own integrity and opinions, and resolute enough to stand for them as necessary.
Philip Baker, on the other hand, is a creature, a wholly owned subsidiary
of another man, and thus not an acceptable match for the female Worthy
Southron.

Baker's public vilification of Delia after she rejects him is the impetus
for Douglas to defend her honor, and the reason he is delivered to the
hands of the tyrant by his own brother at the end of the novel. On the
penultimate page of the book, it is left to Delia to deliver the final judgment on Van Buren, as her uncle Hugh comes before him to plead for
Douglas's life: "The palace of a tyrant is a prison. There is no mercy here.
No hope for my noble husband. Save yourself. Return home while you
may, and leave me here to share his fate. Our friends *may* rescue us. They
WILL avenge us. But in that cold eye there is no relenting."[35] Although
she is indeed permitted to leave, the nobility of her offered sacrifice is the
note on which the novel ends.

Even more so than Tucker, Jones gave his readers strong female characters in Edith Langdon, Alice Randolph, and, to a lesser extent, Flora
Summers. These are characters capable of independent thought and
action, and are relied upon for such by the men in their lives, respectively, Henry Blount, President Randolph, and General Ruffleton. Even
here the tripartite symmetry of Jones's plot—Southern, Federal, and
Northern—is maintained. None of these women exemplifies the Worthy Southron in woman's garb more than Alice Randolph, who serves
as the female mirror to her father. Alice, in fact, becomes the president's
knight-protector, his so-called Knight of the Velvet Cap and leader of his
unit of bodyguards, the Blue Caps.[36] In that capacity, she quite literally
puts herself in harm's way to protect her father and the Constitution that
he represents. Alice is the protector of Monticello as it falls to the British and the defender of the president's Amherst Castle stronghold in the
Blue Ridge Mountains. She is, as her father says repeatedly, the marble to
his flesh and blood, the rock upon which the solidity of his character and
defense of the Constitution is based.[37]

If the juxtaposition of the Worthy Southron and Demon Yankee was
the first element of the imagined Confederacy shared by these authors,
then the Silent Slave was the second. In the imagined Confederacy, slaves

spoke not for themselves but in the service of their masters, and were therefore metaphorically silent. For Tucker, Jones, and Ruffin, as for later Confederate adherents, the dream of independence and liberty was based on a social and economic foundation of black labor. In *The Partisan Leader*, Tucker includes slaves in his conception of familial relations in Virginia. Given that Nat Turner's revolt had occurred just a few years before Tucker wrote his novel, it is interesting that he was perfectly ready to countenance the idea of a black man with a gun. Before he escaped to the Carolinas in advance of the Van Burenite army of observation, Bernard Trevor had used his faithful slaves—his Black Watch or *sidier dhu*—to capture a party of federal troops sent to arrest him.[38] According to the mysterious Mr. B—, "'They . . . are one integral part of the great black family, which, in all its branches, is united by similar ligaments to the great white family.'"[39] The "similar ligaments" mentioned are those of the fostering relationship of "mammy" and her children. Tucker deals with this issue in rapid-fire fashion, dispensing with the peculiar institution in the conventional way by asserting that the Yankee has "not the qualities which would enable them to comprehend the negro character . . . [their] disinterested devotion, . . . [and] unsophisticated heart."[40]

Slaves are less integral to *Wild Southern Scenes*, but at one pivotal moment they do swing the balance of power from the North to the South. As the Northern and Southern armies maneuver for advantage, a new threat emerges from the West. General Fell, a political adversary of President Randolph who believes that his old enemy is betraying the South and that he can better safeguard Southern interests by allying with Ruffleton, raises an army of 250,000 slaves in "the South-west" and marches to join forces with Ruffleton at the James River. The night before battle, the Southern/Federal commander, General Toler, is secretly approached by his former slave Scipio, now a captain in Fell's army. Scipio reports to his former master the general dissatisfaction in Fell's ranks and the intentions of the slaves to return home. The next morning, the slave army turns on Fell and so the war is ended. Toler even attempts to offer Scipio his freedom in return for this service, to which the faithful slave replies, "Now don't say that, Massa John. Don't say I shall hab my freedom, Massa John; I want to be wid you all your life, and I won't be free no how you can fix it." Immediately prior to this outburst, Toler had expressed the relationship between slave and master in terms highly reminiscent of the words of Tucker's Mr. B—: "Scipio, I know you love me. We were boys together, almost like brothers—and indeed the slave in the South is more like a member of his master's family than the free negro of the North is like a freeman."[41] Again, the Silent Slave—denied authentic voice and in service to the purposes of the white master class—is included in the great family of the South.

Perhaps the pivotal role of the Silent Slave in *Wild Southern Scenes*, given voice and yet voiceless at the same time, is in an exchange in a chapel between a nameless runaway slave and the British envoy, Lord Slysir. Slysir surprises the fugitive, who is in hiding, and promises that "the Northern people and the British will make a free man" of him. The slave indignantly replies that he is returning to Alabama, having "had 'nuff" of abolitionist promises. As he puts it before leaving, "I ran away in de under-ground railroad las year—and got sick od de Norf. Dey starbed me, and wouldn't give me physic when I was sick—and now dey's got a gulleting dat chops off people's heads!"[42] While this is a transitory moment in the novel, it does two things. In the fictional world, it speeds Lord Slysir's conviction that the Northern promise of black freedom is hollow and not welcomed by the slaves. In the real world, however, it concisely articulates the Southern fiction about black freedom in the North—a life of privation, suffering, and racism that is inferior to the Sambo-like image of the happy slave on the plantation. Whether knowledgeable Southerners actually believed this pabulum is debatable, but there is little doubt that they worked very hard to convince themselves, and the rest of the world, that it was true.

As noted in the brief narrative exposition of Ruffin's text earlier in the chapter, slaves are important objects in *Anticipations of the Future*. Given that this novel was written as a collection of letters, slaves in Ruffin's world are even more silent than usual, voiced as they are at third or fourth hand through the pen of a foreign newspaper correspondent. In common with Jones, Ruffin's slaves are mobilized by Northern abolitionists and yet ultimately refuse to fight for their own freedom, preferring the certain kindness of their masters to the uncertain mercies of those who would see them cast aside and left "free." Ruffin is more openly racist than his literary peers with respect, for example, to the supposed natural reluctance of African Americans to labor, yet even he acknowledges the expected martial utility of slaves, at least as laborers and artillerymen behind the lines. According to Ruffin, in these capacities the slaves "soon become as zealous partizans and as hostile in feeling to the northern enemy, as any citizens—and might well be relied upon as soldiers, unless incapacitated by their natural and constitutional cowardice."[43]

The most important service of the loyal Silent Slave in Ruffin's narrative, however, was to betray the intentions of his more susceptible peers who had been confused and beguiled into doing the bidding of abolitionists. Owen Brown's attempted slave insurrection in Kentucky, complete with the pikes made infamous by his father, is betrayed by a small band of slaves who desert him after enlisting precisely in order to be able to return home from Canada, to which they had previously run away. The fondest wish of these deserters is to return to slavery, indeed any slavery, "rather than to continue free and starving with cold and hunger at the North." A similar plot to raise the slaves in Maryland is betrayed by another deserter, who balked at the news that whites—including those dear to him among his master's family—were to be slaughtered as part of the rebellion.[44] Here, the fullest reign of the Haiti scenario is given voice: if given the opportunity, Northern abolitionists will whip up slave ignorance and superficial dissatisfaction with their stations into an orgy of violence and racial bloodshed. The Demon Yankee would attempt to spread the virus of his fanaticism across the South. For Ruffin, it seems, the fictional hope was that loyal slaves would betray these attempts, but the real-world hope was that secession and a Southern Confederacy would render these concerns moot. In either case, such incitements to slave violence are clearly coded as being outside the American political tradition to which these authors subscribed.

The third shared element of the imagined Confederacy, after the juxtaposition of Worthy Southron and Demon Yankee and the undergirding force of the Silent Slave, was the idea of Confederate Americanism. The notion that the seceded South was the true inheritor of the legacy of the American Revolution comes through most clearly in a reading of the history upon which these three novels purport to be based. In *The Partisan Leader*, Tucker is careful to represent a particular historical vision. Given his background as a jurist of some distinction and the son of a Revolutionary War veteran, it is striking to the modern reader the extent to which Tucker's story places Virginia in fictional 1849 in the position of the North American colonies in the real 1770s. The story starts out with a group of rifle-armed men "chiefly clad in half-dressed buck-skin," and includes at least one brief aside on the superiority of the rifle over the musket, echoing the tradition of the frontiersman's Kentucky rifle.

More centrally, Martin Van Buren is repeatedly described in monarchical terms, as "King Martin, the First," for example, or as one who had Owen Trevor "consecrated to the purple," or even in his own words as Douglas Trevor's "too partial sovereign." More than that, however, this homegrown King George III seems guilty of exactly the same crimes of which the colonials accused the original in the Declaration of Independence. Many of the specific charges laid against the British dealt with their interference in colonial self-government. Van Buren not only sends federal troops to meddle in Virginian elections but is also revealed to be hoping that the Virginia House of Burgesses, "this superfluous State Legislature, this absurd relic of *imperium in imperio*," will "abolish itself." As Van Buren muses, "We can then restore them all the benefits of real and efficient local legislation, by erecting these degraded sovereignties into what they ought always to have been—municipal corporations, exercising such powers as we choose to grant."[45] Other charges dealt with imperial interference in colonial justice, and we see here that Van Buren has convened his own Star Chamber, an extra-constitutional Court of High Commission chaired by the mercenary Judge Baker and intended to deal with the president's enemies outside the inconvenient channels of due process and defendants' rights. Finally, of course, George III was accused of having "kept among us, in times of peace, Standing Armies without the Consent of our legislatures." Van Buren's "army of observation" in Virginia serves as an exact analogy.[46]

While we may infer from Tucker's background and interests that he was moved by the comparisons of Van Burenite tyranny to British oppression in the late colonial period, the comparison is never explicitly drawn by the author. While we can see *The Partisan Leader* as a justification of revolution, in the Lockean tradition, we must assume that Tucker expected his audience to be moved by the familiar, by the experiences learned from parents and grandparents and the lessons taught by the repeated public and private commemorations of the Revolution.[47] History works beneath the surface of this narrative, but it works on the expected audience just as profoundly as do Tucker's evocations of place and family. Tucker, therefore, laid out for his readers sufficient allusions for them to properly understand that Van Buren's actions were manifestly un-American, while the Virginian heroes of the piece were the true Americans.

Similarly, in *Wild Southern Scenes*, we might expect that readers would be attuned to the curious mélange of Puritan excesses during the

English Civil War, British monarchical tyranny during the American Revolution, and French republican bloodletting presented by Jones as the natural state of the unrestrained North. President Randolph and the Southern Confederacy were clearly coded as American, while General Ruffleton and his Northern allies appear as foreign and un-American, both in place and action. Besides Ruffleton's elevation as Lord Protector in the Cromwellian sense, he goes from the "Protector" to the "Lord Protector" to "his Highness" and finally to "his Royal Highness" as his delusions of grandeur become less and less restrained. Significantly, Ruffleton never insists on those titles; instead, they are coined by his toadies and sycophants.[48] So, we see the lack of American republican backbone on the part of Northerners.

Ruffleton's reliance on British aid marks him out as a Tory of the Revolutionary era, but his reliance on the French guillotine to maintain "order" in the North marks him out as going far beyond what even Tories were capable of—although of course the excesses of the French Revolution occurred after the American Revolution had concluded. Jones jokingly has his characters refer to the guillotine as "the Republican platform," thus making the connection to real-world politics apparent to his readers. The height of Ruffleton's Francophile Toryism comes when we discover that his stalwart ally, the Reverend Blood, has been mistakenly guillotined after a clerk transposed Blood's name with that of the man he accused on the death warrant.[49] Ruffleton's functionary, Windvane, admits to signing the warrant without reading it, thus condemning Blood to his ironic fate. Summary justice, carried out casually, would not have impressed Jones's readers as an American tradition; quite the opposite in fact.

While readers might justifiably condemn Ruffleton's unrestrained tyranny, they would have had to acknowledge that he was following the abolitionist mob as much as he was leading it. Toward the start of the novel, after Senator Langdon is captured in Philadelphia, he is displayed in a cage and forced to eat for the amusement of the crowd, as though he were a carnival sideshow act. Yet his treatment is mild compared to that meted out by the Reverend Mr. Fire, condemned as "an infernal Puritan" by Jack Bim. As the avatar of the mob, Fire imprisons journalists, lawyers, publishers, and others in cages and forces them to endure humiliating and ridiculous punishments for the edification of the unwashed. For example, a Southern fire-eater is caged with "a jackass eating hay" and forced to brush "the flies from its ears, with his handkerchief," all the while "cursing the ass . . . and the mob."⁵⁰ This scene, reminiscent almost of the Roman circus, serves as clear notice that on one side is the rule of law (and, of course, the rule of constitutional as well as statute law), and on the other is the rule of the demagogue and the unrestrained mob. One is American, the other is not. By their actions, and the actions of their opponents, the nature of Confederate Americans are known.

Ruffin's choices with respect to the structure of his novel leave the least room for the sorts of scenes that make up the sinews of Confederate Americanism in the works of Tucker and Jones. Yet, there is no doubt that Ruffin's Seward shares a commonality with Tucker's Van Buren and Jones's Ruffleton. Each is driven by the allure of personal ambition and aggrandizement, and each has forsaken whatever loyalty to the Constitution they may once have felt. Each uses abolitionism as a mere tool, and none really has any authentic or heartfelt stake in ending the institution of slavery. Their quest to usurp the Constitution and subjugate the South is simply about the exercise of their personal power and their individual predilections toward tyranny, autocracy, and dictatorship. Each is a melodramatic villain, and each is defeated—or at least we assume Van Buren would have been had Tucker finished his story—by a combination of overarching, stalwart Southern opposition and a failure to convince their sectional peers that, in the end, the conflict was worth the effort. Ruffin's Seward, for example, discovers too late that with the exception of "fanatical abolitionists," no Northern "volunteers offered their services for distant localities, and for invasion of the South." Contrast that with the willingness of Southerners to fight to defend their country against Northern invasion.⁵¹ True Americans, it seems—Confederate Americans in this case—allow others to live in peace but are stirred to action when threatened.

It is unlikely that these novels—with the possible exception of *The Partisan Leader*—were widely read during the secession crisis. Certainly, Ruffin did not believe he had reached a wide audience.⁵² Yet, it is a fair assessment to say that the resonances between these works and the later elements of wartime Confederate nationalism suggest that they were reflective of the zeitgeist of an imagined Confederacy. What makes *The Partisan Leader* especially interesting in that respect is its republication in both the North and South as the secession crisis and war unfolded. *The Partisan Leader* was first published in 1836 to relatively modest acclaim.[53] But it was rediscovered by both sides early in the Civil War, being first reprinted in New York in 1861 and then in Richmond in 1862.[54] As both reprint editions contain brief introductions that sought to situate the work in the broader context of the war, it is possible to lay Northern and Southern conceptions of this work alongside each other. Interestingly, two of the three modern reprint editions—the Gregg Press's 1968 facsimile and Hugh Holman's 1971 North Carolina edition—reprinted the "Explanatory Introduction" from the 1862 New York edition, while the third modern version—Carl Bridenbaugh's 1933 Knopf edition—reprinted neither of the 1860s introductions. So the Southern version, with its introduction by the Reverend Thomas A. Ware, has long been available only in Rare Book Rooms, in microfilm form, or since 1999 on the Web via the University of North Carolina's *Documenting the American South* project.[55]

For the anonymous author of the introduction to the 1861 Rudd and Carleton New York edition, Tucker's work was prima facie evidence that "our country is suffering from the effects of a conspiracy unparalleled in the history of mankind," that "the fratricidal contest into which our country has been led is not a thing of chance, but of deliberate design." According to this version of the past, after the defeat of nullification in the early 1830s, Southern secessionists successfully infiltrated and came to dominate the Democratic Party, leading it to pursue aims "purely Southern and sectional," including the annexation of Texas, the Mexican War, and the "evil enginery of Lecomptonism." Once the democracy had served its purposes, it was "ruthlessly rent . . . asunder." For this commentator, Beverley Tucker had served as the ideologue of the coming revolution, the man with the blueprint for secession and war, the dark visionary who had foretold "nearly every important point of the great conspiracy" and for whom "the Jeff. Davises, Yanceys, Pryors, Rhetts, Letchers, etc." had "done little else than servilely to follow out the programme sketched for them in this remarkable book." The commentator seems to willfully miss Tucker's focus on Northern economic oppression as the root cause of secession, and instead notes that Tucker eschewed abolitionism as a cause. Therefore, "Tucker seems to have been unable to make out the semblance of a good case" for secession as anything other than a tautological necessity.[56]

In at least one way, Rev. Thomas Ware, writing to introduce the

1862 West and Johnson Richmond edition, agreed with his anonymous Northern counterpart—Tucker had "substantially foretold the great leading features of the history" of the past quarter-century. For Ware, however, and apparently for the late Judge Tucker as well, who was quoted through an acquaintance in Ware's introduction, those "leading features" were the product of defects in the "Yankee character," defects that Ware did not feel the need to explicate, as presumably being well-known to his audience.[57] In fact, Ware seems to take for granted that his audience did not need to be led point by point through Tucker's prescience, and that his republication of the work—and he never acknowledged that Rudd and Carleton had beaten him to it—"would tend to illustrate the necessity of our position, to vindicate the justice of our cause, and to intensify Southern patriotism."[58]

Ware actually devoted a considerable portion of his introduction to a trip he had made to Patrick County, Virginia, the reputed location of events foretold in *The Partisan Leader*. In the course of the visit, he had met one Saunders Witt, a local character of some reputation who had featured (as Christian Witt) in the opening scene of the novel, and who was related as recalling Judge Tucker's pilgrimage to the region in the mid-1820s. Ware seems to recognize, as Tucker had, the importance of place, family, and history in this conception of Southern identity. In his conversation with Mr. Witt, Ware notes,

> I could but regard him with a kind of romantic veneration, as a *real* character in a great prophetic story, whose thrilling events have been essentially fulfilled, and in the realization of which, evincing the same characteristics and endorsing the same sentiments which it was supposed he would maintain. All that I learned from his neighbors tended but to show that precisely such circumstances as those supposed would probably have developed precisely such a character as he is presumed to have sustained.[59]

What is interesting here, of course, is that both Ware and his anonymous Northern counterpart saw Tucker's conception of Southern character and motivations as being essentially unchanged, remaining trapped at the point of nullification in the 1830s, without any awareness of how the intervening quarter-century had radicalized both sections and split them further and further apart as the years wore on—a process of radicalization that we see quite clearly when we lay the relative gentility and possibility for redemption of *The Partisan Leader* against the no-compromise extremism in defense of liberty extant in *Anticipations of the Future.* Thomas Ware, and for that matter Saunders Witt, wanted to believe that not only could Tucker's narrative have come to pass but that it would come to pass, that Southerners would act in the ways that Tucker had prescribed for them in the 1830s, and that as a consequence they would emerge from the war victorious. The Northern commentator would not have endorsed such a conclusion, but he certainly seemed to agree that Southerners had acted in the manner Tucker described in the intervening period.

This then is a debate about "character," a word mentioned explicitly by Ware in the Richmond edition and implied throughout the introduction to the New York edition. For the former, this was about the perfidy of the Demon Yankee, or the "Yankee character": his propensity to lie and dissemble, to bribe and defame honorable men, and to interfere in those matters that were none of his concern. For the latter, much the same can be said, except about the Southerner. The Southerner worked in the dark to undermine the Union, without a clear intellectual rationale for doing so other than that he could. The Southerner infiltrated politics—as though he were in some way exterior to the American body politic—and sought to bring about his nefarious ends through shadowy, underhanded machinations. In both cases, there is at least an implied dichotomy that one side is honorable and open, working in the public arena to engage in an honest debate about policy, while the other is dishonorable and furtive, working behind the scenes to bring their enemies down. But a debate about character is also a debate about identity, about what it means to be American. In both cases, as indeed in the case of Tucker, Jones, and Ruffin themselves, identity is not just something internally imagined; it is also a manifestation of the way one is imagined in and by the world, and the way that one imagines that world. The Southern identity of Tucker, Jones, and Ruffin, as indeed is the case for the nascent Confederate identity that emerged after the publication of their novels, is one of innocence opposed to Yankee guilt, gentility opposed to Yankee barbarism, reason opposed to Yankee caprice, and liberty and democracy opposed to Yankee tyranny and crypto-monarchism. These ideas were at the heart of the Confederate imagined community.

Literature does not make nationalism in and of itself, but it can express manifestations of the nationalist zeitgeist. If, as we have seen, the

Confederate Constitution offered a roof under which nationalism could develop, then literature, perhaps, helps furnish the rooms beneath that roof. The literature discussed in this chapter was an early and somewhat limited attempt to rhetorically manifest a Confederate future, but it contained within it seeds that could bloom once the independent Southern future of which Tucker, Jones, and Ruffin wrote came into being.

3

"The Pledge of a Nation That's Dead and Gone"

The Confederate Nation on the Face of Money

Representing nothing on God's earth now
And naught in the waters below it,
The pledge of a nation that's dead and gone
Keep it, dear friend, and show it
Show it to those who will lend an ear
To the tale that this paper can tell
Of liberty born of the patriot's dream,
Of a storm-cradled nation that fell

SIDNEY ALROY JONAS,
"The Lost Cause" (June 2, 1865)

Any nation must meet a variety of conditions before its self-determination can be fully realized. We have discussed to this point the need for a national frame of government—in the American tradition enshrined in a written Constitution—as well as a national literature, and we will discuss the need for settled territoriality and military defense, those areas in which the Confederacy most signally failed. A fully realized nation, however, also requires a stable national economy and monetary system. In that respect as well, the Confederate American experience was problematic. The burdens of war pressed hard on the civilian populations of the Confederate states, and bread riots shook Southern cities, beginning at the end of 1862 in Greenville, Alabama, and spreading into Georgia, South Carolina, North Carolina, Virginia, and even Texas through the subsequent months.[1] Prices of household goods started to rise exponentially, and wages were by no means keeping pace.[2] Fissures started to appear as well in Confederate politics, as Vice President Alexander Stephens "was spending less and less of his time presiding over the Senate and more and more time at home in Georgia condemning President Davis's alleged usurpations of power in general and those that limited the state's rights of Georgia in particular."[3]

Certainly, Confederate economics were not a positive factor in the quest for independence and nationhood. As with so much else related to wartime Confederate nationalism, however, it is important to look past the failures and try to discern what was intended, rather than what was achieved. On the face of their Treasury notes—analogous to a certain extent to modern banknotes—purveyors of Confederate nationalism depicted a changing image of their new nation, one that shifted as the war progressed from antebellum visions of an agrarian and peaceful Worthy Southron accompanied by the faithful Silent Slave, to a bellum vision of a more martial and distinctively Southern Confederate American in defense of one's cause and nation. The change over time seen in this venue delineates a portion of the progression of the imagined Confederacy from its antecedents to its wartime form.

Reviewing the history of Confederate currency and reading them as a unified text, several conclusions are immediately apparent. In particular, even casual observation indicates that the iconographic tone of banknote designs changed dramatically with the fifth congressional issue of currency in October 1862. Prior to that time, the dominant images on banknotes suggested a collection of attributes that connect under the heading of the virtues of the Worthy Southron and an antebellum vision of Confederate Americanism. Under this umbrella are three subcategories: Classical and Allegorical Allusions, Commercial Agriculture, and American History.[4] This iconographic trend points to the conclusion that the South was a peaceful agrarian nation with strong roots in the traditional American virtues—liberty, justice, and commerce. These last ideas are significant, first because Southern virtues were often buttressed with identifiably American images, and second because the images of agriculture depicted tend to be commercial in nature.[5] This is not something we habitually associate with the Southern plantation system, as it is easy to focus on the inequities of slavery and the paternalistic overtones of pro-slavery rhetoric and forget that planters were in business to make money.

As Lacy K. Ford Jr. noted in his seminal work, *Origins of Southern Radicalism,* Southern agriculture was basically profitable, and planters were rational economic investors who diversified their holdings into commerce and industry as well as slavery.[6] This coincides with the image of the South and the Confederacy that emerged in the currency issues of 1861 and 1862, but challenges the historiographical school that argue that planters were quasifeudal seigneurs locked in a premodern economic system. Such a debate is beyond our scope, but we must concede that the prevalence of railway trains, ships, sailors, and the allegorical figures of Commerce and Moneta suggest the sort of South for which James De Bow agitated on the pages of his *De Bow's Review* rather than the South of the more genteel *Southern Literary Messenger*.[7]

More than anyone else, Eric Helleiner has theorized about the linkages between what he refers to as "territorial currencies" and national identity. For Helleiner, the issue of currency was deeply relevant to nineteenth-century "nationalist policymakers":

> At the level of iconography and naming, policy makers recognized that exclusive and standardized coins and notes might provide an effective vehicle for their project of constructing and bolstering a sense of collective tradition and memory. By reducing transaction costs within the nation, a territorial currency was also seen to facilitate "communication" among citizens. Because trust plays such a large role in the use and acceptance of modern forms of money, it was thought that territorial currencies might encourage identification with the nation-state at a deeper psychological level. And finally, territorial currencies were increasingly associated with national sovereignty both in a symbolic sense and because they could be used to serve the national community as tools for activist national macroeconomic management.[8]

Of those three things—monetary iconography as a vehicle for collective tradition, currency as a facilitator of national communication, and currency as a tool of national sovereignty and economic policy—this chapter will focus on the first and, to a lesser extent, the second. In those areas related to effective economic policy, Confederate fiscal efforts failed miserably, and in all likelihood contributed materially to the blossoming popular disillusion with the war and the Confederacy. The exigencies of a wartime economy that was not especially strong in the first place, as it turned out, prevented Confederate national currency from fulfilling Helleiner's last function. But from the point of view of iconography, currency mattered as a marker of national self-image.

The Union recognized this fact quite directly. Helleiner points to the creation of the national banknote system under the auspices of the National Currency Act of 1863. In the next two years, over $205 million dollars worth of these notes were issued.[9] For our purposes, however, what is interesting are the self-consciously nationalist ambitions of the act's supporters. For example, Senator John Sherman "hoped that the new notes could be used in a symbolic way to enhance a 'sentiment of nationality.'"[10] Spencer M. Clark, the chief clerk of the U.S. Treasury, similarly insisted that the new banknotes be designed in such a way as to ensure that those handling and viewing them were imbued "with a National feeling."[11] According to Helleiner, the result was that the "new notes were emblazoned with detailed vignettes of personalities (e.g., Columbus, Franklin, Washington), events (e.g., the signing of the Declaration of Independence, the Battle of Lexington, the pilgrim's landing, the baptism of Pocahontas, the surrender of General Burgoyne) and symbols (the flag, the eagle, the Capitol) that were seen as seminal to the history and image of the nation."[12] The intent was to put historical images daily in the hands of Americans, both to reinforce preexisting ideas about nationhood and to prompt questions about those scenes and symbols that were unfamiliar.

So we should not take the iconographic value of banknotes for granted. We only have to empty our pockets currently to see how prevalent they remain as symbols of nation. Issuing banks and national finance ministries are very much aware that the way they represent themselves on currency is one of the most important ways that their national image will be transmitted to their own populace and to foreign tourists and businesspeople. The faces, places, and things that adorn currency matter. When the U.S. Department of the Treasury decided in 1929 on the currency designs still in circulation, a special committee "determined that portraits of Presidents of the United States have a more permanent familiarity in the minds of the public than any others." This bland statement disguises the fact that the "familiarity" in question was the familiarity and utility of depicting the only elected official in the country with a national constituency. Exceptions to this presidential rule, like Alexander Hamilton and Benjamin Franklin, were sufficiently "well known to the American public" so as to meet the familiarity test.[13]

The recent trend in the scholarship is clear: the iconography of money matters.[14] Yet the study of Confederate banknotes has largely been left to numismatists. It is true that Confederate banknotes suffered from poor production values, shoddy paper supplies, initially unoriginal designs, distribution problems, easy counterfeiting, and runaway inflation. But if we view Confederate money as one among many texts of Confederate nationalism, one that in intention at least was expected to be widely circulated and handled daily, then we see a text that at first powerfully reinforced the tropes of the Worthy Southron and the Silent Slave. The Confederacy of this vista was initially commercial, agrarian, and peaceful, and only became martial under the provocation of Northern aggression. At the same time, given the understanding that slavery provided the bedrock foundation to this commercial, agrarian economy, it is noteworthy that the laboring slave was a relatively silent partner, believed to be working diligently but not immediately foregrounded. As the war progressed, and particularly by late 1862, this focus on an antebellum Worthy Southron faded, replaced by a wartime vision of a Confederate America.

In the past decade, two significant museum exhibits began to refocus academic and media attention on the iconography of Confederate-era currency. The Civil War Center at Louisiana State University hosts a virtual exhibit entitled "Beyond Face Value: Depictions of Slavery in Confederate Currency," and the College of Charleston's Avery Research Center for African American History and Culture hosted a more traditional exhibit of paintings drawn from the vignettes on Confederate-era currency entitled "Color of Money."[15] The primary focus of these exhibits was the widespread use of images of African American slaves on such money. Both exhibits include sixty or more individual representations from around the Confederacy.

This, however, rather misrepresents the numismatic terrain. For while images of slaves are prevalent on Confederate-era currency, they represent only a small fraction of the vignettes depicted on Confederate currency.[16] That is to say, currency issued by many of the state and local authorities—or, Confederate-era currency—gloried in its depiction of slaves. National currency issued by the Confederate government—Confederate currency—however, reinforced the notion of the Silent Slave. This subtle distinction is important. In the mid-nineteenth century, various authorities—national, state, and local—issued currency, and the exhibits at Louisiana State University and the College of Charleston do not necessarily differentiate by source. Currency issued by state and local authorities, called here *Confederate-era currency*, presents a rather different picture from that issued by the national government, *Confederate currency.* We concentrate on the latter, using the record of national Confederate currency issues as a text upon which to read the changing course of Confederate nationalism during the war.

What we find is that slavery was a relatively minor part of a broader iconographic terrain that celebrated the peculiarly Southern virtues of the Worthy Southron. On the banknote issues of 1861 and 1862, images with these attributes dominate. In late 1862, 1863, and 1864, however, the picture changes, and images of antebellum Southern virtues start to disappear in favor of a new iconographic terrain that was particularly Confederate in tone. So scenes of Greek goddesses, allegorical figures, commercial agriculture, and the occasional slave vanish in favor of state capitols, Confederate politicians, and military vignettes. This reflects a shift from a prewar, Southern conception of nationalism to one tempered by the exigencies of war. On the one hand, this effect was part of a deliberate attempt to use currency as a means of inculcating nationalism, along the lines discussed by Eric Helleiner. In the fall of 1862, the Confederate Treasury Department sought new artwork for their banknotes, largely to make them less easy to copy but at least partially, as Guy R. Swanson puts it, to help "the Confederacy towards defining itself as a nation. . . . [P]aper currency therefore became an effective tool with which to educate Confederates about their country," an idea that echoes the sentiments of U.S. Treasury official Spencer Clark.[17]

On the other hand, there were two problems. First, the economic woes of the Confederacy during the war badly blunted the effectiveness of the nationalist tool of currency. Second, the Confederate self-image relied on the Worthy Southron's innocence to explain why the South was embroiled in the war in the first place. From the point of view of the text of Confederate currency, it was impossible to concede that the Worthy Southron was inadequate to stem the tide of Northern hostility, that the foundations of the Confederate nation were not up to the task at hand. As we shall see in a subsequent chapter, once all you have left to sustain your national experiment is force of arms, the exploits and (hopefully) the successes of your generals and soldiers, you face the conundrum that no general, no army, however brilliant, however courageous, however determined, wins every battle. Over time, in the Confederate case, they won increasingly fewer and fewer battles, and that took its toll.

So Confederate politicians in the early years of the war faced the problem that, while they appeared confident in the underpinnings of their new nation—reflected both in the political certitude over the rightness of their constitutional experiment and in the bold imagery on their currency—they had actually built their national house on a foundation of sand. Their initial conception of Confederate nationalism was ill-suited to wartime tasks. Had the Confederacy been defining itself in time of peace and without a martial enemy, the symbols and concepts shared with that enemy would not have been so problematic. Similarly, symbols that were too universal to be distinctive, or else proved in practice to be divisive rather than unifying, were a significant issue in the context of a war for national survival. George Washington and Liberty represent the first category, Justice and Commerce the second, and slavery the third. As the war progressed, Confederate nationalists searched for a unifying theme to their cause, one that could paper over the class divisions that threatened to tear the Confederacy apart. Could the images adopted by the Confederacy have worked had the war gone differently? Perhaps. But in the short term, they could not accomplish what force of arms did not. In the longer term, however, currency survived as a tangible, collectible manifestation of the once Confederate nation.

So, if we look at Confederate-era currency, or the currency created at every level in the South during the Civil War, then the contentions of the "Beyond Face Value" and "Color of Money" exhibits are quite applicable. Historian and curator Harold Holzer, writing an introductory essay to the Louisiana State exhibit, argues that the appearance on Confederate paper currency "of iconic reminders of the economic foundations of the Confederacy—specifically the cotton industry and the slave labor system that supported it—tells much about the white South's unapologetic reliance on slavery to sustain itself. . . . Much more than the remnants of a shattered economy, these artifacts open a rare window onto the Confederacy's view of itself, and they deserve our attention as artistic and political, not just financial, currency."[18] Similarly, W. Marvin Dulaney, historian and director of the Avery Center, placed the issue in a contemporary context for the *New York Times* when he said that "we hear a lot these days about how the Confederacy was really about states' rights and not slavery. But the currency itself tells the truth. It shows how they saw us, and how they wanted to keep seeing us."[19] All true, but focusing exclusively on slavery when we view Confederate currency misses a good part of the richness of that record. Knowing that slavery was the bedrock of your cause, and physically showing off that knowledge, are two very different things. The realization that the Silent Slave was standing at the right hand of the Confederate master, or working in the fields to further the Confederate war effort, was a vital underpinning of the Confederate self-image. As the war progressed, however, and as the iconographic terrain of Confederate currency shifted, the slave as a visual symbol of the Confederacy faded from view.

Considering what the currency tells us about the record of Confederate nationalism, we should honestly admit that many Southerners did not share Major Jonas's sentiments, quoted at the beginning of the chapter, about "the pledge of a nation that's dead and gone." As the war progressed, that pledge rang increasingly hollow. Wartime Confederate currency was not legal tender in the modern sense, and increasingly was not acceptable as a form of payment to many Confederate citizens.[20] Instead, Confederate banknotes, or officially Treasury notes, promised to pay the holder interest at a set date in the future, usually after the cessation of hostilities. The first congressional act issuing such notes, in March 1861, promised interest "at the rate of one cent per day for every hundred dollars issued," redeemable one year from their printed dates. The sixth such act, in March 1863, promised payment "six months after the ratification of a treaty of peace."[21] Not surprisingly, Confederate Treasury notes were a risky investment.

Confederate Treasury notes did not start out as currency per se either. They started out as a means to raise money, and as people started to use them more as pseudo-legal tender, the Treasury obliged the populace by printing more. The changing nature of Confederate currency—from investment to form of payment—is evidenced by the fact that the first issue included notes in denominations of $1,000, $500, $100, and $50, while most of the subsequent issues had nothing larger than $100 and several denominations smaller than $50, with notes in the amount of $2 and $1 issued after April 1862. The first issue's $1,000 note is the only one of that denomination, and only one other $500 note was ever issued, in February 1864.

Paradoxically, the more popular Confederate Treasury notes became as a form of currency and as an expression of national ardor, and the more ubiquitous they became within the Confederate states, the more they undermined the Confederate Treasury's attempts to practice fiscal responsibility. The problem was that the need to finance the war effort lay at the heart of Confederate currency issues. The Confederacy relied heavily on the issue of Treasury notes, a measure that accounted for perhaps a half of total wartime revenue. In seven installments, the Confederate government authorized over a billion dollars in Treasury note issues.

But the amount actually printed probably dwarfs that authorized, and certainly dwarfs the amount of paper circulating in the Union states. Grover C. Criswell Jr. estimates that the amount printed under the 1864 act, for example, may have exceeded the authorized amount tenfold. Arlie R. Slabaugh speculates that the same act produced "about a billion dollars" in printed currency.[22] Add to that the issues of the several states and local banks, not to mention Union attempts at counterfeiting, and the amount of money circulating in the Confederacy during the war easily topped two billion dollars. Claud Fuller estimates a circulation rate by 1865 of $225 per capita, compared to an estimated $11 per capita before the war, a twentyfold increase.[23] It must have been quite hard, especially in the more densely populated areas of the Confederacy, to avoid routine, perhaps even daily contact with these images of the Confederacy.

Relying on the printing of money to finance a government is inherently inflationary, a phenomenon exacerbated by the exigencies of war. In May 1861, a sack of salt cost 65 cents. In October it cost $7, an almost elevenfold increase in just five months. According to Eugene M. Lerner's figures, the general price index of the Confederacy rose by only 27 percent in that period.[24] Not surprisingly, the situation in the later years of the war was worse. In 1863, a pound of meat cost $1, a year later a pound of bacon cost between $6 and $6.50. A barrel of flour rose in price fivefold from $50 to $250, and meal rose sevenfold from $5 a bushel to $35.[25] Of course, regional differences existed, but the general pattern is of spiraling and uncontrolled price increases that made the purchase of many goods impossible for a family dependent on a private soldier's pay of $11 a month. These are important caveats that strongly affect the possible reception of the nationalist message embedded in Confederate banknotes. We should be careful, therefore, not to overstate the case.

The first issue of Confederate banknotes, authorized in Montgomery, Alabama, in early March 1861, demonstrates the general trend. The images chosen to adorn these first six Treasury notes reflect the general pattern that would continue for another eighteen months: images of agriculture, including slaves and cotton, combined with visions of justice, liberty, peace, and freedom, all leavened with political icons of the United States being claimed by the Confederacy as its own. The $50 bill

(T-6) issued at Richmond under the authority of the March 1861 act is archetypal in this respect.[26] It depicts Minerva and Ceres seated on a cotton bale, flanked on the left by Justice and on the right by a portrait of George Washington. Minerva was the goddess of peace and defensive warfare, Ceres the goddess of agriculture and civilization, and George Washington the inaugural president of the United States. Couple that with the cotton bale the goddesses are using for a seat, the factory in the distance, and the figure of Justice, you have in allegorical form the text of Confederate President Jefferson Davis's inaugural address.

In that speech, given on February 18, 1861, he began by noting his hope that the beginning of the South's "career as a Confederacy may not be obstructed by hostile opposition to our enjoyment of the separate existence and independence which we have asserted, and, with the blessing of Providence, intend to maintain."[27] He followed this plea that the Confederacy be allowed to depart the Union peacefully and with amity with another, pointing to the manner in which the South had honorably discharged its obligations to the United States:

> Sustained by the consciousness that the transition from the former Union to the present Confederacy has not proceeded from a disregard on our part of just obligations, or any failure to perform every constitutional duty, moved by no interest or passion to invade the rights of others, anxious to cultivate peace and commerce with all nations, if we may not hope to avoid war, we may at least expect that posterity will acquit us of having needlessly engaged in it.

History would lay the blame for any impending war, he hoped, upon the Northern aggressor, thus echoing the association of Minerva with defensive warfare. He then pointed out that the economic life of the South, its very rationale for existence, was safe and secure under the Confederate government: "Our industrial pursuits have received no check. The cultivation of our fields has progressed as heretofore." The factory and cotton bale in the image reinforce this sentiment.

Davis's closing remarks are worth quoting in their entirety, for they encapsulate his hopes for the Confederate nation:

> It is joyous, in the midst of perilous times, to look around upon a people united in heart, where one purpose of high resolve animates and actuates the whole—where the sacrifices to be made are not weighed in the balance against honor and right and liberty and equality. Obstacles may re-

FIG. 1. $50 Bill (T-6), March 1861

tard, they cannot long prevent the progress of a movement sanctified by its justice, and sustained by a virtuous people. Reverently let us invoke the God of our fathers to guide and protect us in our efforts to perpetuate the principles which, by his blessing, they were able to vindicate, establish and transmit to their posterity, and with a continuance of His favor, ever gratefully acknowledged, we may hopefully look forward to success, to peace, and to prosperity.

He saw a united people, buoyed by the justice, virtue, and righteousness of their cause. He saw a people engaged in the pursuit of industry and agriculture who merely wished to be left alone after escaping the tyranny of a governmental structure that had "been perverted from the purposes for which it was ordained, and had ceased to answer the ends for which it was established." In short, he sought to lay claim to the terrain of Revolutionary American nationalism—through his reference to "our fathers." Davis's message—historically flawed though it was—converged with the images depicted on that one Confederate Treasury note. The Confederacy was an agricultural nation, a commercial nation, a just nation, and an American nation.

The other notes issued in March 1861 reinforced these themes. The very first Confederate Treasury bill, the $1,000 authorized on March 9, 1861, depicts John C. Calhoun and Andrew Jackson flanking a central plate bearing the words "Confederate States of America" (T-1). Both were Southern, Calhoun from South Carolina and Jackson from Tennessee, and yet both were national at the same time. Calhoun had been a federal representative and senator, cabinet member, vice president of the United

FIG. 2. $1,000 Bill (T-1), March 1861

States from 1825 to 1833, and the intellectual father of the Confederacy. Jackson was Tennessee's first federal representative after it gained statehood in 1796, the victorious general at the Battles of Horseshoe Creek in 1814 and New Orleans in 1815, the first governor of the Territory of Florida, and the seventh president of the United States from 1829 to 1837. Coincidentally, and ironically given the later relationship between Confederate President Jefferson Davis and his vice president, Alexander Stephens, Calhoun and Jackson vehemently opposed each other on the issue of nullification in the early 1830s, while Calhoun still served as Jackson's vice president. The images of these men were immediately identifiable, meaningful to the populace, and tangibly associated with the South.

In contrast, the $500 bill in the March 1861 Montgomery issue focused on agriculture, depicting a scene described as "cattle crossing a brook" (T-2). In the background, a railway train crosses a bridge. In the left panel, Ceres beckons the South onward. The scenes were peaceful and classical, speaking to a pastoral South in which people (and livestock) minded their own business and wanted to be left alone. The $100 bill features a railway train being loaded in the center panel, with an image of Minerva on its left (T-3). The $100 bill issued concurrently at Richmond was quite similar, featuring a slightly different railway scene in the center, Minerva to the right, and the allegorical figure of Justice to the left (T-5). Finally, the $50 bill issued at Montgomery provides a vignette of African American slaves hoeing cotton (T-4). Throughout this issue, we see images of agriculture and commerce, justice and peace, buttressed by industry and the iconic weight of Cincinnatus.[28]

FIG. 3. $500 Bill (T-2), March 1861

FIG. 4. $50 Bill (T-4), March 1861

The images of slaves represented in these early issues fit the script of the Silent Slave. For example, in both T-4 (March 1861) and T-29 (September 1861), slaves are depicted working in the cotton fields.[29] In T-4, they are planting and hoeing; in T-29, they are harvesting. In both cases, they are working in sight of the plantation house but in neither are they overseen by whites. Insofar as can be discerned, they look relatively well dressed, well fed, clean, and content. They are hard at work, without direction or supervision, and no whips, chains, shackles, or other physical manifestations of the punitive side of the institution of slavery are visible. These slaves are silently enlisted in service of their masters' cause, but the vision they represent is the same one we have already identified: peaceful and prosperous agriculture.

The issues of July 1861, September 1861, and April 1862 added forty-

FIG. 5. $10 Bill (T-29), September 1861

two types of Treasury notes and increased the circulation of Confederate paper currency more than 400-fold, but they largely conformed to the iconographic pattern established with the March 1861 issue. New figures appeared in addition to the staples of Minerva, Ceres, Washington, and cotton agriculture. Tellus, the goddess of the Earth, supports Washington on a $50 bill authorized in May 1861 (T-8). A three-masted sailing ship of the type used to transport cotton to its overseas markets adorns a $20 bill of the same issue (T-9). The figure of Liberty graces $10 and $5 bills, both with eagles in attendance (T-10 and T-11). Another slave vignette, this time of loading cotton into a cart, is featured on a $100 bill authorized by the August and December 1861 amendments to the May act (T-13). That note also shows a sailor leaning against an anchor. Moneta seated by a treasure chest takes center stage on the $50 bill of that issue, supported by two sailors to her left (T-14). This list could go on at considerable length, but the point remains clear: the images depicted on Confederate currency of 1861 and 1862 consistently presented an iconographic portrait of the South that embraced the values of commerce and agriculture, and the virtues of liberty and justice.

Another notable feature of these early notes, and one that prefigures later changes in the iconographic terrain, is the depiction of Confederate notables. Jefferson Davis rests on a $50 bill issued under the amended authority of the May act, while Alexander Stephens gazes out from the center of one $20 bill of that issue and supports an image of the allegorical figure of Industry seated between a beehive and Cupid, the god of love, on another of the same denomination (T-16, T-20, and T-21).

Robert M. T. Hunter makes the first of what would become ten appearances on Confederate Treasury bills on a $10 note of the amended May issue (T-24). Christopher G. Memminger accompanies Hunter on another $10 bill of that issue, and would appear eight times in total, leading Minerva by one in terms of frequency (T-25). Hunter was a Virginian, a former member of that state's House of Delegates, a three-term U.S. senator, and the Confederacy's second secretary of state from July 1861 until March 1862, at which point he was elected to a seat in the Confederate Congress. Memminger was a German émigré to South Carolina, the respected chair of the committee that drafted the Provisional Constitution of the Confederacy, and the secretary of the treasury from February 1861 to July 1864.

Not surprisingly, the Confederacy began to mark out its own iconographic territory more clearly as the war progressed. The first $2 bill issued by the Confederacy, authorized in April 1862, depicts Judah P. Benjamin to the left (T-38). Benjamin had just completed a term as the Confederacy's secretary of war from September 1861 to March 1862, before becoming its third and last secretary of state. But the central image, commonly called the "Personification of South Striking down Union," is particularly fascinating. It appears to be a robed figure with a sword held high, looming over another figure, reclining and holding a shield. It also appears as though a bird, which could easily be an eagle, is joining the attack. Even the symbol of the United States apparently cannot stand its own perfidy. In this case, however, popular opinion as to the nature of the image was faulty. In the case of the personified Southern victory, numismatists have identified it as a vignette of Hercules freeing Prometheus from the eagle set there by Zeus to peck at his liver for eternity in punishment for his opening Pandora's Box and unleashing evil on the world.[30]

Just as the T-6 note referenced above can function interpretively as an allegorical companion to Davis's Inaugural Address, so can this T-38 note—repeated twice more as T-42 and T-43—function as an allegorical interpretation of what was wrong with Confederate banknote imagery: it gave out mixed messages. On the one hand, the South struck down the Union, but on the other, Hercules freed Prometheus from the eagle. The two are antithetical. Abstract notions like agriculture, commerce, justice, and liberty, and concrete politicians like George Washington and Andrew Jackson, represented a paradoxical message for Confederate nationalism because they were at the same time images of the enemy. Nationalism

FIG. 6. $2 Bill (T-38), April 1862

functions partly through its identification of the other and the depiction of that other in ways that are unlike the national self. The early rendition of Confederate nationalism, seen in the T-6 note's embrace of commerce, agriculture, industry, and peace, sought to grasp the same iconographic terrain as the Union, and that made difficult the ability of the Confederacy to appear distinctive.

The symbols that should have functioned as emerging markers of Confederate unity proved flawed, thus they took a backseat to other images after October 1862. Pictures of slaves for example do not appear after the T-41 issue of April 1862. This is a manifestation of the emerging fear among leading Southern politicians that slavery was a double-edged sword. A very real class schism developed in the Confederacy because of the war. Whatever the truth of the matter, some common Southerners felt that the Confederate government was ignoring their plight and exploiting them in order to defend slavery, an institution from which they were purposefully excluded. There can be little doubt that a similarly real difference in attitude to the war existed between the poor, who were reduced to a subsistence level of real hardship, and the rich, who had to forego ice cream and wear calico dresses instead of silk. Even more damaging to the image of the Confederate government was the furor raised over the infamous Twenty Negro Law. Passed in October 1862 to combat fears of slave insurrection in the aftermath of the first Emancipation Proclamation, this act permitted the exemption from military service of one white man for every twenty slaves. Although it only affected a small number of Southerners, it quickly became a powerful symbol for the common people that the war was being fought by them on behalf of the planters.[31]

While Abraham Lincoln's political acumen papered over such divisions in the North, Jefferson Davis was a very different sort of politician. It is notable that, while his image does not disappear from Confederate currency as do images of slavery after 1862, he was not emphasized on Confederate currency to the extent one might expect, given the U.S. Treasury's 1929 comment about the familiarity of presidents and their suitability for use on currency. After all, Davis was an antebellum figure of national dimensions, a hero from the Mexican-American War, and a former cabinet member and senator. In his tenure as Confederate president, however, he was not a unifying figure. The animosity, and even outright hostility, evident in the relationship of Davis and Vice President Stephens was simply a symbol of disharmony in the Confederacy generally. Davis fought relentlessly with his cabinet, with Congress, with state governors, and with generals. All of those groups fought among themselves and with each other. Beneath all of this, ordinary Southerners came to increasingly feel neglected, betrayed, and alienated from the very institution created to safeguard their way of life.[32] President Davis worked, above all else, for the independence of his nation, but that goal had decreasing immediacy for many white Southerners as mere survival became paramount.

In their quest for a distinctive symbolic text of nationalism, Confederates faced a conundrum in the first eighteen months of the war. Not only were the images they used not obviously Southern, but they were also in some cases the same images being used on Northern, or even Canadian, currency. For example, the railway train centered on the $100 bill issued at Montgomery in March 1861 (T-3) was concurrently used by the American Bank of Baltimore, Maryland. Another railway image, this time on a $50 note issued in August and December 1861 (T-15), was being used by the Westmoreland Bank of New Brunswick, Canada. The cattle crossing a brook on the $500 Montgomery issue (T-2) was shared with the North Western Bank of Warren, Pennsylvania.[33] Many more designs were concurrently in use by other Southern banks, and still others had enjoyed a wide usage in the antebellum period.

This is at least partly a function of three things: the Confederacy refused to recognize the United States's copyright laws, which would have prohibited such borrowing; the Confederacy needed to print money in a hurry and skilled lithographers and engravers were scare, so they used those plates that already existed; and at least at the outset of the war, the same company produced Northern and Southern banknotes at the same time. One company, the National Banknote Company of New York, produced the entire first issue of Confederate Treasury notes. After the war broke out, the New Orleans office of this company, where the March 1861 notes were actually produced, seceded from its parent company and established itself as the Southern Banknote Company. Production soon shifted to Virginia and South Carolina where companies like Hoyer and Ludwig, Keatinge and Ball, and B. Duncan took up production. Edward Keatinge was coincidentally an employee of the American Banknote Company recruited by the Confederacy at the outbreak of war.[34]

This lack of originality does not invalidate the basic point: that the iconography of Confederate banknotes produced through the issue of T-48 in October 1862 represents the embrace of a prewar notion of Southern nationalism. In fact, the continuation of banknote images from the antebellum period into the Civil War reinforces it. While the early designs were copied out of necessity, the emergence of new production companies after May 1861 and the simple passage of time strongly suggests that the copying was partly convenience and partly because the imagery did reflect the Southern image of itself in the early years of the war.[35] As the South laid claim to the real American nationalism, it is not surprising that the two ideas of America—Northern and Southern—overlapped.

In late 1862, starting with the T-49 note, the iconographic terrain of Confederate banknotes shifted markedly. The old staple images disappeared. Ceres, railway trains, steamships, and Liberty all appear on the types issued in April and September 1862, as they had on the previous three issues. None of them reappears after October 1862. The vision of the Worthy Southron and an antebellum Confederate Americanism articulated in the first years of the war also went away, replaced by a more martial, distinctively Confederate vision of Americanism. The first $100 bill of that issue (T-49) depicted Lucy Holcombe Pickens in the center, with a pair of soldiers to the left, and former Secretary of War George W. Randolph to the right. Pickens was the so-called "Queen of the Confederacy," first among Southern belles and the wife of Francis Pickens, the secessionist governor of South Carolina whose order to fire on the *Star of the West* on January 9, 1861, as it tried to approach the besieged Fort Sumter technically started the Civil War. Lucy Pickens's popularity went beyond her portrayal on Confederate currency as a South Caro-

FIG. 7. $100 Bill (T-49), October 1862

lina regiment named itself the Holcombe Legion in her honor. Randolph was a grandson of Thomas Jefferson, a general, and a veteran of a six-month tenure at the War Office before being named Confederate envoy to France just prior to Congress's authorizing this currency issue.

This wholly Confederate note—actually the first one that was un-ambiguously Confederate in tone, excepting two 1861 issues depicting Jefferson Davis and Alexander Stephens alone (T-16 and T-21)—was ac-companied by a reissue of the T-16 depiction of Davis on the $50 bill (T-50). The $20 (T-51), $10 (T-52), and $5 (T-53) bills started a pattern that was to persist until the end of the war, accounting for eight types in total. In the center, they featured Confederate state capitol buildings: Nashville, Tennessee, on the $20 bill; Columbia, South Carolina, on the $10; and Richmond, Virginia, on the $5. In addition, they carried por-traits of Alexander Stephens, Robert Hunter, and Christopher Mem-minger, respectively, on the right. This pattern was slightly distorted by the 1864 $10 bill (T-68), which replaced the Columbia capitol with a de-piction of horse artillery at the gallop. Two small denominations com-pleted this issue: a $2 bill bearing the likeness of Judah Benjamin and a $1 bill depicting Clement C. Clay, a distinguished Confederate sena-tor and former U.S. senator. All of these types were reissued in 1863 and 1864.

As noted, this shift in iconographic tone was quite deliberate. Confed-erate Treasury officials requested new designs from their note suppliers, both to reduce the incidence of counterfeiting and to meet the changing needs of the Confederate nation itself. Several of the important compo-

FIG. 8. $20 Bill (T-51), October 1862

nents of the Worthy Southron virtues icon group were flawed to one extent or another. Some were too closely associated with the Union, others were insufficiently unifying. Also, the watershed battles of Shiloh in April and Antietam in September 1862 convinced people that the chances of the Civil War's ending soon were remote. Given the imperatives incumbent upon the Confederacy—maintaining support for a government that was sustaining itself in time of war via methods that are never especially popular, first with taxation and later impressment—it is little wonder that older, more genteel images gave way to newer, more martial depictions. Minerva had served her time, as this was no longer wholly a defensive war but a hard war for the survival of the white Southern way of life.

Fundamentally, the fatal flaw of Confederate nationalism was its parochial nature. Unlike contemporary insurgent nationalisms in Europe, it had no history of religious or linguistic difference to distinguish it from the enemy. It had no anchor that was external to the present conflict. Therefore, as the war went against the Confederacy, for reasons that in practice had little to do with its nationalism, it became the snake that swallowed itself. In particular, the iconography of Confederate nationalism became inextricably tied to the fortunes of military leaders. In the end, the Confederate nation had nothing except military victory to sustain it.

The obvious subjects for depiction on Confederate currency, perhaps, were the military leaders of the South, whose pictures adorned so much else of the published record of Confederate nationalism. Yet, with one exception, none of the emblematic military leaders of the Confederacy ever

FIG. 9. $500 Bill (T-64), February 1864

adorned its money. Neither Robert E. Lee, Albert S. Johnston, Joseph E. Johnston, Pierre G. T. Beauregard, Braxton Bragg, John B. Hood, nor even George E. Pickett ever appeared on a Confederate banknote. The one exception was Thomas J. "Stonewall" Jackson. He featured on what has become the most famous Confederate banknote, the $500 bill of the February 1864 issue (T-64). On one side sits Stonewall Jackson, on the other the Great Seal of the Confederacy resting on "a pile of war munitions consisting of a bugle, a drum, a cannon, and a stack of muskets," and surmounted by the battle flag of the Army of Northern Virginia, the infamous Southern Cross.[36] The seal features an equestrian statue of George Washington surrounded by a belt bearing the motto *Deo Vindice*. Jackson was dead by the time this note appeared, having fallen to what we would today call "friendly fire" at the battle of Chancellorsville in May 1863. While this note has become emblematic of the Lost Cause, it was in fact completely atypical of the types of Treasury notes produced during the war.

We can speculate a little as to why no other Confederate generals—with the tenuous exception of George Randolph, who was depicted in civilian dress—were shown on Confederate currency. Living generals were problematic because they might die while serving as national emblems, and the Confederacy only had two dead generals of any note, Jackson and Albert Johnston, who fell at Shiloh in April 1862. Of the two, Jackson was far more popular and well-known. He was also less than a year dead when he started to appear on Confederate currency, and thus the national wound of his passing was still raw. Add to that the Great Seal,

FIG. 10. $10 Bill (T-68), February 1864

produced at great expense in England and never actually used for its intended purpose during the war, and here you have another allegorical interpretation of the Confederacy's national terrain.[37]

Martial scenes might have replaced the pastoral depictions of the South as the war progressed, but, so far as we can tell, just two military scenes appeared on Confederate Treasury notes. The first were the two soldiers depicted in the lower left corner of the Lucy Pickens note discussed above (T-49, issued in December 1862 and reissued in April 1863 [T-56] and February 1864 [T-65]). The second was on the $10 bill issued in February 1864 (T-68). That bill shows R. M. T. Hunter on the lower right; the central image depicts horse artillery at the gallop. Arlie Slabaugh suggests that this was an adaptation of Carl Nebel's 1851 painting of the battle of Buena Vista during the Mexican-American War.[38] If Slabaugh is correct, then it is a depiction of a unit of the 3rd U.S. Artillery commanded by Major Braxton Bragg. While Bragg was one of only six full generals in the Confederate Army by the time this note was issued, he was relegated in February 1864 from a line command to an advisory portfolio, and was often the butt of jokes. In short, if this is indeed an adaptation of Nebel's painting, it was by a German, depicting an action of the U.S. Army, and featuring a unit commanded by the least of the Confederacy's generals, from the point of view of their impact on the nation's self-image. Insofar as it lends weight to the script of Confederate nationalism, this particular image was deeply problematic.

Nationalism can function at the level of allegory. Intangible symbols offer connections to tangible allegiances and concepts. In the case of the

T-6 bill in 1861, its allegorical relationship is to Jefferson Davis's stated hopes for peace and amity between the Confederacy and Union. For the T-38 bill in 1862, we see the ambiguity of the Confederate nationalist message, and with the T-64 bill in 1864, we can see what the allegorical representation of the Confederacy could have been on the face of its Treasury notes but which it never really was. The peaceful and innocent Worthy Southron was never effectively replaced by a more martial, distinctively Confederate set of symbols in this venue.

Currency serves a somewhat different purpose than does a constitution or, especially, literature. While a constitution is associated with the strength of a political system, the solidity of the polity moves far more slowly than does the solidity of the economy. Following Eric Helleiner, currency serves multiple functions—monetary iconography as a vehicle for collective tradition, currency as a facilitator of national communication, and currency as a tool of national sovereignty and economic policy. Confederate currency failed in the last of those goals, which could not help but to undermine the success of the first two. That being the case, had the Confederacy survived as a national entity, it at least had a symbolic text extant on the face of its Treasury bills that could have established a longer-term sense of collective tradition and national communication. Currency might then have been part of the wider imagined community of the Confederate nation, as, to an extent during the war years, it was.

4

"Thoughts That Breathe and Words That Burn"

The Confederate Nation in Wartime Literature

Southern Independence has struck the lyre as well as un-
sheathed the sword. That it has inspired many a song no less
truly poetical than intensely patriotic, our newspapers amply
testify. But the newspaper can only give an ephemeral life to
"thoughts that breathe and words that burn." The book embalms if it does not immortalize.

WILLIAM G. SHEPPERSON,
War Songs of the South (1862)

The role of white Southern writers in imagining a Confederate America
before the Civil War began is clear. We might anticipate finding a continuation of that imagining in the war years, and we would not be dis-
appointed. Confederate writers were living the creation of an imagined
Confederate America, and they recognized, perhaps without consciously
realizing so, that the written word plays a powerful role in creating, defining, and sustaining the nation. It is not, to be sure, a sufficient condition on its own, but it comes very close to being a necessary one. In
October 1862, M. Louise Rogers, a correspondent of the *Southern Illustrated News,* announced to her readers that "history affords no account
of the national happiness, peace and prosperity of any country which did
not have a pure, elevated and high-toned *home* literature; and no phi-
losopher ever wrote a line containing more truth than he who said, 'Show
me a nation's ballads, and I will make its laws.'"[1] Six months later, in April
1863, the editor of the *Southern Field and Fireside* noted with some ve-
hemence that the development of a Southern literature of note was "no

trivial subject. Literature is the only power which can give immortality to a people."[2]

Eight months later still, in January 1864, Frank H. Alfriend, the new editor of the *Southern Literary Messenger,* writing to introduce himself to his readers, went into considerably more detail on the subject. In his characteristically purple prose, Alfriend drew a connection between independence and mature nationhood on the one hand, and a distinctive national literature on the other: "Where is the nation," he asked, "which in any age, in any department or arena of action, has ever attained a position of eminence or even respectability among its compeers, that is not under the heaviest obligation of gratitude to its Historians, its Poets, and its Novelists?" Using this rubric, he compared the "intellectual vigor and sagacious diplomacy of the more cultivated Gaul and Briton" with the "brute strength" and crudity of Russia. International reputation, and even world power, in Alfriend's eyes, seemed to rest upon intellectual achievement as much as anything else. So, for Alfriend, it was obvious that, save the Confederacy's "physical ability" to successfully prosecute its war for independence, "the all important interests of Southern Literature . . . overshadows all others in importance, requires immediately the active intervention of all of its friends, if we would prevent its utter prostration."[3] For Alfriend, the construction of a literary Confederate Americanism was the most important task facing the nation save the military defense of its independence.

Even while these commentators were discussing the relationship of nation and literature at the meta level, a number of white Southern writers—now writing as Confederates—were engaged in producing literature that dealt with the themes of the ongoing conflict. This literature, written during the war and commenting on the war, represents an integrally creative part of Confederate nationalism. The same themes evident in other arenas of such production are replicated and reinforced in the writings of the Confederate literati during the Civil War. Taking this variant of wartime Confederate literature as our text, we can identify a clear set of juxtapositions of the white Southern self and its others. Five pairs in particular stand out: liberty and abolitionism, freemen and hirelings, pure-bloodedness and ethnicity, civilization and barbarity, and the white voice and black silence.[4] On the one hand, the Confederate literary self—which fits with the trope of the Worthy Southron—is imagined as a champion of liberty, in this case meaning a champion of the rights of individual and community self-determination, the right to live one's life as one wishes, disregarding controls imposed external to the community, and presumably, although this is generally left unstated, whiteness, maleness, and the right to own, use, and dispense property in slaves. The Worthy Southron is not an ethnic American—by which we can infer that he is a pureblooded, Anglo-Saxon American, whatever that means—and he is a paragon of civilization, which is coded in turn as distinctly Southern.

On the other hand, the Northern other—analogous to the Demon Yankee—is imagined as a fanatical abolitionist, one who wants both to abolish slavery for his own selfish and arrogant ends and to abolish liberty as well. This Demon Yankee is either ethnic—Irish or German in the main—or willing to stoop so low as to employ ethnics to do his foul bidding. As such, the Northern other is barbarous or willing to use the barbarous to his own ends. If civilization is coded as Southern, then its polar opposite, the demise of civilization into barbarity is coded as Northern. The final result will be the same: the destruction of a white Southern way of life that is taken to represent purity, civilization, and grace, in short, a Confederate America that fights to protect itself from the rapacious opposition of Northern agitators.

The Worthy Southron has another counterpoint in this literature, one that is both a companion to self and yet other at the same time. This is the juxtaposition, internal to the Confederacy, between the white master or mistress who speaks for him- and herself, and the Silent Slave who is spoken for. There are multiple levels of racial silence the historian can peel off from this genre. The physical production of the journals and books, or the ink and paper, was at least in some part the product of black labor, slave or free, and in any case, the very money that changed hands as the words found their way into print was deeply implicated in an economy based on the forced exploitation of black labor. Along with this physical silence—those workers never found a voice in this process— there was a deafening literary silence. Given that most of the characters in these various novels are middle-class or better, we know that they would all have had servants, that almost all the servants would have been African American, and they would in all probability have been slaves. Yet they are silent, invisible, in these narratives. When slave voices are heard, they are puppets for their masters, mouthing the words and ideas that their owners and their collaborators wished them to utter. By design, the authentic slave voice is totally silent in this literature.

This chapter analyzes the creation of national identity in literature, especially novels, of the Civil War South. This literature, often published in Richmond or Mobile, was produced less for a specific local community and more for an abstract body of Confederate readers. Study of these Confederate novels opens up a valuable window onto the process by which some Confederate literary elites tried to articulate the founding principles of their nation in a fictional form. Literature is essential for an analysis of nation-building's multiple levels because it straddles the artificial boundary between the intelligentsia as nationalist producer and the citizen as nationalist consumer (one model of nationalism-in-formation): author and reader cooperate in the shared act of writing and reading, distant in time and sometimes in understanding, yet united in the creation of a shared meaning.

So, at the same time that members of the Confederate opinion class were calling for the production of a distinctive, national literature of the new Confederate nation, members of the literati were writing exactly that. The conundrum faced by the former, however, was that nothing ever seemed to be good enough to meet their high standards. In spite of the literary outpourings of the war years, much of it published in the pages of the very journals calling for a literature of nation, no commentator seemed ready to claim that contemporary Confederate literature had achieved the heights of which they dreamed. In the very same article in which he strenuously advocated the importance of a national literature, Alfriend of the *Southern Literary Messenger* asked, "Are the indicators encouraging of a thorough and healthful awakening of the Southern mind upon this most important subject?" His answer? No. "We see nothing to justify such a conclusion. True, an unwonted activity is exhibited in the production of a certain species of literature which, so far as its tendencies extend, is more to be dreaded than even absolute ignorance."[5] Alfriend feared that this type of "mere temporary efflorescence of the popular mind," as he colorfully described it a few months later, would lead to the "insidious growth of a spurious literature whose noxious fruits, once permitted to reach maturity, will render the mental soil barren to the culture of the bloom and beauty of the health-giving and life-inspiring productions of True Learning and Genuine Virtue."[6] One has to wonder whether even Charles Dickens or William Makepeace Thackeray—both popular in the antebellum South—would have met Alfriend's exacting standards had they been fellow white Southerners. Probably not.

More than this, both *De Bow's Review* (in late 1861) and *Southern Punch* (in early 1864) wondered aloud if the Confederacy was actually capable of this sort of literary independence. In both journals, commentators explicitly associated the development of "great" literature with the development of commerce and manufacturing, something they found lacking in the contemporary Confederacy.[7] For *Southern Punch,* the thesis that the war itself would catalyze literature was dubious at best:

> It is said that the war will give a new impetus to Southern literature, and that hereafter we shall see its sun rise over the waste of waters splendidly. We confess that if experience teaches anything, it teaches us to receive these promises with skepticism. In all this broad South, we find that for a century and over, under fine auspices too, that Southern literature was an unsubstantial thing, and more, not much is to be hoped for when the startling fact is before us, that never in our history has such a feature as an Art Gallery been seen.[8]

This promise of a future literature, however, could do nothing to bolster the actual Confederate nation in its struggle for independence from the Union.

In at least one case, a member of the opinion class was also a member of the literati. In the first two months of 1864, poet Henry Timrod, acting as a columnist for the Columbia *Daily South Carolinian,* expounded on what he saw as the potential, problems, and challenges facing Confederate authors.[9] To begin with, Timrod professed to see the same sorts of literary opportunities identified by Alfriend and his peers. In a column published on January 14, 1864, Timrod noted that "the great and troubled movement through which we are passing has stirred the Southern mind to an unwonted activity. No pre-eminently great man, indeed, has arisen amid the turmoil, but the people are beginning to think with an independence which they never evinced in their former provincial position. . . . [W]e think we perceive the national mind struggling to find fit and original expression."[10] Timrod, it seemed, perceived the first stirrings of a literature of nation, one he was too modest in which to place himself.

These notions of literary "independence" and "originality" were themes that Timrod had articulated before, in 1859 in *Russell's Magazine* for example, and the first of which at least appeared to be widely shared among his peers.[11] But it was not enough for Timrod that white Southern writers should start to free themselves from Northern publishing houses and Northern audiences; it was not enough that they begin to develop Southern locations and characters. What Timrod wanted was originality of style. As he had put it in 1859, "To be an American novelist, it was sufficient that a writer should select a story, in which one half of the characters should be backwoodsmen, who talked bad Saxon, and the other half should be savages, who talked Choctaw translated into very bombastic English."[12] Almost certainly thinking of the works of James Fenimore Cooper or William Gilmore Simms, Timrod was distinctly underwhelmed.

This quest for literary independence and originality was not a new development in the United States, or in the American South. It was also not news that it was an uphill struggle. Writing in 1847, Timrod's mentor, William Gilmore Simms, had peevishly noted that "the South don't care a d—n for literature or art."[13] Some modern scholars have questioned whether "the South" was actually a meaningful intellectual community in the antebellum period at all. Writing on Southern Romanticism, Michael O'Brien suggests that the South "was a provincial culture anxious to invent and legitimate itself." That act of invention, we might suggest, was a necessary precursor to any unified sense of white Southern regionalism or Confederate nationalism. O'Brien also notes, quite tellingly for the creation of the trope of the Demon Yankee, that absent a true "core against which to rebel," white Southerners had to invent one. They invented a Boston of fanatical abolitionism and tyranny, which was "a gross overestimation of the cultural power of New England to mold American opinion, but it was a necessary invention."[14] The point here is that, in spite of the lamentations of the white Southern opinion class, a literary culture was developing in the antebellum period, and it gained a form of coherent expression during the war years.

In a similar vein, antebellum literati had sought to emancipate themselves from the British literary world at the same time as they reprinted and repurposed foreign texts to their own ends, sometimes commercial, and sometimes nationalist in nature.[15] Paul Giles in particular articulates a Revolutionary-era relationship between Americans and the British that very much echoes the Civil War–era relationship between the South and the North. Giles argues that in the "years on either side of the Revolution British and American cultural narratives tended to develop not so much in opposition but rather as heretical alternatives to each other."[16] Fundamentally, the same claim could be made of Northern and Southern cultural narratives in the antebellum period, and it was from that relationship that Southern literary critics were seeking to free themselves, at the same time as they doubted their ability to complete the task. Just as the newly independent American colonists struggled to emancipate themselves from the British cultural shadow, so the newly independent Confederates desired to emancipate themselves from the weight of Northern American cultural expressions. They sought an immortal Confederate America through the power of literature, to repeat the sentiments of the editor of the *Southern Field and Fireside* quoted at the start of this chapter.

For Henry Timrod, however, writing five years after his *Russell's Magazine* essay in 1859, the possibility for Southern literary settings remained unimpressive: "It would be quite possible for a southern poet to write a hundred odes to the Confederate flag, or for a Southern novelist to fill his book with descriptions of Southern scenes, and yet be un-Southern in every respect."[17] For Timrod, what mattered above all else was originality: "There is but one way to be a truly national writer, and that is by being a truly original writer. No one who does not speak from himself can speak for his country, and therefore, no imitator can be national."[18] Furthermore, as he continued this theme in later columns, the current condition of the South, embroiled in war and revolution, was a superb breeding ground for a future national literature but was not conducive to the contemporaneous development of the same.

At the end of February 1864, Timrod noted that "thought now flows mainly but in one channel, and boils along in too turbulent a stream to be confined within the limitations of polished prose or harmonious verse." So the implacable tides of political nationalism were, in fact, an impediment to the development of the sober reflection of literary nationalism, though Timrod did believe that the current turmoil would provide fruitful material for a later generation of poets and novelists: "While . . . the tumult of revolution is undoubtedly incompatible with the composition of poetry; it operates, on the other hand, not without much salutary effect upon the poetical genius. In the very excitement which seals for awhile the poet's lips, he is receiving an education which shall bear the noblest fruits in the future."[19] Herein lay the conundrum for Timrod and his peers, the same paradox that lurked beneath the entire wartime project of Confederate nationalism—only once the war was won and independence secured would the time come for the development of what most commentators agreed was the real essence of a mature nationalism.[20] Was the immortality of Confederate nationalist literature to be that of vibrant life in the present or the cold grave in the future? By Timrod's definition, writings about the war, published during the war, could not be considered "literature" in the highest sense, nor could they be considered the fit outpourings of the genuine mind of the South. So what were they? What then can we make of the "mere temporary efflorescence of the popular mind," as Frank Alfriend described the literary efforts of his wartime contemporaries? Should we be as quick to dismiss this genre?[21]

Whatever the literary merits of this body of work as history, as an expression of an imagined Confederate Americanism, as an act of creating the mythic present, wartime Confederate literature is invaluable. Wartime Confederate literature did reflect a rose-tinted understanding of the society in which it was rooted, and it was unabashedly patriotic and even nationalistic. From the point of view of the historian of wartime Confederate nationalism, these are its strengths as a documentary source. In *The Imagined Civil War*, Alice Fahs notes that a wartime literature that has often been dismissed, derisively, as "popular" was in fact "vitally important in shaping a cultural politics of war."[22] Fahs's central point, made specifically with reference to the poetry of the pseudonymous Tyrtaeus in the *Charleston Tri-Weekly Mercury*, makes very clear the ways in which wartime Confederate literature "did not just reflect a new united nationhood; it attempted to imagine such unity into being rhetorically."[23] The lines of Tyrtaeus:

> Nor shall Tennessee pause, when like voice from the steep,
> The great South shall summon her sons from their sleep;
> Nor Kentucky be slow, when our trumpet shall call,
> To tear down the rifle that hangs on the wall![24]

echo those of Henry Timrod in "A Cry to Arms:"

> Ho! Woodsmen of the mountain sides
> Ho! Dwellers of the vales!
> Ho! ye who by the chafing tide
> Have roughened in the gales!
> Leave barn and byre, leave kin and cot
> Lay by the bloodless spade;

Let desk and case, and counter rot,
And burn your books of trade.[25]

Tyrtaeus's political geography and Timrod's use of terrain serve the same rhetorical purpose, to convince readers in diverse environments and locales that they have something in common.[26] The very idea of a Confederate nation, binding together the diverse and widespread South, faced an uphill battle of the imagination, and it was in that arena that wartime Confederate literature played a significant role.

So what exactly constituted these acts of rhetorical and imaginary creation? What were the components of Confederate Americanism and its nation as seen through the eyes of its literati? As noted above, these novels collectively lay out for the modern reader a pattern of rhetorical self and other: clear oppositions of liberty and abolition, freedom and dependency, purity of blood, civilization and barbarity, and white voice and black silence. Writing largely in the middle years of the war—1862, 1863, and 1864—and principally about the origins of the conflict, Confederate novelists betrayed their belief that, at least for the North, the American Civil War was very much a war to abolish the peculiar institution and the Southern way of life. This understanding existed, of course, in spite of the later historical understanding that for many Northerners, it was initially about anything but slavery. The reverse was rarely explicitly admitted, that the South was fighting to preserve slavery, but what is liberty in this case, if not anchored to the specific privilege at issue, the right of white men to own slaves?

The defenders of liberty are also cast as freemen in comparison to the Northern hordes, who are usually characterized as "hirelings." A freeman chooses to defend his community and way of life; he does so voluntarily and out of a sense of honor, duty, patriotism, or nationalism. A hireling does none of these things; he defends someone else's way of life for monetary reward, out of a mercenary sense of materialism and nothing more. The underlying belief here appears to be that the real abolitionists were not personally fighting; they were sending hireling proxies into battle for them. Two other juxtapositions reinforce this notion—the abolitionist hireling is understood to be both ethnically different and of an alien sensibility. Generally, these Northern hordes—a common trope—are ethnically Irish or "Dutch" (that is, German, from "Deutsch") and as such barbarous and insensible to the polite and humane rules of civilized warfare. Slaves and women both, the South's two vulnerable classes of noncitizens, are repeatedly subject to the Northerners' ravenous depredations. Southerners by contrast are all gentlemen, regardless of class and background, and are scrupulously observant of the norms of civilized behavior. When they are not, in recognition of the fatal flaw in the tragic hero, they always repent at the end. Little is ever said about Confederate white ethnicity, except the underlying assumption, seen in contrast to the repeated ethnicization of the enemy, that "Southern" must itself be an ethnicity of pure and noble derivation.

So, in short, this is a war between good and evil, a war forced on the peaceful Southern land, its inoffensive people, and its unobjectionable way of life. This vision comes through clearly, for example, in the replacement lyrics for a proposed Confederate national anthem penned by St. George Tucker early in the war.[27] In the second verse of this song, Tucker laid out what seemed to him to be the causes of the burgeoning conflict; the broadside containing the lyrics is dated just two weeks after the start of the war in April 1861:

> How peaceful and blest was America's soil,
> 'Till betrayed by the guile of the Puritan demon,
> Which lurks under Virtue, and springs from its coil,
> To fasten its fangs in the life-blood of freemen.
> Then loudly appeal to each heart that can feel,
> And crush the foul viper 'neath Liberty's heel;
> And the Cross of the South shall forever remain
> To light us to freedom and glory again.[28]

Here we have the theme of the Northern other, in the "Puritan demon," juxtaposed to Southern freemen and therefore presumably not free itself. This demon is the betrayer of America's soil and will be defeated by the crushing heel of liberty. In short, this is the Southern script for the war, their self-justificatory explanation for their own innocence in opposition to Northern perfidy. They, the South, are the aggrieved party here.[29]

The last verse of Tucker's anthem maps out the future, much as the last verse of Francis Scott Key's hymn did for the United States in 1814. In Tucker's version,

> And if peace should be hopeless, and justice denied,
> And war's bloody vulture should flap its black pinions.

> Then gladly to arms, while we hurl in our pride
>> Defiance to tyrants and death to their minions,
> With our front in the field, swearing never to yield,
>> Or return, like the Spartan, in death on our shield,
> And the Cross of the South shall triumphantly wave
>> As the flag of the free and the pall of the brave.[30]

Or, as Key put it, writing at Fort McHenry in September 1814,

> Oh! thus be it ever, when freemen shall stand
>> Between their loved homes and the war's desolation!
> Blest with victory and peace, may the heaven-rescued land
>> Praise the Power that hath made and preserved us a nation.
> Then conquer we must, for our cause it is just,
>> And this be our motto: "In God is our trust."
> And the star-spangled banner forever shall wave
>> O'er the land of the free and the home of the brave![31]

This distinction runs to the heart of Confederate Americanism, in literature or anywhere else: there is a world of difference between the flag flying over the home of the brave, and the flag acting as the pall of the brave. On the one hand, the flag welcomes home the still-living defender of the free; on the other, it decorates his coffin and consoles his grieving relatives and friends. Tucker's vision is of a hell in which Southern bravery and fortitude might carry the day but at a tremendous cost; Key's vision is of a land blessed by peace and justice, looked over favorably by the Almighty. One is a vision of unyielding defiance, struggle, and possibly heroic defeat; the other, a vision of just conquest and victory. Both, however, are visions of a nation, of an America, challenged.

William Shepperson's choice of words in the quote that opens this chapter offers a similar example: "The book embalms if it does not immortalize."[32] To be immortal is to be exempted from death, to be remembered in fame everlasting; but to be embalmed is to have one's mortal shell—and that alone—preserved from the decay of the tomb. An immortal walks among us still, an embalmed corpse is forgotten in its dusty mausoleum—which would any author prefer, immortality or embalming? The flag as pall and the book as embalmed make the same negative point about the future of the South. This sense of tragedy is seen again in a comparison between two of the most popular songs of the war, North and South. For Northern audiences, Julia Ward Howe's "Battle Hymn of the Republic" aggressively bound the Creator to the Union cause and denied the possibility of defeat:

> I have read a fiery gospel writ in burnish'd rows of steel
> "As ye deal with my contemners, So with you my grace shall deal;"
> Let the Hero, born of woman, crush the serpent with his heel
> Since God is marching on.
> He has sounded forth the trumpet that shall never call retreat
> He is sifting out the hearts of men before His judgment-seat
> Oh, be swift, my soul, to answer Him! be jubilant, my feet
> Our God is marching on.[33]

By contrast, Daniel Decatur Emmett's "Dixie" wistfully entreats its listeners to "look away, look away," to "take my stand to live and die in Dixie."[34] Just as with the gulf between Key and Tucker, between Shepperson's twin fates for Confederate literature, so the song that inspired the Union called on God to smite others, while the song that inspired the Confederacy called on Southerners to die (at least by implication) for their homeland. Northerners told others to die and expected to be remembered in glory, Southerners expected to die themselves and be remembered in tragedy.

One can push such comparisons too far, and most of St. George Tucker's literary contemporaries did not overtly share his dark vision of the coming conflict. But they very much did share his vision of the Southern self and the Northern other. In Sally Rochester Ford's novel *Raids and Romances; or, Morgan and His Men* (1863), General Morgan's first appearance in the text is accompanied by a description bordering on the adulatory—his horsemanship is elegant, his features "bespoke daring and determination," his mustache is "trimmed with exquisite precision," he is handsome and immaculately clothed, and he manifests both "manly dignity" and "graceful ease."[35] In short, he is the sort of man you would want to call on your daughter. His men and his Cause are blessed on high, and their conduct will only be that befitting civilized gentlemen: "Did not the pitying eye of the Lord Jehovah look down upon this brave band of patriots, and have the wrongs these freemen then endured come up before Him in remembrance, when defeat and panic and route have overtaken the insolent oppressor?" These are men who actually guard the property of Unionists with the "same fidelity" as they guard the property of their friends and neighbors.[36]

Ford also made it abundantly clear that Morgan and his men were chivalrous gentlemen in contrast to the barbarous and depraved Yankees. Almost from the first, the northern foes are seen as "hordes of blue-coated Abolitionists," whose "polluted feet [are] desecrating the streets of our city." They are the "jail-birds and wharf rats" commanded by men who are "coarse, [and] vulgar . . . devoid of honesty and patriotism; destitute, indeed of every thing but bombast and selfishness." These are men who shoot stretcher-bearers and torment prisoners of war: "Such was the brutality and heartlessness—such the entire destitution of every emotion of humanity in the hearts of these vulgar, stinking wretches, that they jeered and scoffed, and with low and cruel mockery taunted their helpless prisoners."[37]

More than these venal crimes of lowborn men, however, the hordes of Abolitionists are not even Americans. For Ford, writing of events just a few years past, the Union soldiers were "ignorant Irish and Dutch Lincolnites, who cared no more about the Constitution and the laws, in whose name and by whose authority they claimed a right to practice their outrages, than did the perjured tyrants at Washington."[38] Moreover, these outrages are described by the author in luminous detail:

> The Federals proceeded to Gallatin, but found no Confederates upon whom to be revenged. But their insatiable cruelty must be gratified, and with that the fiendishness characteristic of the Yankee soldier, they sought out the aged and peaceful citizens, and dragged them from their homes, to incarcerate them in their wretched dungeons.
>
> From house to house these armed wretches proceeded, bursting open doors, rushing from room to room, using revolting language to unprotected females, dragging forth, with abuse and cruelty, old men whose only crime was daring to oppose such inhuman proceedings, and a government that would sanction and support them. . . .
>
> A squad of fifteen of these armed ruffians, with demonic yells and imprecations, rushed upon the Masonic Lodge, drove in the door, and with the fury of madmen, upset and broke chairs, tables, desks, dashed the fragments about the room, threw the Bible from the window, dragged forth the paraphernalia of the order, and scattered it wildly about the streets.[39]

In every sense of the word, Union troops do not act like civilized human beings, like free men, like good republican men, like Southrons. Instead, they insult ladies, abuse the elderly, and desecrate the holiest of books. They can sink no lower.

Similar themes infect the work of other authors as well. Augusta Jane Evans dedicated her 1863 novel *Macaria; or, Altars of Sacrifice*:

> To this vast legion of honor,
> Whether limping on crutches through
> The land they have saved and immortalized,
> Or surviving uninjured to share the blessings their
> Unexampled heroism bought, or sleeping dreamlessly in nameless
> Martyr-graves on hallowed battle-fields whose
> Historic memory shall perish only with
> The remnants of our language.[40]

Those gallant boys fought the "hireling hordes of oppression," and the scenes of carnage at the end of each battle (First Manassas, in this case) were the "fruits of the bigotry and fanatical hate of New England, aided by the unprincipled demagoguism of the West; such were the wages of Abolitionism, guided by Lincoln and Seward . . . such the results of 'higher law,' canting, puritanical hypocrisy."[41]

For Mary Jane Haw, in her novel *The Rivals* (1864), the Federals were "hordes of ruthless and barbaric hirelings," set out to oppress the free men of the South "in consequence of a long course of political chicanery and corruption, grasped by a set of *fanatical demagogues*, who declared that noble Constitution 'a covenant with death and an agreement with hell,' and who were pledged to use the whole power and resources of the country to rob and oppress a large and important part of it." Here again the Federals were represented by "dirty Dutchmen," only capable of communicating through "a volley of coarse oaths, uttered in broken English or low Dutch, and enforced by rude, menacing gestures." These Yankees are despoilers of graves, inveterate thieves, and abusers of the very slaves they are ostensibly supposed to be freeing. The tragic hero of the piece, turncoat Virginian Walter Maynard, retains his commission in the U.S. Army at the outbreak of hostilities for purely mercenary reasons— Americans are incapable of patriotism for their own country it seems, a sentiment only felt by true Southerners for their nation. Denied the advancement his Southern heritage and martial proficiencies anticipate, Colonel Maynard is redeemed by dying, in best melodramatic fashion, advancing on Richmond in June 1862. By this point,

He would have gladly sacrificed fortune and fame to stand by Charley Foster's side among that noble band of self-sacrificing Southern patriots, whose valor and heroism challenged his respect and excited his highest admiration. Thus, while the deadly missiles were flying around him, he scarcely heeded them; for conscience, lately aroused, was lashing him with a whip of scorpions for his treachery to his friend and to his country. For some time past he had been oppressed with a fearful presentiment of approaching death; and while he felt life to be a burden, his soul recoiled in horror from the thought of standing in judgment before a just and righteous God.

Maynard thanks the Lord for the Confederate victory, is forgiven by his friend and the woman they both love, and dies, having "sinned and suffered his last on earth."[42] It is hard not to caricature the melodramatic evil and simplistic binaries between Southern good and Northern evil that are articulated in these pages, but the pervasiveness of the same tropes suggests something more at work.

The master of this genre, at least in the sense of hyperbolic patriotism if not literary merit, was James Dabney McCabe. In his novel *The Aid-de-Camp* (1863), General Beauregard serves the same function that General Morgan had for Sally Ford. The first time the reader sees him, through the eyes of McCabe's protagonist Edward Marshall:

> He was sitting at a table, glancing over some papers, but rose as the gentlemen entered. . . . There was much of benevolence and good humor in the expression of his countenance, and through every action there breathed a quiet dignity which at once won the respect and confidence of all persons. You felt at a glance that he was born a soldier. It was impossible to see him without admiring him, and it was equally impossible to know him without honoring and loving him. Uniting that warm and genial disposition which at once endeared him to all, with that brilliant military genius which has ranked him among the greatest Generals of the age, it is not strange that every Southern soldier's heart should throb with devotion, and his eye glow with pride, when he hears the magic name of Beauregard. It is to him the embodiment of chivalry and patriotism.[43]

At the same time, Lincoln and his cronies were creating an army of the "scum of the North and West . . . mustered into the Federal regiments," a mob of "half armed and miserable specimens of humanity" masquerading as soldiers of the United States. The villain of this piece, a Phila-delphian by the name of Henry Cameron, kidnaps Marshall's one true love, Mary Worthington, after she rejects his odious suit. Cameron, with the obligatory hair "black as night" and a "foul and sinister expression about the mouth," conceives a dastardly plot to force Miss Worthington to marry him in order to save her beau, whom Cameron has had arrested on trumped-up charges of treason. She has the obvious choice, marry the villain to save her love from execution or watch him die. She escapes through the usual machinations of deus ex machina, as Cameron's wife, whom he has tried to cast aside in favor of Worthington, releases her from captivity at the last minute. She then conspires to free Marshall from jail, because it never occurs to his brutish captors that anyone might smuggle in rope and "a set of burglar's tools."[44]

Yet the execrable McCabe reserves his choicest vitriol for the chief conspirator himself, President Abraham Lincoln. In most of these nov-els, the chief Lincolnite usually watches the proceedings from the safety of Washington, D.C., like a spider in the center of its web. But in *The Aid-de-Camp*, Lincoln has a bit-part role. On his way from Baltimore to Charleston in April 1861, Edward Marshall stops in the capital to visit his friend, Mr. Wheeler, "an old gentleman who had long enjoyed the confi-dence of those high in authority, and nearly every President, irrespective of party, sought his advice and confidence. He was known to be a strong friend to the South, and had passed unnoticed by President Lincoln."[45] Wheeler takes Marshall through a secret tunnel into the White House and thence by a series of secret passages to a concealed viewing gallery overlooking the Cabinet room. So, on April 7, 1861, young Edward Mar-shall gets to see the Republican Cabinet in action. His descriptions of the protagonists, juxtaposed with that of Beauregard, make abundantly clear the two species of men with which we are dealing. Where Beauregard is benevolent, warm, dignified, honorable, and chivalric, creating love, devotion, and patriotism in his wake, Lincoln and his gang are uncouth, ignorant, sinister, knavish, and serpentine, only trawling behind them oppression, ambition, deception, and unbridled self-interest.

We first get to see the president with his feet on the table, and his "whole appearance was expressive of great awkwardness, and there was about him . . . a dejected and careworn look upon his countenance, and an eager, uneasy gleam in his dark eyes . . . at once suggestive of fraud and ignorance." Secretary of the Treasury Salmon "Chase was a fair specimen of a keen, shrewd Yankee sharper. The quick, piercing eye, the restless and uneasy air, the mocking and sinister mouth, all told of trickery and deceit." Postmaster General and native Marylander Montgomery Blair "was dark and gloomy. A bitter and malignant expression constantly hovered upon his countenance. . . . His manner towards the President was a strange mixture of fawning servility and contemptuous hate." Secretary of War Simon Cameron had about him "an air of defiant boldness and accomplished knavery which at once convinced the gazer that the man was a great villain." Secretary of State William Seward, the greatest villain of all, "the master spirit of the Cabinet, the true Ruler of the Union," impresses Marshall with his "calm, cold face, in which not a particle of color was visible. . . . There was something fascinating in his appearance, but it was the fascination of the serpent, that made the gazer shudder as he looked upon him. One felt that he was a man utterly destitute of principle and integrity, that ambition was his God, and that he feared nothing, scrupled at nothing, in his efforts to gratify his absorbing passion."[46] These men are either villains themselves, immoral knaves, or willing dupes of an insidious and morally and politically corrosive force. How can they successfully prosecute such an iniquitous war against the gallant and stoic South?

The topic for the evening's discussion on April 7, as overseen by Marshall, was the need to manufacture a war with the South to satisfy the presumed desires of the Northern electorate and the depraved ambitions of Seward, the sinister Grand Vizier standing behind a master—Lincoln—who, as he himself puts it, wished he had never been elected: "Here's a pretty night's work, d—n the luck; I wish I had never been elected; but I must stick to it. Seward says we must run the machine as we found her, if we bust her; and I'll do it." Seward's plan is to attempt to reinforce Fort Sumter, expecting a Southern military response, which will then "arouse the Northern and Western States, and we will be able to mould them as we will. It is necessary to sacrifice the garrison of Fort Sumter for the effect that it will have upon the Free States." And lest the reader be unclear, the point here is not the preservation of the Union but the preservation of Republican political power, or, as Seward puts it, in the absence of a war:

"We must go out of power . . . if we yield to the South, the people will drag us from power. There is a strong anti-slavery sentiment in the country, which will sustain us in a war with the South, and we can work upon the Unionism of the people. There is no retreat for us, gentlemen," he continued emphatically. "We are pledged to carry on the war against slavery, and we have tried the ballot-box long enough. We must now use the sword."

The end result of this war, which Secretary Cameron admits will be "long and bloody," will also be "advantageous to us as individuals, and in the end we will conquer the South. We have greater resources, more men and material, and we shall finally hold the Southern States as conquered Provinces." Seward ends the meeting by calling the president a "fool," admitting that what they are about is "a d—d rascally piece of business. But we can't help ourselves," and then departing, stage left, for a brandy with his puppet chief executive.[47]

In this overseen exchange among the Northern conspirators-in-chief, we see encapsulated many of the themes characteristic of the genre. Abolitionism is but a tool of the power-hungry, the South is innocent of any aggression and the victim of Northern plots and machinations in which perfidious politicians are willing to sacrifice the lives of their own soldiers in order to manufacture a casus belli. Clearly, the disrespectful, brutish, and self-interested Republicans would not know gentlemanly and civilized behavior if it walked up to them in the street and called them out. The comparison between the fictive Northerner and the fictive Southerner in these novels could not be clearer: the Demon Yankee meets the Worthy Southron and is bested by him. Furthermore, the Northerners are a debased shell of their region's former glories. The true Americans are the Confederates who watch them, guard against their inequities, and ultimately fight to resist their tyranny. There is nothing noble or worth emulating in Lincoln's Cabinet room or in the ranks of the Union Army. Yet, everything that is worth preserving, everything of the true American nation, is to be found in the ranks of gray.

Presumably the brandy to be shared between Seward and Lincoln would be served by one of the White House's servants, and there is a fair chance that servant would be an African American. Yet such a person is not present in this scene. In fact, such people, whether slave or free, are rarely present in any of these novels.[48] On rare occasions, African Americans did serve as part of the backdrop to the story, as grooms or servants or musicians. For example, in Haw's *The Rivals,* we see "a negro groom, much encumbered with satchels and carpet-bags, brought up the rear of the cavalcade," and "a couple of negro fiddlers occupying a little platform in the hall between the doors opening into each room." We also learn that "the Misses Maynard owned no servant except an elderly man and his wife, a half grown boy, and some younger children; and they were not able to hire."[49] In Napier Bartlett's *Clarimonde,* we hear at one point that "a sedate quadroon servant announced that a carriage was waiting."[50] In Evans's *Macaria,* we learn from Mr. Campbell, "I have a negro to attend to my office, make fires, etc."; from Electra Grey that she is "going down next week with Uncle Eric, to consult with the overseer about several changes which I desire made concerning the negroes"; and from Irene Huntingdon about the fact "that negro labor is by no means so profitable in factory as field seems well established."[51]

On a few occasions in these novels, slave characters are given voice, but that voice belongs to the white literary puppeteer—the slaves themselves still remain silent, their putative voice given them by their white literary creators and put to the service of the same cause as the white characters. The clearest example of this comes in Mary Jane Haw's *The Rivals.* For Haw, a black character actually serves as a pivotal plot device in the overarching story of Walter Maynard's apostasy and deathbed conversion back to the Confederate cause. Miss Emeline Maynard's elderly servant is given full voice by his creator, and he—"Uncle Tom he would have been called anywhere else in Virginia, but the Misses Maynard called him Uncle Thomas"—was first used by Haw to show full black complicity in the Southern system of manners.[52] Uncle Thomas becomes visibly upset when Charley Foster tries to usurp his duties, telling the slave servant that there is no need to brush his coat as he can do it himself. In reply,

> said uncle Thomas, with dignity, straightening up his bent figure, "I'm never too tired to wait on my young master's visitors. I don't hurt myself with work; I ain't obliged to work; nobody ever says work to Thomas. But things here ain't on as grand a scale as I was always used to, and there being so many fewer colored folks than I was raised with, and not so much company with the white folks as used to be, I gets sorter lonesome, and jest works for company like, and to set the youngsters a good example and teach 'em industrious habits."[53]

Here Haw—through Uncle Thomas—argues that this sort of elderly house servant only works because he wants to, that no one makes him, and that he does so out of a sense of loyalty and obligation to his owners and a desire to replicate such good habits in succeeding generations. As we will see shortly, one of Haw's chief complaints, as expressed through her slave character, is that more recent generations of African Americans do not share Uncle Thomas's work ethic and sense of responsibility.

Uncle Thomas appears again in the narrative during the war, when Colonel Maynard's regiment has advanced sufficiently to bring the almost-deserted Poplar Lodge house within Union lines. Maynard, looking for some evidence of inhabitation, overhears a "genuinely pathetic" prayer from his aunt's former servant:

> "O, Lord, deliver us! Good Lord, save us. O, Lord, arise in our defence. Drive back these Philistines that have come up against us—these worse than Egyptians, that rob and despoil us. Let loose upon them the thunder-bolts of Thy wrath. Grind them under the chariot-wheels of Thy justice. Scatter them as chaff before the wind.—Smite them as Thou didst the hosts of Sennecharib. Overthrow them both horse and rider into the Red Sea of thy destruction.
>
> "And Thou, O Lord, who seest the little sparrows when they fall upon the ground, and hearest the young ravens when they cry to Thee, take knowledge of Thy unworthy servant Thomas. Suffer him not to perish, but give him this day his daily bread. Thou who didst send the ravens to feed Elijah in the wilderness, succor poor Thomas. O Lord, have mercy."

We discover that when the aunts left for Richmond, Uncle Thomas "was left here, by my own request, to take care of the things." So we see that Uncle Thomas was so loyal and responsible that he would willingly risk his life in defense of his mistresses' property and presumably their honor as well. After Maynard makes his presence known, Uncle Thomas tells him that he is "'Miserable! miserable! ruined!'" and again, Thomas's primary concern is for the property and propriety of his mistress. His primary grievance is with the depredations of the blue-coated barbarian hordes:

> "Thousands would'nt repair the damage; and we havn't got a cent. . . . Thousands wouldn't replace what we've lost; every living thing eaten up; every green thing devoured by these blue-legged locusts; the house pulled all to pieces; the fences all burnt; the horse stolen; the very furniture that used to stand in your grandfather's drawing-room taken for firewood. God knows I tried to save something; but they cussed me, called me a 'Rebel nigger,' and threatened to stick their bayonets in me. I asked 'em was that the way

for gemmen to behave; and they cussed me again, and asked me what did I know 'bout gemmen. I told them I had been raised with gemmen, and by gemmen that wouldn't 'a had a Yankee to black thar boots; and at that, one that they called the corporal, knocked me down."

Colonel Maynard then suggests that Uncle Thomas had been "impertinent" and therefore received appropriate chastisement. Uncle Thomas indignantly replies, "'La! Mars Walter . . . they ain't no better'n niggers, nor so good, in my opinion. All that will turn 'ginst thar marsters and go with them, and lie and steal for them, it's 'hail fellow, well met,' they are gemmen; but them that stays with their marsters and mistresses that has raised 'em, are infernal niggers!" We also discover that while Southern soldiers had been bivouacked in the neighborhood for more than a week, they had stolen nothing; it apparently only took the Northern troops three days to completely wipe the countryside clean of movable loot.[54]

Another slave from the surrounding region, one John, known as Smith's John to indicate his position in the community, comes in for particular complaint, as it appears that their previous dealings had predisposed John to see Thomas come to the unfavorable attention of the invaders. For the Haw-voiced Thomas, John is the archetypal slave who "turn 'ginst thar marsters." John, who in Thomas's eyes is coincidentally "the grandest rogue and liar in the county of Hanaracco" and "a grand rascal," encourages the soldiers, "tellin' them that I guided the 'Rebels' 'bout here, and fed thar pickets." It turns out that John's intelligence is absolutely correct, though Thomas does not think John actually knew that and was instead just guessing, because, for Thomas, the real issue in this episode is payback: John "owed me a grudge for catchin' him stealin' Miss Judith's turkeys last winter, and carryin' him before the magistrate. He got thirty-nine lashes then."[55]

This episode is pivotal to the plot, for it enables Maynard to learn that his relatives have been disgraced by his behavior, that he is the shame of the family, no better than "a Benedict Arnold, a Judas Iscariot, a renegade." This gets him started on the road to his eventual battlefield, deathbed recanting.[56] From our point of view, however, it illuminates neatly the place of the slave in this fictive Confederate America being built by Haw and others. Not surprisingly, slaves that put their owners first, who risk their lives in the defense of whites, who betray their community to safeguard white property are the model. The slave who seeks freedom, who chafes at the petty indignities and fundamental injustices of chattel slavery, is the "grand rascal." Not only, therefore, is the voice of the slave silent in this narrative of a nationalist and independent Confederacy, but their very personhood is submerged beneath the assumed needs of the white story. And if the slave himself does not desire freedom, as Uncle Thomas and his ilk clearly do not, then the "hordes of blue-coated Abolitionists" are merely acting out of some internal, narcissistic need to impose their norms and practices on others.[57] Demon Yankees—abolitionists and Lincolnites all—are breaking this Union for their own self-aggrandizement. Worthy Southrons could not allow themselves to believe anything less.

The pervasiveness of these tropes of liberty and abolition; of free Southrons and hired Federals; of depraved, ethnic Northerner soldiers and ethnically pristine Southern gentlemen; of civilization and barbarity; and of white noise and black silence is striking. The same themes and juxtapositions run through much of the admittedly small genre of Confederate wartime literature. On the one hand, as commentators like Daniel Aaron have remarked, this understanding of the present conflict was fatally flawed. By the time these novels started to see public light, often as serials in literary periodicals like the *Magnolia Weekly* and the *Southern Illustrated News* in 1862 and 1863, the mythic present they depicted was evaporating like an early morning mist. And Confederate literature faced the same nationalist challenge of every other sphere of indigenous cultural production in the wartime South—if the conflict was such a clear and evident example of good and evil, why was evil winning? Confederate nationalists and the texts upon which they relied could not satisfactorily answer that question. And at least in part they could not satisfactorily answer the question precisely because the mythic present they had created and in which they preferred to live was obscuring their gaze. They could not see the trees of the war for the forest that was their nationalism. On the other hand though, as we have noted in previous chapters, whether or not the Confederate nation was successful, there was created a distinct sense of Confederate nationalism in the South during the Civil War, and this literature was instrumental in that endeavor. As we said at the end of chapter 2, literature does not make nationalism in and of itself, and it most certainly does not win wars for independence. But the nationalist ideas that flowered in this literature were at the heart of the Confederate conception of self and, had the outcome of the war been different, would, it seems safe to say, have taken root.

5

To "Surpass All the Knighthood of Romance"

Soldiers as Paragons of Confederate Nationalism

In the nature of things, . . . among a people begirt by enemies
. . . there is a deeper pathos, a loftier poetry in the incidents
of yesterday's battle-field than belong to the most tuneful
measures, while Jack Morgan and Jeb Stuart surpass all the
knighthood of romance.

Southern Illustrated News (1862)

We have made the point repeatedly that, had the Confederacy in some
way prevailed in the war, the foundation had been laid for the development of a mature Confederate nationalism. Although the nation it
created had a longer timeframe with which to work than did the Confederacy, the United States that emerged out of the Revolutionary War, and
particularly the figure of General George Washington, provides an earlier example of a similar phenomenon. Don Higginbotham argues that
Washington self-consciously capitalized on his wartime emergence as
"the most visible and meaningful sign of American cohesion throughout
the independence struggle," and that "nation-building had been his mission as early as 1776." Higginbotham concludes, "In this case, a man who,
like the hedgehog, knew one big thing, and that was national unity."[1] Unlike his later Confederate peers, Washington had the advantages of victory in his war for independence, time to establish a nation, and purpose.
It is not unreasonable, however, to suppose that Robert E. Lee may have
emerged in the aftermath of a Confederate victory to fulfill a somewhat
analogous role. In a more expansive study, Sarah Purcell argues that
"military memory, especially memory of the Revolutionary War, is really
at the heart of American national identity." She suggests that "by focusing

on a few central heroic figures, martyrs like Joseph Warren, Americans looked beyond the immediate battlefield and created remarkable symbols of patriotism which they thought to be worthy of remembrance and commemoration."[2] As we shall see, if you switch the name Joseph Warren for that of Stonewall Jackson, you have a remarkably similar phenomenon occurring in the Confederacy. The living Washington and the dead Warren served to cement a particular vision of national unity and sacrifice in the imagination of Americans in the 1770s and 1780s. In like manner, the living Lee and the dead Jackson instilled ideas of a mythic present of a Confederate America in the minds of white Confederates during the war years. This latter instance occurred at a much accelerated pace, as the Revolutionary War lasted some six years to the Civil War's four, and of course the insurgents won in the former case and thus had the postbellum time and space necessary to build a national polity, which the Confederates did not.

As the ever ebullient Joseph Addison Turner put it from his plantation in rural Georgia, a few months from the end of the war,

> We love the south still, and are determined, if fate so ordains it, to die by her. . . . But die, the South will not. . . . The darkness which surrounds her, will break, and roll away: and . . . she will stand forth in her might, and the nations shall know, and feel her power.
>
> This will be so, if the sons of the south will be but true to her. Many of them must bite, as many have bitten the dust. . . . But by and by, peace will come with healing in her wings, and with earth's immortal sons shall be written the names Lee, and Beauregard, and Jackson, and Johnston, and Forrest, and Hood, and thousands of others, as brave, though not as distinguished as they.[3]

For Turner, as for any who remained loyal to the Confederacy and its goals, those heroes of the battlefield were all that kept the blue-clad wolf from the door. Yet Turner's words contain the implication of a divide between the project of nationalism and the project of nation. By January 1865, it seems rather unlikely that Turner believed the Confederacy would win the war, but he did believe that "the South . . . will stand forth in her might." As we noted in the introduction, five months later, in May 1865, Turner remained convinced that Confederate nationalism could survive, even if the Confederate nation had not. Given the relative victory of the South during Reconstruction, it is hard to argue that it did not, albeit in a very different manner than that seen after the American Revolution.

On April 9, 1865, "earth's immortal son," Robert E. Lee, surrendered to Ulysses S. Grant at Appomattox Courthouse in Virginia. Two weeks after that, on April 26, another "immortal son," Joseph E. Johnston, surrendered to William T. Sherman at Durham Station in North Carolina. Richard Taylor surrendered the remaining Confederate forces east of the Mississippi at New Orleans on May 4, and Edmund Kirby Smith surrendered the trans-Mississippi army on May 26. Stand Watie, the last Confederate general to formally lay down arms, did so on June 23, two and a half months after Appomattox.[4] At long last, the Civil War was over, although contrary to modern received wisdom it did not entirely end at Appomattox. Lee's surrender was instead the beginning of the end, and its modern prominence marks the immense shadow cast by Lee and the Army of Northern Virginia on Civil War history.

Moving backward in time to a point prior to these surrenders, it is apparent that the ability of the Confederate nation to achieve the immediate goal that mattered—political independence—was in the hands of the Confederate military, especially its army. Therefore, it is not surprising that from a relatively early point in the war, the putative makers of Confederate national opinion recognized this fact and incorporated it into their burgeoning nationalist project. A nation needs heroes, and a nation in creation during wartime potentially has them at hand in the person of victorious generals. In the case of the Confederacy, its officers were the Worthy Southron personified—noble, chivalrous, self-sacrificing, loyal, and honorable. A nation seeking to constitute itself through war, as the Confederacy did, might tend to concentrate on the virtues and achievements of its military men. As might be expected in the midst of a war, the Worthy Southron came to be depicted wearing cadet gray with stars on his collar and an Austrian knot of braid on his sleeve.

This use of military men to create a mythic present for the purposes of nationalist exploitation carried with it considerable dangers. On the one hand, military victory, political independence, and national consolidation were symbiotically linked together. While in theory the Confederacy could have achieved a favorable outcome to the war through extra-military ends, that would only be possible if Southern soldiers were able to exert sufficient battlefield pressure to convince Northern politicians—or even European statesmen—that a negotiated settlement was a safer solution than the specter of military defeat. On the other hand, the necessary reliance on the military both to achieve victory in the real world of the battlefield and the mythic world of nationalism created a feedback loop. The ability of nationalist expressions to buoy popular convictions about the course and conduct of the war—and particularly about the level of sacrifice required to achieve independence—was directly tied to military success. It could not, therefore, reasonably be expected to compensate for military failure. So, the mythic present of the Confederacy depended for its continued existence on everything going according to plan, and in battle, the plan only survives until the first shot is fired. What is true, however, is that the ability of the Confederacy to secure victory, and the ability of the Confederacy to achieve a sense of distinct nationhood, while obviously linked, were not entirely the same thing. As we have shown, a sense of Confederate Americanism clearly existed in several realms of cultural expression that relied on a fictional military to convey their message. What we turn to here is the role the actual military played in that process.

In the forefront of this effort to bind together the Confederate nation and its military men was the *Southern Illustrated News*. The Richmond publishing house of Ayres and Wade issued the first copy of this journal in September 1862. Just a week earlier, General Lee's forces had bested John Pope's Federals at the Second Battle of Bull Run (or Manassas), and just two days before the first appearance of the *Southern Illustrated News*, on September 4, the Army of Northern Virginia had started to cross the Potomac River in its invasion of Maryland. It is in times like these, when the project of national independence seems closer to reality than to a dream, that the production of nationalist ideologies and symbols becomes absolutely vital.

So, in their inaugural comment on "The Times," the editors of the *News* noted that this was a critical period for the Confederate nation, with hopes high and spirits buoyed by repeated victories against seemingly inferior Union generals:

> From the dark gloom of despondency, our people have been elevated into the clear sunlight of hope. Light has literally come out of darkness, confidence has succeeded to a state very nearly resembling despair, universal cheerfulness has assumed the place of general depression. In such a condition of the public mind our journal makes its appearance, like an emana-

tion from an atmosphere brilliant with anticipations of prosperity yet to come.[5]

Military victory and the Worthy Southron generals brought hope, light, confidence, good cheer, and the prospect of future success. The corollary, of course, was that military defeat, and the generals who provide it, bring despondency, darkness, despair, depression, and the prospect of future subjugation. The rhetorical dualism of the *News* mirrors the conundrum that lies at the heart of the relationship among the nation, its nationalism, and its military—the rewards are great, but the risks are greater still. For a nation in creation, like the Confederacy, all or nothing rides on this thin reed of hope.

With the benefit of historical hindsight, we know that the *News* was chasing rainbows when it forecast such a bright future for the Confederacy's national project. Early September 1862 was in fact just a fleeting interlude before the meat grinder of Antietam (or Sharpsburg) and the issuance of the Emancipation Proclamation, events that changed the tenor of the war—and the country—forever. In this brief historical moment in the fall of 1862, however, we can see the centrality of the Confederate military to its national endeavor. It was not lost on the editors of the *News* that the future prosperity to which they looked would come at the hands of the Confederacy's "great leader, and the gallant army which he commands"—that is to say, General Robert E. Lee and the Army of Northern Virginia.[6]

Historians have noted this connection among generals, their armies, and the nation they were fighting to prolong, although scholars sometimes choose to narrow it. For example, Gary W. Gallagher notes in *The Confederate War* that, "often preoccupied with Jefferson Davis and government institutions, historians interested in Confederate nationalism have failed to analyze Lee and his army as critical agents that engendered unity and hope." He goes on to argue that "the written record . . . affirms incontrovertibly that Lee and his soldiers influenced Confederate hearts and minds. . . . Well before the close of the war, Lee and his army had come to embody the Confederacy in the minds of many white southerners."[7] As we shall see, Robert E. Lee and the Army of Northern Virginia certainly figured prominently in attempts to create a sense of wartime Confederate nationalism, at least by the end of 1862. But it was, in fact, the person of Stonewall Jackson who seemed to capture a particular place in the emotional center of the Confederate nationalist project, and it was the death of Stonewall, at Chancellorsville in May 1863, that really brought into sharp focus the tenuous and potentially dangerous relationship among the military, the nation, and its nationalism.[8]

Twenty years before Gallagher's work, Thomas L. Connelly, writing of "Lee in His Time" in *The Marble Man*, noted that "the Confederate populace was convinced that it possessed several 'great military masters.' There were other men who rivaled and sometimes surpassed Lee in popularity."[9] Specifically, Connelly suggests that Stonewall Jackson was Lee's "main competitor for hero status," but Connelly also notes that at certain times Pierre G. T. Beauregard, Joseph E. Johnston, and Albert Sidney Johnston all appeared preeminent in the Confederate military pantheon.[10] Other scholars have pointed to the pivotal roles of such luminaries as Jeb Stuart, John Singleton Mosby, Turner Ashby, Nathan Bedford Forrest, and even, improbably, Edmund Kirby Smith.[11]

This list is potentially endless, not so much because any individual Confederate general or even ordinary soldier was preeminent over the others in the creation of Confederate nationalism, though some were clearly of first importance, but rather that the idea of the Confederate military leader sui generis was of vital importance to the ideological health and mission of the fledgling nation. We can follow this idea down to the local level, to see, for example, the status enjoyed by Martin Witherspoon Gary and Matthew Calbraith Butler as general officers in Edgefield, South Carolina, both of whom rode their wartime military prominence to postwar political leadership.[12] Military leaders were national figures experienced in the local communities, and it is no surprise that each community, each district, each state had its own favored sons, its own localized Worthy Southrons, just as it is no surprise that the Confederacy itself had those to whom it ceded the utmost in devotion and expectation. In particular, Lee and Jackson appear as lynchpins of this wartime nationalist production, the general for the ages and his doughty and tenacious lieutenant.

Yet a focus on Lee and Jackson should not lead us to ignore the sheer volume of poetry, prose, and other commentary lavished on various and sundry Confederate military figures. Regardless of the identity of its subject, the sheer volume of this literature provides ample evidence of the often overblown and unrealistic esteem in which various segments of the white Confederate population held their military figures. General Beauregard, for example, inspired poetry from two of the South's foremost men of letters, William Gilmore Simms and Paul H. Hayne. In late 1862, the *Southern Literary Messenger* published a song to the Creole general by Simms:

> The South, with meet reward,
> Will bring thee tribute, honour,—raise to fame, Beauregard:
> She will shine thee in her story,
> And proclaim to ages hoary
> How thou'st led her on to glory
> And find her cry of battle in thy name, Beauregard:
> Beau-fusil, Beauregard!
> Beau-canon, Beauregard!
> Beau-sabreur et beau soldat, Beauregard, Beauregard!"[13]

Two years later, when the possibilities for Southern success at arms were rather dimmer, the *Magnolia Weekly* printed Hayne's sonnet to Beauregard:

> Where'er such pregnant powers, in part or whole,
> We need to save us—there, invincible chief,
> Summoned by Heaven and thy loved people's voice,
> King like thou comest! lift thine eyes! rejoice!
> Fair Liberty! and golden-winged Relief,
> Fly on before, till victory's thunder roll
> On some great field, shall justify thy choice![14]

In both cases, the ultimate fate of the nation, and the implicit cause for which it was fighting, were inextricably bound up in the person of a single military leader. For Simms and Hayne, the notion of Beauregard as the archetypal Worthy Southron meant both that the South would celebrate him—Simms's "She will shine thee in her story" and Hayne's "Summoned by Heaven and thy loved people's voice"—and that his personal character would repay that celebration—Simms's "How thou'st led her on to glory" and Hayne's "till victory's thunder roll / . . . shall justify thy choice." The South would choose the Worthy Southron, and the Worthy Southron would lead the South to victory.

Similarly, in November 1864, *Southern Punch* printed an anonymous poem to commemorate Nathan Bedford Forrest's implacable assault on the foes of the Confederacy:

In carnage and flame they are victors still,
With the blood of the "Yank" they are drenching the hill—
Their rifles so true whence the death-shots go,
'Tis the Southrons who revel in chase of the foe. . . .
The Southron who saw Sherman's rear swept away,
Shall for ages of triumph remember this day,
Nor weep for his brothers, who bought with their blood
Their fatherland's freedom—the purchase was good;
His altars shall smoke, and his goblets o'erflow
To the Southrons who died in chase of the foe.[15]

There is far less of the honor and glory in this poem than in the odes to
Beauregard, either because of the changed dynamic of the war or because
of the more bloodthirsty reputation of the subject, but in any case, the
underlying message is the same—blood, sacrifice, and leadership will win
the freedom of the Southern land, whether rejoicing in liberty or bath-
ing in blood. In this case, substituting for the almost bloodless glory of
Simms's and Hayne's Beauregard, the mythic Forrest would drench the
landscape in "the blood of the 'Yank,'" and thus offer martial sacrifice
for "the Southrons who died in chase of the foe." For this was the other
conundrum embedded at the heart of the Worthy Southron as military
hero of the Confederacy—many would fall in service of their cause. For
the imagined Forrest, more so than the imagined Beauregard, blood sacrifice would substitute for personal glory.

To be fair, not everyone was as starry-eyed over the military hero, but
only one general frequently served as the butt of humor—Braxton Bragg.
For example, less than complimentary odes to Bragg appeared in *The
Countryman* and *Southern Punch* in late September 1863 in the immediate aftermath of Bragg's victory at Chickamauga. In the satirical entry in
the former, "Bragg the nag" makes an appearance:

Hurrah for Bragg,
The fastest nag,
That's yet been on the field, sir:
He kicked old Rose,
With such hard blows,
It made the Dutch horse yield, sir. . . .
This cunning rat
Has made us all change tunes, sir:

> But should again
> He fail amain—
> Ah! then, we'll curse him soon, sir.[16]

Three days earlier, in *Southern Punch*, a far more biting assessment appeared:

> Some said you had a wooden head,
>   And other people said
> That you had only brains enough
>   To find the way to bed. . . .
> The hero of a hundred fights
>   Alas! you never won;
> Victorious in retreats toward
>   The setting of the sun;
> Kentucky, Tennessee, will soon
>   Be both 'reclaimed,' we know,
> If you shall lead our soldiers, Bragg.[17]

Bragg exemplifies the danger expressed by the *Southern Illustrated News* that in these men, all was invested and much was expected—but what if they were unable to live up to the hopes placed upon them? Bragg, in particular, exemplified that dilemma and was lambasted for it. In this case, his lack of success demonstrated that this particular Southron was not Worthy at all.

To cement the role of the military in its conception of the Confederate nationalist project, the first issue of the *Southern Illustrated News* featured an extensive portrait of Stonewall Jackson on its first page. Virtually every subsequent issue of the journal highlighted another military portrait. For the *News,* the generals and the nation ran together, the martial Worthy Southron personifying the imagined Confederate nation. This first issue of the *News* made clear the dualistic problem of employing military men as nationalist heroes. On the one hand, they promised great victories, and a consequent growth of patriotism and loyalty as well as the ultimate promise of independence. But on the other hand, they carried the potential for defeat, disillusion, subjugation, and even death. This comes through, for example, in the respective attitudes of the *News* to leading Confederate and Union generals. While Stonewall Jackson was a soldier of God and the Southern republic, John Pope, the recently defeated Union commander, "*came*—and the poultry was swept by his sword, / Spoons, liquors and furniture went by the board; . . . / He *conquered*—truth, decency, honor full soon, / Pest, pilferer, puppy, pretender, poltroon."[18] The comparison between the two men could not be clearer: one was a Worthy Southron, the other a Demon Yankee. The former was a righteous warrior of the Divine, the latter a common thief and mean-spirited wretch. A nation at war lives or dies on the qualities of its military—an obvious statement to be sure, but one that had important implications for the burgeoning nationalist project of the Confederacy.

The *News* cast itself as a literary journal devoted to the fight for "our intellectual, as well as political independence," as one of their correspondents put it, and so they tended to see the stories of the war through a literary and intellectual lens.[19] In their inaugural "Salutatory" welcome to new readers, the editors of the *News* pointed to the power of battlefield stories to inspire, a power that "mere literary or artistic novelties" could not match. As they put it, "there is a deeper pathos, a loftier poetry in the incidents of yesterday's battle-field than belong to the most tuneful measures, while Jack Morgan and Jeb Stuart surpass all the knighthood of romance."[20] Or as George W. Bagby of the *Southern Literary Messenger* would later phrase it, "If the blood of martyrs be the seed of the church, the blood of heroes is the life-giving dew to the germs of liberty."[21] So Confederate military prowess loomed large as a unifying factor, something Southerners could gaze on with pride. Modern observers know that this was built on the sandy foundation of a few victories over poorly led foes, but those victories proved an ample fabric from which to spin a nationalist mythology with only a toehold in strategic realities.

From the outset, however, this mythology of victory was tenuous and undermined by the continuing possibility of defeat at the hands of the Federals. This points to the danger of creating a mythology at the same time as its story plays out. Another article, appearing on the same page of the *News* as the "Salutatory," makes this clear. Under the heading "Resting on Their Laurels," the editors admonished unnamed generals for letting fame and success go to their heads. As the writers put it,

> It is curious to observe that so soon as opinion crowns some of our generals with a little airy fame, they deem their fortune made and their duty ended. They forget that their scrap of good deeds past are being put in a huge wallet at Father Time's back, along with the other "alms for oblivion," and that,

whilst they feast their ears on the few lingering echoes of popular applause, even then they are in danger of going quite out of fashion, and like a rusty mail, hanging "in monumental mockery."

So, in this telling, the Worthy Southron has entered into a compact with the imagined Confederacy and must always remember that he is the servant of the nation and not the other way around. Glory in the service of the nation is the soldier's duty, while glory in the service of the self is his trial to avoid. Yet, the disapprobrium of public opinion was not the most important thing here, neither for the nation nor the Cause. The key was that the people—for whom the *News* presumed it could speak—had serious and weighty expectations of their generals, which the generals would disappoint at their own peril. As the *News* concluded this short piece, the authors noted that, from some of the Confederacy's leaders, "who are endowed with every quality of nature with which the hero should be gifted, every thing is demanded."[22] A military victory was expected from the Worthy Southron, along with conduct appropriate for a Southern gentleman, and ultimately independence and enduring nationhood.

A similar attitude toward the relationship of the military and the nation is seen at approximately the same time in the grandfather of Southern literary journals, the *Southern Literary Messenger*. In a late summer edition in 1862, in the aftermath of General George McClellan's failed Peninsular Campaign and the end of the Seven Days battles at Malvern Hill, the *Messenger*'s editor, George W. Bagby, noted that the people of Richmond had invested casual and complete faith in the ability of their soldiers to defend them. As he put it, "When the battle, which was to decide the fate of the Confederate capital, perhaps of the Confederacy itself, began, they took it very coolly, and went on about their business. They said, 'Jackson's come, and we know how it is going to end.'"[23] In fact, of course, the tardiness of Jackson's corps in moving to support General A. P. Hill at Mechanicsville on June 26 had led to a slaughter of Confederates, with casualty ratios four to one in favor of the Union in that engagement.[24] But it was Jackson's reputation, won in the Shenandoah Valley a few months earlier, that buoyed the spirits of the inhabitants of Richmond and cowed the susceptible McClellan.

Bagby chose to interpret the unflappable Richmonders as "apathetic rather than Yankeefied—'enthused' to madness by every little success." His own attitude toward Jackson, however, betrays the possibility of an alternate explanation—supreme confidence rather than apathy. For Bagby, Jackson was "that go-ahead, really great fighter—the pride and joy of the people . . . that true patriot, pure Christian, invincible soldier."[25] Bagby's faith in Stonewall was unshakable, and Bagby unconsciously projected that certitude onto the people of his city—but that of course raises the conundrum mentioned earlier, what happens when such an invincible, such an "immortal son," is found to be vincible or mortal?

The time-honored tradition of the martyred hero—which Stonewall certainly would become—provided one route out of that conundrum. But there were other fallen heroes for Confederates to mourn. Turner Ashby, one of Jackson's cavalry commanders, died in early June 1862 during the infamous Shenandoah Valley campaign. Almost immediately, the *Southern Literary Messenger* published a twenty-verse paean to his death. This poem covered much of the script of Confederate nationalism to that time. Ashby's troops caused the Northern "hireling legions turn to fly," and of course, "To Freedom's sons the victory." The poem ends with the hope that, "Sacred the soil that wraps his clay, / Where weepers dash their tears away, / To think upon the coming day / That brings *revenge* for ASHBY!"[26] Later in the same edition, a shorter ode by John R. Thompson expressed more long-ranging sentiments: "Throughout the coming ages, / When his sword is rust, / And his deeds in classic pages, / Mindful of her trust—/ Shall Virginia, bending lowly, / Still a ceaseless vigil holy / Keep above his dust!"[27] In the first place, the martyred hero belongs to the present, as he represents an opportunity to inspire immediate revenge as the troops march out to do battle in the weeks and months after his death. In the second place, the martyred hero belongs to the future past, as he represents an opportunity to memorialize the cause to those who were too young, or not yet born, when it lived. The present martyr however is also a visceral reminder that the Cause demands blood in the here and now.

Another lesser-known martyr was Lieutenant Colonel Joseph V. Scott of the 3rd Virginia, who apparently died heroically at Malvern Hills in July 1862. He was the subject of a John Harry Hartman "Tribute" in the *Southern Illustrated News* the following October. In this case, martyrdom was specifically linked to the cause of nation: "The pride of a nation which valued thy worth; . . . / And Peace shall bequeath to the sons of the free, / A home and an anchor 'neath 'Liberty's Tree.'"[28] In this case again, blood and sacrifice would ensure the future safety of peace and liberty.

But, one must ask, was the future benefit to Colonel Scott's family and community worth the cost? That was one of the essential purposes of the Confederate nationalist narrative, to make the Cause worthy of the sacrifice and loyalty it demanded of Southerners.

This need for martyrs could also have ironic consequences. Felix Zollicoffer was a Confederate brigadier general killed at the battle of Fishing Creek (or Mill Springs) in January 1862. Later that spring, in April, the *Southern Literary Messenger* published the obligatory poem to the fallen hero, by one H. L. Flash. According to Flash, Zollicoffer was "First in the fight, and first in the arms / Of the white-winged angels of glory, . . . / And nothing on earth remaining, / But a handful of dust in the land of his choice, / A name in song and story, / And Fame to shout with her brazen voice, / 'DIED ON THE FIELD OF GLORY.'"[29] In point of fact, Felix Zollicoffer died because he lost track of where he was on the battlefield. He was shot after he rode into Union lines thinking they were his troops. He died trying to order those same Union troops not to shoot at Confederate troops, who he thought were their comrades. Zollicoffer may indeed have been a hero, but he was also supremely unlucky and perhaps a little foolish. Yet to match the script, he had to fit into only one box—martyr to the Cause.

Zollicoffer was not prominent enough to merit a feature spread in the *Southern Illustrated News,* but many of his peers did enjoy such prominence. The centerpiece of the *News,* the thing that cemented its commitment to the Confederate nation and its putative military heroes, was the paper's ongoing series of front-page portraits of leading military figures. Many of these were, as the name of the journal might suggest, illustrated with engravings of the men under discussion. The first engravings were small head shots, but starting with Turner Ashby in the sixth issue, they presented the occasional cavalier-like pose on horseback. Starting with Robert E. Lee in the nineteenth issue in January 1863, the *News* offered full-page portraits of the generals complete with accompanying artillery pieces and Confederate flags.[30] After Lee, such luminaries as Albert Sidney Johnston, Lloyd Tilgham, James Longstreet, and Pierre Beauregard were feted with full-page spreads. A few exceptions to this domination of the front page by generals—and the occasional naval officer—occurred, most notably by "Vicksburg, Mississippi" in the ninth issue and "The Society of Women" in the fifteenth.[31] But even when the front page was taken, portraits of generals continued in the interior pages, with Braxton Bragg and Jeff Thompson featured, respectively, in these instances. And in a pre–mass media society, we should not undervalue the power of images like these to make their points and stir a sense of patriotism and nationalism.

The first issue of the *News* contained, just under its masthead, a profile of Stonewall Jackson, and Jackson's career illustrates the dangers of relying on the military as exemplars of national virtue. According to the *News*, Stonewall was immune to the "prejudice and bigotry of rank," was a soldier's soldier and a leader "daunted by no danger, exhausted by no toil, caught by no stratagem." Perhaps more than all of this, he was marked by a "rigid remembrance of Divine power."[32] In short, in terms of temperament and character, he was perhaps the perfect expression of the Confederate general. Jackson also inspired literary flourishes from the correspondents and contributors to the *Southern Illustrated News*, including Hard Cracker's "Foot-Cavalry Chronicle" and "Jackson's Foot-Cavalry"; "Stonewall Jackson's Way," supposedly found on the body of a sergeant in Stonewall's brigade; and Virginia Norfolk's "Over the River," allegedly based on Jackson's last words. As Hard Cracker notes, "The foe had better ne'er been born / Than get in Stonewall's way." In another poem, the same author continues,

> No wonder that the Yankees run,
> > And will not stop to fight;
> For we've no need of sword or gun—
> > They cannot stand a *sight*.
> Our long hair floating on the wind,
> > Like witches in Macbeth—
> They know they dare not lag behind—
> > We'll have their—shoes, or death.[33]

Jackson's troops, and Jackson himself, were seen as just a little bit magical in what they were able to accomplish against their Northern foes. In fact, Stonewall appeared to inculcate more devotion from the partisans of the *News*, and indeed other Southern periodicals, than any other individual.

And yet Stonewall was human, and his mythic status was ultimately disfigured by his death by friendly fire in May 1863 after the battle of Chancellorsville. Instant reaction to Jackson's death, published in *The Countryman* just a few weeks after the battle, suggested the depths of the tragedy. For one aspiring poet, Jackson's death represented, "The heaviest blow / That ever rent a nation's heart, / Is that which laid our chieftain low."[34] For another, Jackson's death was cause for lamentation:

> His warrior-soul its earthly shackles broke
>> In the full sunshine of a peaceful town;
> When all the storm was hushed, the sturdy oak
>> That propped our cause, went down.
> Though his alone the blood that flecks the ground,
>> Recalling all his grand, heroic, deeds,
> Freedom herself is writhing with the wound,
>> And all the country bleeds. . . .
> The MOSES of the South![35]

For George Bagby, writing in the *Southern Literary Messenger* in June 1863, Jackson's death represented the fact that "our idol has been taken from us. . . . JACKSON leaves a void which no man can fill."[36] After all, who can replace the "Moses of the South"?

Joseph Turner of *The Countryman* favorably compared the unassuming manner of Stonewall's death to those of Alexander the Great, Hannibal, Julius Caesar, and Napoleon Bonaparte. According to Turner, none of these notables suffered an end fit for the lives they were purported to have led nor for the legendary status they were to occupy in the annals of military history—except for Stonewall. Alexander died in "a scene of debauch"; Hannibal died "by poison administered by his own hand—unlamented, and unwept, in a foreign land"; Caesar was "miserably assassinated by those he considered his nearest friends"; and Napoleon "closed his days in lonely banishment—almost literally exiled from the world."[37] In contrast, Stonewall died "without ambition, and . . . in peace," giving all his earthly glory to God and, in his last minutes, commanding his subordinates to ensure that they cared for his soldiers.[38] Of course, we know, as Turner either did not or else preferred to ignore, that Jackson's death was just as pointless and wrapped in as much tragedy as any of the famous deaths of military heroes against which his was compared.

Bagby of the *Messenger* did report that Stonewall was the victim of Confederate fire, but he managed to absolve the soldier who committed that deed by commending Stonewall's immortal soul to God in some act of need on the part of Heaven: "Looking to all the antecedents of his death, we are forced to the conviction that this God given leader was taken away by the all-wise Giver for beneficent reasons. His hour was come; his work was done. Let us bow humbly to the sad decree." So neither Federal nor Confederate shot nor "the cold bandage" that caused his pneumonia were the cause of Stonewall's demise; his was the call of angels presumably to do battle against an even greater foe than the North. As Bagby concluded his dirge, "Jackson belongs to no State, and not even to the South! His place is with Tell and Bruce and Kosciusko—champions of freedom for the oppressed of all lands and every age."[39]

Interestingly, immediately above Bagby's "Editor's Table," he placed a poem titled "No Such Thing as Death," which whimsically noted that

> "There's no such thing as death!"
> That which is thus miscalled,
> Is life escaping from the chains
> Which have so long enthralled;
> 'Tis a once hidden star,
> Piercing through the night,
> To shine in gentle radiance forth
> Amid its kindred light.[40]

For Bagby, the answer to the question posed by Jackson's death for the Confederate nation and its self-declared cause of liberty and freedom for the oppressed everywhere—naturally indicating a rather monochromatic definition of oppression—was to look upward to the heavens and accept the fate that the Almighty had ordained.

Not all of his contemporaries could be so sanguine, and in fact, Bagby himself considered the question of what would come next, arguing that Jackson's "imperishable spirit lingers in the breasts of his soldiers. His courage and steadfast faith in the cause, still inspire the people in whose defence he died. They owe it to his spotless memory to make good the holy cause in which he perished, and by God's blessing, they will not prove recreant to the sacred trust."[41] The Lord giveth, and the Lord taketh away.

Other writers wanted more concrete answers, and in particular sought to consider the impact of the death of Jackson on Lee, the Army of Northern Virginia, and the fate of the Confederacy. In its edition of August 29, 1863, the *Southern Illustrated News*, partly in an effort to publicize a book on Jackson published by Ayres and Wade, devoted its front page to "Recollections of Stonewall Jackson." Their opening comments drive home the point that military heroes who die in the service of the current nation, rather than in the past, present a particular problem to the development of a sense of nationalism:

JACKSON IS DEAD.

Seldom have words penetrated more deeply to the heart of a great nation. The people of the Confederate States had begun to regard this immortal leader as above the reach of fate. He had passed unhurt through such desperate contests; his calm eyes had surveyed so many hard fought battlefields, from the commencement of the combats to their termination, that a general conviction of the hero's invulnerability had impressed every heart—no one could feel that the light in those eyes of the great soldier would ever be quenched.

And yet it got worse, for the *News* then discussed the vital link between Jackson and Lee, now broken by Jackson's demise: "Lee is the exponent of Southern power of command; Jackson, the expression of its faith in God and in itself, its terrible energy, its enthusiasm and daring, its unconquerable will, its contempt of danger and fatigue, its capacity to smite, as with bolts of thunder, the cowardly and cruel foe that would trample under foot its liberty and religion." And then it got worse still, for in the view of this author, Stonewall "was no accidental manifestation of the powers of faith and courage. He came not by chance in this day and to this generation. He was born for a purpose."[42] Yet this man was dead—at the hands of his own soldiers, though the *News* never appeared to report this fact. Certainly, there was the hope that "his fiery and unqualifying spirit would survive in his men," but that was little more than wishful thinking.

The Confederacy had lost a man apparently born to deliver them victory, a man who was the arm of God and General Lee on the battlefield and the expression of the South's martial characteristics. How could the Cause survive his demise? And in the case of the *Southern Illustrated News*, with so much of the nationalist spirit and vigor invested in this one figure, how could its vision of Confederate nationalism survive? The *News* appeared to offer no answer. For ordinary Confederates, however, the answer may have lain in their individual acts of commemoration. For instance, when Jubal Early's troops were marching through Lexington, Virginia, in June 1864, they marked in their diaries and letters their passage past the grave of Stonewall Jackson. As Aaron Sheehan-Dean puts it, "The image of successful Confederate soldiers paying homage to their fallen leader could be repatriated and absorbed into the emerging national culture."[43]

Some historians have noted that Jackson's tragic death disassociated him from the reality of the Confederacy's ultimate defeat, and thus made his canonization by the advocates of the Lost Cause easier than his sometimes checkered record as a general might warrant. While that may be true, it should not lead us to underestimate the very real impact his death had for the Cause, for the Confederacy before its surrender necessitated the creation of a Lost Cause myth.[44]

Modern historians are sometimes similarly susceptible to hyperbole over Stonewall's demise. For example, Robert K. Krick ends a very detailed discussion of the exact circumstances of the general's death with an anthropomorphic obiter dictum on the martyring power of ballistics:

> The five [projectiles] that tore human flesh in Jackson's group were fiendishly effective. Six of Jackson's eight escorts escaped untouched. The relatively immense target that the general bestrode, Little Sorrell, remained unhit. As though vectored specially toward Jackson, three bullets missed every impediment and every other target, dodged precipitous laws of averages, and mortally wounded Lee's right arm. Nothing could have done more harm to the Army of Northern Virginia and to the nascent nation for which that army was the sturdiest underpinning.[45]

Both the contemporary *News* and the modern historian Krick seem to forget that Jackson's demise came about two years before the end of the war, and that there was a lot of hard fighting, the outcome at that point uncertain, between the death of Stonewall and the dissolution of the Confederacy.

In particular, we should not forget that Lee, "the exponent of Southern power of command," remained alive and at the head of his army. So what of him? Part of the problem seems to be that, although they mouthed platitudes about the relationship of Jackson and Lee, the editors of the *News* and other periodicals appear to have seen the fate of the Confederacy bound up more in the former than the latter. So the position of Robert E. Lee in the military pantheon of the Confederacy is something that needs attention.

In the inaugural issue of the *Southern Illustrated News*, Lee was described as "our great leader" and "our gallant leader"; his befuddlement of McClellan before Richmond in the Peninsular Campaign was held to contain "some of the most splendid combinations known to the art of war, the conception of which has placed the author in the first rank of generals."[46] Similarly, a few months earlier, for George Bagby of the *Southern Literary Messenger,* Lee's "reputation now overshadows all others."[47] Later issues of the *News* continued this theme of hyperbolic praise. Introducing their portrait of Lee in the nineteenth issue of the journal in January 1863, the editors of the *News* noted that "the achievements of General Lee form the most remarkable chapter, not only in the history of the present gigantic war, but in some respects, in the entire annals of war itself."[48] Again, they pointed to the Peninsular Campaign as a brilliant episode in the career of the Confederacy's "distinguished chieftain." When the *News* featured Lee on its front page in October 1863, it quoted Union general Winfield Scott describing Lee as "'the greatest military genius in America, myself not excepted.'"[49] The paper also ranked him among the greatest generals in the history of the world, alongside Epaminondas of Thebes, Julius Caesar, Gustavus Adolphus, Frederick the Great, and Napoleon Bonaparte.[50] So there is little doubt about the position of Lee as far as the *News* was concerned.

Yet a few factors should give us pause. In the first place, the *News* misreported Lee's name throughout its entire publication run—he was always Robert Edmund Lee rather than Robert Edward Lee. This is a minor point but still suggestive. More significantly, while Stonewall Jackson was the general portrayed in the first issue of the *News,* Lee was the nineteenth. Before the *News* turned its attention to the "great leader," it profiled John H. Morgan, Sterling Price, Turner Ashby, Ben McCulloch, Joe Johnston, Braxton Bragg, Leonidas Polk, A. P. Hill, William Cabell, Bankhead Magruder, Nathan Davis, Jeff Thompson, Frank Cheathem, and two naval officers, Commander M. F. Maury and Admiral Franklin Buchanan. Possibly the answer to this conundrum is as simple as the lack of a suitable engraving of Lee—the one used in the January 17, 1863, issue was taken from a decade-old photograph, described as the only one "extant" of the general.

But it also may be that Lee's reputation in late 1862 and early 1863 was not as stellar as the *News* seemed to imply. On the one hand, he was its greatest chieftain, but on the other, he was only a year removed from being "Granny Lee," the timid and frustrated military advisor to the president.[51] If Lee was so central to the Confederacy's national project, and what the *News* said never wavered from this analysis, why was his profile printed after so many others, including at least three of his subordinates in the Army of Northern Virginia?

It is also worth noting that Lee inspired little of the literary output from the contributors to the *News* that Jackson did. Jeb Stuart had a poem or two in his honor, and even—improbably—Joe Johnston had one ode penned to him, but never Lee. Paul Hayne's poem to Stuart suggests that the South,

> drink to a spirit as leal and true
>> As ever drew blade in a fight,
> And dashed on the Tyrant's lines of steel
>> For God, and a Nation's Right!"

John Thompson's poem to Johnston commemorates his "exile" to the Department of the West, concluding, "One flash of his sword when the foe is hard prest,/And the Land of the West shall be free!"[52] Whether this represents the editorial inclinations of the journal, or the colorlessness of Lee's popular image, is uncertain.

Lee did feature in omnibus odes to putative Southern heroes, such as John Esten Cooke's "The Song of the Rebel," but the *News* failed to feature any poems in which Lee was the sole focus. For example, the last of Cooke's thirty-three verses read,

> So a health to *Stonewall Jackson*,
>> To *Longstreet* brave as steel—
> To *Stuart* with the fearless soul,
>> A knight from plume to heel.
> And last to *Lee*, our General,
>> Beneath whose flag we go
> To test the edge of Southern steel
>> On a vulgar, brutal foe.

The first ten verses of this epic memorialized Stonewall Jackson, then two serenaded James Longstreet, eight more rhapsodized Jeb Stuart, then in quick succession Cooke threw out the names of William Barksdale, Maxcy Gregg, Thomas R. R. Cobb, Richard Garnett, Albert Gallatin Jenkins, John Rogers Cooke, James Kemper, John Bell Hood (who garnered a verse of his own), and many others, before finally turning to

Robert E. Lee in the twenty-seventh verse. Lee received five verses, three less than Stuart and half as many as Jackson.[53]

Although not in the *News,* there was one poem devoted to Lee alone, published in the *Magnolia Weekly* and the *Southern Literary Messenger* in late 1863. Although titled "Lee," this ode never mentioned the general by name. According to A. J. Riquier, Lee was

> First of a race of heroes, whom the Fates—
> Wielding the wonders of an Iron Age—
> Have reared to pace its ocean bounded stage,
> And wield the thunder of the patrician States
> On cannon smitten seas and mountain gates.
> Chief among chieftains!—christian soldier, sage—
> Whose truth grows loftier for the conflict's rage,
> And when the victor's laurel wreath elates—
> Thy genius and thy virtues have been made
> People's heritage! and doubly crowned,
> Thy Fame shows Richmond wrenched from ramparts round, With ghastly gunners in trenches laid
> Then points exultant to the fiery ball
> That hurled their kin through Shenandoah's vale.[54]

Compare this rather somber assessment to the flights of poetic fancy inspired by even Felix Zollicoffer, not to mention Stonewall Jackson, and one has to wonder how well Robert E. Lee fit the script of Confederate nationalism.

One clue is found in the language used to describe the two men. Jackson was the heart of the Confederacy's military, representing its "faith," "energy," "enthusiasm," "daring," "contempt of danger," "capacity to smite," and "its unconquerable will." Lee was a military technician of the highest order, but he never inspired the same linguistic flights—he remained a mechanic of the military arts rather than a poet. Jackson was a romantic hero to inspire the generations, Lee rather more mundane, and while always given his due, seemingly never embraced to the same extent. Even at the height of Lee's wartime achievements, his mythic status never rivaled that of Jackson, his subordinate colleague. It is not that Lee was unappreciated as a national symbol of the Confederate cause. As Gary Gallagher has persuasively argued, Lee and his army "became the most important national institution" as the war progressed.[55] It is rather that in this reading of the symbolic text of Confederate nationalism, the martyred Jackson loomed larger.

Gallagher argues that "Robert E. Lee and his soldiers functioned as the principal focus of Confederate nationalism for much of the war."[56] At one level, this analysis supports that conclusion. At another, however, we need to broaden that assertion and understand that the gap between "Robert E. Lee" and "his soldiers" is not perhaps as great as we might imagine. In particular, in the middle years of the war, Stonewall Jackson's position in the military pantheon of Confederate nationalism may have rivaled that of his commander. After Jackson's death, and in spite of his incipient martyrdom, it was perhaps inevitable that attention shifted—as Gallagher so adroitly demonstrates—to the surviving Lee who was, after all, the last best hope of the Confederacy.

We might wonder if Lee's relatively unassuming form and personality did in fact not fit the needs of the script that was being written around him in 1862 and 1863? On October 20, 1862, *The Countryman* repeated a description from the *Charleston Courier* that ended by acknowledging that Lee "holds in the hollow of his hand the destiny of his country."[57] The point of the piece, however, was to describe the plain, handsome, gentle, benevolent, grace-filled, and polite demeanor of the general. Compare that with the descriptions of Stonewall as a prophet of Old Testament proportions—for George Bagby, a "true patriot, pure Christian, invincible soldier," and a champion "of freedom for the oppressed of all lands and every age"; for the *Southern Illustrated News,* as a man marked by a "rigid remembrance of Divine power" and "this immortal leader as above the reach of fate"; and for one unnamed poet, "The MOSES of the South."[58]

Almost all of these poetic and overwrought tributes to military heroes, living and dead, tended to conflate the achievements and importance of the generals with the men that they led. But that was not true of all Confederate nationalists. For some, the individual soldier was from "A noble race, and brave!/Meet for a nation's need;/Ready to die a martyr's death/As to dare a hero's deed;/Marching with firm and steady step/Where their noble chieftains lead."[59] Still more of the nationalist outpourings of the wartime South dealt specifically with the "private in the ranks," as in this August 1863 poem written by an "exile from New Orleans" and published in *Southern Punch:*

History teems with pages bright of heroes who have won
Immortal fame, undying name, resplendent as the sun;
Let valorous deeds ne'er be forgot, give praise where praise is due,
Too oft a nation lands amiss, the faulty for the true.
Standing firm in darkest hour, undaunted, true and bold,
Braving alike noon's scorching rays and midnight's blighting cold,
Deserving most, too oft forgot, a high-toned nation's thanks,
One of nature's noblemen—the private in the ranks.

This poem continued to the effect that "A watchful eye, a listening ear, for front, for rear, and flanks, / Attests the debt a nation owes the private in the ranks," and "His duty done, one boon he craves, a gracious nation's thanks, / Withhold it not—'tis freely given, the private in the ranks."[60]

A few months later, the same periodical printed an ode to "Our Southern Boys." The refrain established the theme that the Southern boys were freely given to the Cause by their mothers, wives, and sweethearts, for whom they were fighting: "Hurrah! for our Southern Boys! / The ladies should adore them! / Hurrah! our flag above them flies, / While Heaven watches o'er them."[61] Yet not every poet or commentator was as blasé about the ability of those left on the homefront to cope with the immensity of battlefield loss. As "Lieutenant Cluverius" put it in the *Magnolia Weekly* in April 1864: "But he was gasping for life—'twas leaving him fast, / And it poured from his side in a red, trickling rill—/ Oh! tell her, he said, as in times that are past, / Tell her, oh yes, that I am loving her still."[62] Falling somewhere in between, an anonymous "Private in Gray" asked rhetorically in October 1862:

Who have we here?
On this glorious bier,
Though the trumpet of fame
May ne'er sound his name—
As calm shall he rest
As the plaudited chief,
(On the kind mother's breast
That can sooth every grief,)
He fought as a hero; what more can be said
In the praise of the glorious, living or dead?[63]

These twin themes of noble sacrifice and blood-soaked loss are an inevitable part of any attempt to bind battle and soldiers to a cause. The question, as it was for the Confederacy during the Civil War, is whether the Cause is worth the price.

There seemed little doubt as to the nature of the Cause, "To fight for God and native land!"[64] Or, as C. Toler Wolfe wrote in the *Southern Illustrated News*, "For your native land ye died, / On the bloody field of fame; / Ye have won high immortality, / And an undying name."[65] During the Confederacy's military high tide, in the fall of 1862, Susan Archer Talley reminded readers of the differences between the Cause of the South and that of the North:

> Ye fight for a tyrant's flag—
> Ye bow to a tyrant's laws;
> *We* stand serene in a freeman's faith—
> In a freeman's holy cause.
> We know in the conflict's hour
> That our God is in our van:
> Solemn and sure our faith remains—
> Conquer us if you can![66]

But as before, given all of this, what message did defeat send? If the Confederate cause was so just, so true, what did it mean when Confederate arms were inadequate to meet the task, when the hireling hordes of voracious Lincolnites prevailed?

What happened, for example, when the valiant Confederate was forced to surrender, when their mantra—at least according to James Dabney McCabe—should be "no surrender"? As McCabe suggested to the readers of the *Southern Illustrated News* in late 1862:

> Go tell your chief we'll die at our posts—
>> Mississippians never surrender. . . .
> O! men of the South, may the same proud cry
>> Nerve your arms to deeds of glory; Ye may fall, but your gallant
>>> sufferings
> Shall live in your country's story.
>> And maiden, and mother, and sister, and wife,
> Though it ring your hearts so tender,
>> E'er teach your loved ones like heroes bold
> To die, but "never surrender."[67]

Only seven months later, those same defenders of Vicksburg were surrendering to the Union Army.

Alan T. Nolan's discussion of the "idealized Confederate soldier" in the context of the Lost Cause myth makes this point, that the reality of the Confederate soldier was one that balanced devotion to the Cause with, for example, mass desertion long before the military efforts of the Confederacy became hopeless.[68] Social historian Maris Vinovskis has estimated that approximately one in every eight Confederate soldiers deserted, and that only 20 percent were ever returned to the colors.[69] Even worse, the soldiers who did remain loyal and present for duty—and therefore the Confederate nation itself—proved incapable of protecting the homes of Southerners from the enemy's troops. For example, in 1863, a single Union cavalry raid into Confederate Arkansas captured 1,000 horses and mules; large numbers of cattle, sheep, and hogs; and a considerable quantity of grain. In addition, 1.5 million bushels of corn, .5 million pounds of bacon, 3 tanning yards, 5 mills, and 60 river flatboats were destroyed. In 1864, General Philip Sheridan's cavalry in the Shenandoah Valley captured or destroyed 808 barns, 57 grain mills, 4 sawmills, almost 2 million bushels of wheat, 500 barrels of flour, 1,347 head of cattle, 1,231 sheep, 725 hogs, and hundreds of tons of straw and fodder.[70] The scale of this campaign was immense, and virtually no area of the eastern Confederacy was spared its effects.

In general, though, it is no surprise that in a culture that tended toward self-romanticization then and now, the exploits of dashing heroes might be essentialized and elevated to mythic status. Yet that same hero needed a villain against which to measure himself, and in the North, Confederates convinced themselves they had another worthy of the title. In an October 1862 article entitled "The Yankee Spirit of Rapine," the *Southern Illustrated News* accused the Federals of desiring "extermination, and all the horrors of indiscriminate emancipation," reenacting the "worst days of the Terror in France," and threatening to "deluge the whole land with blood!"[71] This was what Northern generalship would bring the South, from Pope's cowardly poltroonery to "Hunter the Hound" and "Butler the Beast."[72] Southern generalship, by contrast, was urbane, civilized, sanctified by the Lord, and expressive of the best features of Southern society and culture.

At one level, of course, the preservation of Southern independence relied on the efficacy of Confederate soldiers in winning the war, or else in making the Union's attempts to subdue the South so costly that they would quit and sue for terms. This did not happen. As symbols of Confederate nationalism, however, the battlefield exploits of Confederate generals and their soldiers transcended their individual and collective success or failure. Confederate generals were the Worthy Southron personified, and if these men failed to defeat the Demon Yankees, it was merely because they would not stoop so low as to engage them in their own scurrilous tactics. In the eyes of the Confederate nation, there were no Popes, Butlers, or Hunters, only Lees, Jacksons, and Beauregards. And it was the heroic stature of the latter three, even in death in Jackson's case, that provided the symbolic military underpinnings of Confederate America.

Conclusion

The fast pace at which Confederates constructed their nation meant that they continued to tinker with the apparatus of national symbolism right up to the end of the war. The alacrity with which they wrote a Constitution was not matched, for example, in deciding on a definitive national flag, motto, or seal. The official Confederate motto, adopted by Congress in 1863, was *Deo Vindice*, customarily translated as "God will vindicate."[1] The translation of that phrase, however, and the debate over exactly what the motto should mean, suggests rather more complex depths to the relationship between Confederate nationalism and the divine. It also demonstrates that the minute details of Confederate nation-building mattered to their participants. The Confederate House of Representatives originally proposed as the national motto *Deo Duce Vincemus*, or "Under the leadership of God we will conquer." When the Senate took up this proposal in April 1863, Louisiana Senator Thomas Semmes objected, noting that *duce* was "too pagan in its signification," and that *duce vincemus* combined reduced God to

> the leader of a physical army, by means of which we will conquer, or must conquer. If God be our leader we must conquer, or he would not be the God of Abraham, and of Isaac, and of Jacob, nor the God of the Christian. This very doubt implied in the word "vincemus" so qualifies the omnipotence of the God who is to be our "leader," that it imparts a degrading signification to the word "duce" in its relations to the attributes of the Deity.

The idea that an army led by God could *not* be victorious was an oxymoron to Semmes, and yet he did not wish to tempt fate by arrogantly declaring the Confederacy's victory before the fighting had ended. Thus, it would seem, the possibility of defeat on Earth led Semmes to temper his enthusiasm for the original proposal.

Instead of *Deo duce vincemus*, Semmes proposed the phrase *Deo vin-*

dice majores aemulamur, or "Under the guidance and protection of God we endeavor to equal and even excel our ancestors."[2] The latter part of this mouthful was intended to connect with the statue of George Washington that adorned the center of the proposed Great Seal of the Confederacy—Washington being representative of the "ancestors." Semmes's Senate colleagues rejected his strained phraseology and finally settled on just the first half of his phrase, *Deo Vindice.* As Semmes put it, this had multiple meanings that, when combined, spelled only success for the Confederate cause: "Under God as the asserter of our rights, the defender of our liberties, our protector against danger, our mediator, our ruler and guardian, and, as the avenger of our wrongs and the punisher of our crimes, we endeavor to equal or even excel our ancestors. What word can be suggested of more power, and so replete with sentiments and thoughts consonant with our idea of the omnipotence and justice of God?" According to Semmes, the root verb *vindex* can "signify an asserter, a defender, protector, deliverer, liberator, a mediator and a ruler or guardian . . . an avenger or punisher."[3]

At least one prolific Confederate commentator was certain that *Deo Vindice* meant one thing and one thing alone: "God our Vindicator." Joseph Addison Turner adamantly rejected the notion he had read in the *Macon Confederate* that the new national motto had anything to do with either revenge or avenging. Instead, it signified that the Lord would guard and defend the cause of the Confederacy and "be the vindicator of our claims to nationality, and independence."[4] For as Turner implicitly understood, something is customarily avenged by a third party after the death or destruction of the individual or cause. So accepting "God will avenge us" as one among several possible readings for *Deo Vindice,* then Confederates also implicitly accepted the possible defeat of the Cause.

Nineteenth-century scholars loved to dispute the various meanings of Latin phrases, but there is more at work here. *Deo Vindice* as a national motto was a symbol of the Confederate nation, and in this case, as with so many others, Confederates devoted considerable intellectual and physical energy to devising it, debating its significance, and defending it against recidivist challenges. Symbols are the material manifestation of nationalism, and we must take them seriously. Confederate nationalism has itself become a symbol in the years following its defeat. *Deo vindice, resurgam* (or "God will vindicate, I shall rise again") has become a

Fig. 11. Great Seal of the Confederacy

popular motto for neo-Confederates in modern times.[5] And as historian Charles Reagan Wilson so aptly noted in the opening lines of *Baptized in Blood,* the Confederate "nation . . . survived as a sacred presence, a holy ghost haunting the spirits and actions of post-Civil War Southerners."[6]

As a symbol, therefore, one part of the proposed national motto received the unequivocal support of all—*Deo.* To many Confederates, it was clear that God was on their side, and it was just a matter of how best to articulate that truism. The preamble to the Confederate Constitution, for example, differed in some important respects from its forbear, including an assertion of individual state sovereignty that harkened back to the Articles of Confederation, as well as the substitution of "permanent federal government" for "more perfect Union," and the deletion of the desires to "provide for the common defence" and "promote the general Welfare." The most noteworthy change, however, was the invocation of "the favor and guidance of Almighty God."[7]

So, from the very first moment of their national awakening, Confederates expected the favor of the divine. As we have seen in previous chapters, especially with respect to Confederate literature and the role of Confederate generals in symbolizing their nation, the language of the divine was part of the daily lexicon of the Confederate nationalist. Stonewall Jackson's life—and death—for example, were routinely couched in the language of sacrifice and martyrdom. To many, he was the epitome of the Christian soldier. As Daniel W. Stowell notes, however, Jackson's death was interpreted by many devout Confederates as both an internal "spiritual crisis" and a very potent "message from God." Not all Confederates immediately saw Jackson's death as a sign of God's disfavor; some evangelicals thought that the idolatrous worship of Jackson himself as an emblem of the Confederate cause might be at the root of his untimely and tragic death.[8] Religion was undoubtedly important in the symbolism of Confederate nationalism, but scouring the heavens and earth for signs of divine favor or disfavor has been an historically problematic project, and so it was for the Confederacy.

There was one aspect of the Confederate nation, however, that most white Southerners, at least before the war, agreed bore the favor of God— the institution of slavery. As various scholars have noted, as the tides of war turned against the Confederacy, some of those same white Southerners came to wonder whether they had been fallible on this subject. Not all took that route, and some came to see the secular benefits of nation outweighing the secular benefits of slavery. Or, to put it another way, as the war progressed, for at least a few Confederates, faith in slavery and faith in nation became incompatible ends. The Confederate Congress finally recognized this incongruity in March 1865 when it authorized the enlistment of African American slaves as soldiers, with freedom offered as a reward for service. By then, of course, it was too late to make a difference. It is entirely probable that such a policy would not have made much of an impact, however early in the war it was implemented, as there are just too many very reasonable doubts about the willingness of slaves to fight for their masters, whatever inducements were offered. Certainly, posT-Emancipation Proclamation, it seems hard to conceive of such a policy achieving the success it sought. That being said, in many ways the ultimate testament to the existence of a sense of wartime Confederate nationalism is that some Confederates were willing to end slavery if they thought that such a reform would improve the chances of national liberty being preserved. In that sense, while the South certainly seceded to protect slavery, for some, the logic of war and national independence called into question the sacrosanct nature of the peculiar institution.

Bruce Levine has written compellingly about the circumstances that led to "Confederate emancipation," which in his nuanced reading was both contingent and extremely limited in scope.[9] But a close reading of the most fully realized proposal for Confederate emancipation, that of General Patrick Cleburne in January 1864, reveals a strain of nationalist sentiment underpinning the radical notion that slavery should be sacrificed to the cause of independence. We should be very clear that this proposal had an incredibly limited circulation, and that when it was finally adopted in a reduced form by the Confederate Congress, the emancipatory impulse had been largely subsumed by a simple need to increase military enlistments. Stephanie McCurry argues that when Confederate politicians took up the slave enlistment issue in early 1865, they, unlike Cleburne, "believed they could have their cake and eat it too: that they could choose independence and slavery, arm slaves and retain slavery."[10] That truth, however, is not the point being made here. In this reading, Cleburne's proposal—distinct from the congressional action of March 1865—reveals just how deeply some Confederates had drunk at the well of the mythic present.

Cleburne's lengthy proposal, signed by twelve other officers of his division of the Army of Tennessee, laid out a compelling case for the enlistment of slaves—within the context of slavery as understood by its authors. Put another way, if we accept Cleburne's assumptions about the nature of Southern African Americans and their willingness to fight for the Confederate cause, then the case makes sense. If we do not, as the vast majority of modern readers will not, then the case falls apart. What is significant for our purposes, however, is the seemingly casual way in which Cleburne deployed the nation as an ally in his cause. Although he only used the words "nation" or "national" twice in reference to the Confederacy, it is clear to what end his arguments were being made.[11] In his words, "as between the loss of independence and the loss of slavery, we assume that every patriot will freely give up the latter—give up the negro slave rather than be a slave himself." Later in the letter, Cleburne wrote, "It is said Republicanism cannot exist without the institution. Even were this true, we prefer any form of government of which the Southern people may have the molding, to one forced upon us by a conqueror." Finally, in conclusion, Cleburne attempted to conclusively dismiss his future critics, arguing,

> It is said slavery is all we are fighting for, and if we give it up we give up all. Even if this were true, which we deny, slavery is not all our enemies are fighting for. It is merely the pretense to establish sectional superiority and a more centralized form of government, and to deprive us of our rights and liberties. We have now briefly proposed a plan which we believe will save our country. It may be imperfect, but in all human probability it would give us our independence. No objection ought to outweigh it which is not weightier than independence. If it is worthy of being put in practice it ought to be mooted quickly before the people, and urged earnestly by every man who believes in its efficacy.[12]

For Cleburne and his compatriots, national independence was the paramount objective of the ongoing war, and everything—slavery included—needed to be weighed in that balance.

Some Confederates followed Cleburne's assertion that nation should trump slavery. As Joseph Addison Turner put it in *The Countryman* in January 1865, "We have got to abandon this war, or put negro soldiers in our army—one or the other."[13] For others, however, this represented nothing less than the "new heresy." John W. Overall of *Southern Punch* thundered in September 1864, "WE ARE FIGHTING FOR INDEPENDENCE THAT OUR GREAT AND NECESSARY DOMESTIC INSTITUTION OF SLAVERY SHALL BE PRESERVED, and for the preservation of other institutions of which slavery is the ground work."[14] Overall's attitude was more widely shared by the white Confederate population, as demonstrated by President Davis's order that Cleburne's proposal be buried and not spoken of again.

The congressional proposal, even though it was only adopted fourteen months after Cleburne's letter as an act of sheerest desperation, represents the logical conclusion of the ideas of the mythic present. For Cleburne, the Demon Yankee sought to take white Southern liberty and make white men slaves. To answer this crusade, the Worthy Southron needed to be clear-headed about what was worth preserving and what needed to be sacrificed. For Cleburne—ironically, not a native Southerner—the preservation of a Southern form of government and the saving of his country demanded the sacrifice of the institution of slavery to the fires of war and nationhood. And the whole reason this proposal made sense to its proponents was because they appeared to have fully imbibed the symbol of the Silent Slave. The loyal slaves of the white Southern imagination would be willing to fight for their masters, their home, and their freedom. Without this act of the imagination, the entire proposal would have collapsed.

Cleburne's nationalism was not a majority sentiment among his fellow Confederates. Jefferson Davis tacitly recognized that fact as he ordered the general to bury his proposal. But Cleburne's extension of the ideas of wartime Confederate nationalism to demand the sacrifice of slavery was rooted in symbols that were far more commonly held. Had the Confederacy won its independence as a result of the Civil War, a similar process of nation building and the extension of nationalism might have occurred as it did in the aftermath of the American Revolution. We should not regret the reality that such a process never occurred. The mythic present imagined by Confederates, arising out of the antebellum assumptions of white Southerners and finding voice during the Civil War, was simply too far from reality to prevail.

To a great extent, white North American liberty had been conceived as a companion to black North American slavery, and while Northerners had long since moved away from that simple binary, Southerners had not. Yet by the end of the Civil War, the call of independence and self-determination—the siren call of nation, to put it simply—had transcended the liberty:slavery equation for at least a few Confederates. The logic of Confederate nationalism, born in a defense of slavery, had paradoxically moved past that defense. While this is speculation and beyond the scope of this work, it may be that the logic of Confederate nationalism was one factor that enabled white Southerners in 1865 to pivot directly from a defense of slavery to a defense of white supremacy. Confederate nationalism may, in fact, have demonstrated that white Southerners did not need the legal institution of slavery to maintain their dominance.

The end of slavery may have actually helped that pivot, because it eliminated the Silent Slave as a companion trope to the Worthy Southron. While white Southerners certainly continued to talk for black Southerners, the dominant racial idea of Reconstruction became the Feared African, the bumbling, inadequate, corrupt, and, above all else, dangerous, demon of Thomas Nast's cartoons and James Pike's *The Prostrate State: South Carolina under Negro Government*. According to Bruce Baker, "the importance of *The Prostrate State* in shaping the way the nation would remember Reconstruction cannot be overestimated." In addition to centering attention on "'the rude form of the most ignorant democracy that mankind ever saw,'" Pike blamed "'the compulsive power of the Federal authority at Washington'" and argued that the Reconstruction government of South Carolina was one "'that the intelligent public opinion of the State would overthrow if left to itself.'"[15] While the analogies are not exact, it is certainly possible to hear in those words echoes of the Worthy Southron—"'the intelligent public opinion of the State'"—and the Demon Yankee—"'the compulsive power of the Federal authority.'" But the Silent Slave was dead, replaced by a manifestation of "'the most ignorant democracy that mankind ever saw.'" And, underpinning this whole reconstructed conception of the Southern white self, remained the idea of Confederate Americanism—that there was and perhaps is a Southern way to be American.

Notes

Introduction

1. Kentucky Ordinance of Secession, November 20, 1861. The resolution specifically mentions "fifteen states," though only thirteen had seceded. Both New Mexico and Arizona Territories seceded (at Mesilla on March 16 and at Tucson on March 23), but neither was technically a state. *Official Records*, ser. IV, vol. 1, 741.

2. On the nature of time and narrative generally, see Ricouer, *Time and Narrative*. For two studies of the influence of time on Southern and Civil War history, see Smith, *Mastered by the Clock*, and Wells, *Civil War Time*.

3. On the antebellum delusions of both sides, see Thomas, *The Dogs of War*.

4. On the one hand, see Cash, *The Mind of the South;* Taylor, *Cavalier and Yankee;* and McWhiney and Jamieson, *Attack and Die*. On the other hand, see Pessen, "How Different from Each Other."

5. Faust, *The Creation of Confederate Nationalism*, 6.

6. Rable, *The Confederate Republic*, 124.

7. Joseph Addison Turner, "The State of the Country," *The Countryman*, May 2, 1865, 266.

8. Turner, "The Five Points," *The Countryman*, May 23, 1865, 285.

9. Faust, *The Creation of Confederate Nationalism*, 6–7. There have been excellent studies of Confederate nationalism. See Thomas, *The Confederacy as Revolutionary Experience*, and *The Confederate Nation;* Escott, *After Secession;* Beringer et al., *Why the South Lost;* Rable, *The Confederate Republic;* Bonner, *Colors and Blood;* Rubin, *A Shattered Nation;* Bonner, *Mastering America;* McCurry, *Confederate Reckoning;* Bernath, *Confederate Minds;* and Quigley, *Shifting Grounds*. See also Asperheim, "Double Characters."

10. Faust, *The Creation of Confederate Nationalism*, 6–7.

11. Bonner, *Mastering America*, xvi, 254 passim.

12. McCurry, *Confederate Reckoning*, 1.

13. Rable, *The Confederate Republic*, 120–21.

14. Rubin, *A Shattered Nation*, 1, 11, 247.

15. Bernath, *Confederate Minds*, 4, 287. Bernath overturns Faust's assessment that "anything published and disseminated in the initial months of the war had a far greater potential impact than information made public after the severe restraints of

war had been imposed on the southern media. Confederate nationalism was thus inhibited in its ability to grow and change. What was said initially is what was heard most widely" (Faust, *The Creation of Confederate Nationalism*, 17–18).

16. Quigley, *Shifting Grounds*, 5, 173.

17. See, for example, Wyatt-Brown, *Southern Honor*, and Greenberg, *Masters and Statesmen*.

18. McCardell, *The Idea of a Southern Nation*, 3–4, 91.

19. Dew, *Apostles of Disunion*, 54.

20. See, for example, Wallenstein, *From Slave South to New South*, and Williams, *Rich Man's War*.

21. *Jacobellis v. Ohio*, 378 U.S. 184 (1964), Justice Stewart concurring at 197. On his understanding of "hard-core pornography," Stewart wrote, "I shall not today attempt further to define the kinds of material I understand to be embraced within that shorthand description; and perhaps I could never succeed in intelligibly doing so. But I know it when I see it, and the motion picture involved in this case is not that" (available at http://caselaw.lp.findlaw.com/scripts/getcase.pl?court=US&vol=378&invol=184, accessed December 20, 2012).

22. On this latter point, see Burton and Binnington, "'And Bid Him Bear a Patriot's Part.'"

23. Curtin, "The Black Experience of Colonialism and Imperialism," 20.

24. Calhoun, *Nationalism*, 4–5. For other important definitions of nationalism, see Ernest Renan, *Qu'est-ce qu'une nation*, trans. Ida Mae Snyder (Paris: Calmann-Levy, 1882), 26; Anthony Giddens, *A Contemporary Critique of Historical Materialism: II. The Nation-State and Violence* (Cambridge: Polity Press, 1985), 119; Walker Connor, "A Nation Is a Nation, Is a State, Is an Ethnic Group, Is a . . . ," *Ethnic and Racial Studies* 1, no. 4 (1978): 388; Anderson, *Imagined Communities*, 6; Tom Narin, *The Break-Up of Britain* (London: New Left Press, 1977), 348; Greenfield, *Nationalism*, 3; and Zelinsky, *Nation into State*, 4–6.

25. Searle-White, *The Psychology of Nationalism*, 85.

26. Õzkirimli, *Theories of Nationalism*, 206, 208–9, 210–11. Õzkirimli's assertions about the daily reproduction of nationalism echo the ideas of Billig, *Banal Nationalism*.

27. Confino, *The Nation as a Local Metaphor*, 3, 4.

28. Wiebe, "Imagined Communities," 53–54; Wiebe, *Who We Are*, 5.

29. Anderson, *Imagined Communities*, 6–7, 17–40, esp. 40.

30. Cullen, *The Civil War in Popular Culture*, 3.

31. Leonard, *News for All*, 12. Barbara Ellis makes a similar claim for the *Memphis Appeal*, noting that editor John Reid McClanahan was "mindful of the illiterate Grandmother Pugh and those unable to afford a paper who depended on others to read the news and views to them. He wanted parlor and tavern orators to make the rafters sing when they read his work aloud." Ellis, *The Moving Appeal*, 52. Editors also made sure to include enough local news and comments to keep their readers' interest; see, for example, Eleanor Elizabeth Mims, "The Editors of the Edgefield Advertiser: Oldest Newspaper in South Carolina, 1836–1930" (M.A. thesis, University of South

Carolina, 1930), 54. See more generally Ratner and Teeter, *Fanatics and Fire-eaters*, 1–2, 7–33.

32. McPherson, *What They Fought For*, 4; Elisabeth Muhlenfeld, "The Civil War and Authorship," in *The History of Southern Literature*, edited by Louis D. Rubin Jr. (Baton Rouge: Louisiana State University Press, 1985), 182. See also Wiley, *The Life of Johnny Reb*.

33. Cornelius, *When I Can Read My Title Clear*.

34. Machor, "Historical Hermeneutics and Antebellum Fiction," 55, 78.

35. Fahs, "Commentary," 214. See also Diffley, *Where My Heart Is Turning Ever*.

36. While this list is not intended to be exhaustive, see, for example, Silber, *The Romance of Reunion;* Snay, *Fenians, Freedmen, and Southern Whites;* Blum, *Reforging the White Republic;* and Blight, *Race and Reunion*.

1. "At Last, We Are a Nation among Nations"

The epigraph comes from Parks and Parks, eds., *The Collected Poems of Henry Timrod*, 92. Timrod wrote this poem at the Montgomery Convention in February 1861. The *Charleston Daily Courier* printed it on February 23 and 25, 1861, and January 31, 1862. The *Charleston Tri-Weekly Mercury* printed it on September 26, 1861.

1. W. E. Gladstone, speech at the New Townhall, Newcastle, October 7, 1862, printed in *Times of London*, October 9, 1862, 7. D. P. Crook quotes the latter portion of this remark in *The North, the South, and the Powers*, 227–228, as does James M. McPherson in *Battle Cry of Freedom*, 552. (McPherson cites Crook as his source.)

2. Gladstone, ibid. The *Times* recorded that both of these remarks met with the approval of the audience.

3. DeRosa, *The Confederate Constitution of 1861*, 121.

4. Joseph H. Echols, *Speech of . . . Jan. 19, 1865* (Richmond, 1865), quoted in Faust, *The Creation of Confederate Nationalism*, 24.

5. Nieman, "Republicanism, the Confederate Constitution, and the American Constitutional Tradition," 202.

6. Reid, *The Origins of the American Civil War*, 298, 366.

7. A. Featherman, "French Revolutionary History," *De Bow's Review*, March 1861, 288.

8. Murrin, "A Roof without Walls," 346, 347. See also Knupfer, *The Union as It Is*.

9. For a useful sample of this literature, see Hutchinson and Smith, eds., *Nationalism*.

10. To clarify this point, the term "state" as used here refers to the central government, not to the individual states that comprise the subdivisions of the American federal system.

11. Of the eighteen men who served on one or both of the Drafting Committees, seventeen were slaveholders, twelve had served in state legislatures, ten had served in Congress, and six had served time as judges. See Lee, *The Confederate Constitutions*, Appendix A, 154–58.

12. See McCardell, *The Idea of a Southern Nation*.

13. Among those scholars who try to tie kinship and nationalism together, see Van Den Berghe, "Race and Ethnicity," 403, and Robert H. Wiebe, "Reconsidering Nationalism," public lecture, University of Illinois at Urbana-Champaign, September 25, 1996. On the Confederacy in particular, see several works by Orville Vernon Burton: *In My House There Are Many Mansions*, 104; "On the Confederate Homefront"; and "Localism and Confederate Nationalism."

14. For the selling of the Constitution of 1787, see Alexander, *The Selling of the Constitutional Convention*.

15. On this subject, see Frank L. Owsley, *King Cotton Diplomacy: Foreign Relations of the Confederate States of America* (Chicago: University of Chicago Press, 1931); Crook, *The North, the South, and the Powers;* Philip S. Foner, *British Labor and the American Civil War* (New York: Holmes and Meier, 1981); Martin Crawford, *The Anglo-American Crisis of the Mid-Nineteenth Century: The Times and America, 1850–1862* (Athens: University of Georgia Press, 1987); Howard Jones, *Union in Peril: The Crisis over British Intervention in the Civil War* (Chapel Hill: University of North Carolina Press, 1992); Charles M. Hubbard, *The Burden of Confederate Diplomacy* (Knoxville: University of Tennessee Press, 1998); Blackett, *Divided Hearts;* Myers, *Caution and Cooperation;* and Jones, *Blue & Gray Diplomacy.*

16. The initial participants at Montgomery (in order of secession) were South Carolina, Mississippi, Florida, Alabama, Georgia, and Louisiana. The Texas delegation arrived late but participated in the ratification debates. The sources employed in this discussion include the *Charleston Daily Courier, Charleston Tri-Weekly Mercury,* and *Edgefield Advertiser* (South Carolina); the *Huntsville Southern Advocate* (Alabama); the *Augusta Daily Chronicle and Sentinel, Milledgeville Southern Union,* and *Milledgeville Southern Recorder* (Georgia); and the *New Orleans Daily Picayune* and *De Bow's Review* (Louisiana). Also consulted were the *Hannibal Daily Messenger* (Missouri) and the *Southern Literary Messenger* (Virginia).

17. Between February 12 and February 26, each of the above journals (except *De Bow's Review* and the *Southern Literary Messenger*) reproduced the Provisional Constitution. Between March 14 and April 3, each one (with the same exceptions) reproduced the Permanent Constitution. All except the *New Orleans Daily Picayune* had only four pages.

18. Except for Davis, all of these men were delegates to the Montgomery Convention. Smith sat on both Drafting Committees, Stephens on the first alone.

19. The first chair was Christopher G. Memminger, the second Robert Barnwell Rhett Sr.

20. Leonard, *News for All*, 12.

21. *Journal of the Congress*, I, 19. Memminger proposed the motion on February 5, 1861, the second day of the convention. It was the first piece of substantive business addressed. A basic reference for the creation of the Confederate government is Davis, *"A Government of Our Own."*

22. Preamble, Provisional Constitution of the Confederate States of America, *Journal of the Congress*, I, 26, 41.

23. Lee, *The Confederate Constitutions*, 150. Other works in this school include

Carpenter, *The South as a Conscious Minority;* Fitts, "The Confederate Convention," 189–210; Nixon and Nixon, "The Confederate Constitution Today," 369–76; and Leslie, "The Confederate Constitution," 153–65. See also Robinson, "A New Deal in Constitutions."

24. See Nieman, "Republicanism, the Confederate Constitution, and the American Constitutional Tradition"; Don E. Fehrenbacher, "The Confederacy as a Constitutional System," in Fehrenbacher, *Sectional Crisis and Southern Constitutionalism,* 137–86; and DeRosa, *The Confederate Constitution of 1861.*

25. Bland, "The Great Issue: Our Relations to It," *Southern Literary Messenger,* March 1861, 168, 171. The journal identifies the anonymous author as J. Randolph Tucker, attorney general of Virginia (162).

26. Fehrenbacher, "The Confederacy as a Constitutional System," 143, 139.

27. DeRosa, *The Confederate Constitution of 1861,* 5.

28. George Fitzhugh, "Small Nations," *De Bow's Review,* November 1860, 568–69.

29. J. Quitman Moore, "National Characteristics—The Issues of the Day," *De Bow's Review,* January 1861, 43–52; Fitzhugh, "The Message, the Constitution, and the Times," ibid., February 1861, 157–67; "What Is a Constitution?" ibid., March 1861, 304–54; "Thoughts Suggested by the War," ibid., September 1861, 296–305. Those without listed authors are so similar to Fitzhugh's style and position that he may have written them himself. One article in *Southern Literary Messenger,* "Disfederation of the States," February 1861, 118–19, made very similar points.

30. "Disfederation of the States," *Southern Literary Messenger,* February 1861, 119.

31. Fitzhugh, "Small Nations," *De Bow's Review,* November 1860, 568.

32. Ibid., 567. Fitzhugh repeated much of this in "The Message," *De Bow's Review,* February 1861, 157.

33. "What Is a Constitution?" *De Bow's Review,* March 1861, 304.

34. Fitzhugh, "The Message," *De Bow's Review,* February 1861, 159, 162–63.

35. Moore, "Past and Present," *De Bow's Review,* February 1861, 197.

36. "Thoughts Suggested," *De Bow's Review,* September 1861, 297.

37. See, especially, Rable, *The Confederate Republic,* for the importance of parochialism and states' rights as a doctrine within the Confederacy.

38. *Augusta Daily Chronicle and Sentinel,* January 31, 1861.

39. *Huntsville Southern Advocate,* February 13, 1861.

40. *Charleston Tri-Weekly Mercury,* February 14, 1861.

41. B. M. Palmer, "Why We Resist, and What We Resist," *De Bow's Review,* February 1861, 232; "What Is a Constitution," *De Bow's Review,* March 1861, 303–6; Featherman, "French Revolutionary History," *De Bow's Review,* March 1861, 288; Editorial, *De Bow's Review,* 378.

42. *Charleston Tri-Weekly Mercury,* February 14, 19, 1861.

43. *Augusta Daily Chronicle and Sentinel,* January 17, 1861.

44. *Charleston Daily Courier,* January 29, 1861.

45. Rutledge, "Suggestions for a Southern Confederacy," *Charleston Daily Courier,* January 30, 1861. See also Bland, "The Great Issue," *Southern Literary Messenger,* March 1861.

46. Preamble, Permanent Constitution, *Journal of the Congress*, I, 909.

47. Article I, sec. 9.1, 9.2; Article IV, sec. 3.3, *Journal of the Congress*, I, 914, 921.

48. Article II, sec. 1.1, 2.3; Article I, sec. 6.2, *Journal of the Congress*, I, 917, 919, 912.

49. See Nieman, "Republicanism, the Confederate Constitution, and the American Constitutional Tradition"; Fehrenbacher, "The Confederacy as a Constitutional System"; and DeRosa, *The Confederate Constitution of 1861*.

50. Editorial, *De Bow's Review*, March 1861, 378.

51. Letter from L. P. Walker, dated December 14, *Huntsville Southern Advocate*, December 19, 1860.

52. *Milledgeville Southern Union*, January 29, 1861.

53. Ibid., February 12, 1861.

54. *Milledgeville Southern Recorder*, February 12, 1861. A short header announced, "U. S. Constitution Adopted," while lower down the same column, the paper printed the differences between the two documents.

55. *New Orleans Daily Picayune*, February 10, 1861.

56. *Huntsville Southern Advocate*, February 20, 1861.

57. *Milledgeville Southern Union*, March 5, 1861.

58. *Charleston Tri-Weekly Mercury*, April 2, 1861. Two points need clarification. First, I interpret "the fanaticism on the slavery question" as referring to the fanaticism of the North, not the South. Otherwise, we would have one of the most radical Southern papers calling for a diminution of the proslavery effort. Second, we should interpret "the Northwest" to mean the states of the Upper Mississippi Valley, not the Pacific Northwest.

59. *Charleston Daily Courier*, March 16, 1861.

60. Ibid. The order of ratification was as follows (convention vote in parentheses): Alabama, March 12 (87–5); Georgia, March 16 (276–0); Louisiana, March 21 (102–7); Texas, March 23 (126–2); Mississippi, March 26 (78–7); South Carolina, April 3 (138–21); Florida, April 22 (54–0) (Lee, *The Confederate Constitutions*, 123–40).

61. *Charleston Tri-Weekly Mercury*, February 14, 1861.

62. *New Orleans Daily Picayune*, March 19, 1861.

63. Lee, *The Confederate Constitutions*, 130–33, 137.

64. *Augusta Daily Chronicle and Sentinel*, January 30, 1861; February 12, 1861.

65. Ibid. See also February 20, 23, and 24. Ibid., March 8, 16, 19, 28, 24, 1861.

66. D. C. Humphreys, "Thoughts and Suggestions on the State of Affairs," *Huntsville Southern Advocate*, April 3, 1861.

67. *New Orleans Daily Picayune*, March 16, 1861; Lee, *The Confederate Constitutions*, 130.

68. Lee, *The Confederate Constitutions*, 137–38.

69. On such repression, see Durrill, *War of Another Kind*.

70. The reprint history of the Inaugural Address is *Charleston Tri-Weekly Mercury, Charleston Daily Courier,* and *New Orleans Daily Picayune*, February 19; *Huntsville Southern Advocate*, February 20; *Milledgeville Southern Union*, February 26; *Edgefield Advertiser*, February 27. The reprint history of Stephens's impromptu

speech in Montgomery on February 9 is *Charleston Daily Courier,* February 11; *Augusta Daily Chronicle and Sentinel,* February 12; *Huntsville Southern Advocate* and *Hannibal Daily Messenger,* February 14. The reprint history of his Savannah speech is *Augusta Daily Chronicle and Sentinel,* March 24; *Charleston Daily Courier,* March 25; *Milledgeville Southern Recorder,* March 26; *Milledgeville Southern Union,* April 2; *Huntsville Southern Advocate,* April 10.

71. The reprint history is as follows: Smith, *Huntsville Southern Advocate,* April 24; Wigfall, *Charleston Daily Courier,* April 4, and *Edgefield Advertiser,* April 10; Hill, *Milledgeville Southern Recorder,* April 16; Fearn, *Huntsville Southern Advocate,* April 17. Several of these speeches were reprinted from other Southern newspapers, thus suggesting quite a wide dissemination.

72. Alexander Stephens, *Hannibal Daily Messenger,* February 14, 1861.

73. Stephens, March 21, in Wakelyn, ed., *Southern Pamphlets on Secession,* 408. Many of these speeches and letters were reprinted in pamphlet form for even wider distribution.

74. Jefferson Davis, Inaugural Address, February 19, 1861, *Journal of the Congress,* I, 64.

75. Benjamin H. Hill, *Milledgeville Southern Recorder,* April 16, 1861.

76. Robert H. Smith, in Wakelyn, ed., *Southern Pamphlets on Secession,* 213.

77. Thomas Fearn, *Huntsville Southern Advocate,* April 17, 1861.

78. Stephens, *Hannibal Daily Messenger,* February 14, 1861.

79. Davis, Inaugural Address, February 19, 1861, *Journal of the Congress,* I, 65.

80. Smith, in Wakelyn, ed., *Southern Pamphlets on Secession,* 196, 213.

81. Davis, Inaugural Address, February 19, 1861, *Journal of the Congress,* I, 65, 66.

82. Stephens, in Wakelyn, ed., *Southern Pamphlets on Secession,* 403.

83. Smith, in ibid., 196; Hill, *Milledgeville Southern Recorder,* April 16, 1861.

84. Fearn, *Huntsville Southern Advocate,* April 17, 1861.

85. Hill, *Milledgeville Southern Recorder,* April 16, 1861.

86. Smith and Stephens, in Wakelyn, ed., *Southern Pamphlets on Secession,* 197, 403 passim.

87. Fearn, *Huntsville Southern Advocate,* April 17, 1861. The first eight amendments to the Constitution of 1787 became part of the Confederate Permanent Constitution verbatim, forming clauses 12–19 of Article I, section 9. The ninth and tenth amendments, with slight changes, became clauses 5 and 6 of Article VI. The substance of the eleventh amendment became part of Article III, section 2.1, and the twelfth amendment replaced the section it had originally superseded, Article II, section 1.3.

88. Smith, in Wakelyn, ed., *Southern Pamphlets on Secession,* 198–99.

89. Stephens, *Hannibal Daily Messenger,* February 14, 1861; Davis, *Journal of the Congress,* I, 168.

90. "The Belligerents," *De Bow's Review,* July 1861, 70, 76.

91. Stephens, in Wakelyn, ed., *Southern Pamphlets on Secession,* 405.

92. *New York Herald,* February 11, 1861.

93. Rev. J. H. Thornwell, "Our Danger and Our Duty," *De Bow's Review,* May–August 1862, 44, 45. Thornwell was not alone in seeing the Confederate national proj-

ect as one born in conservatism. Writing a few months later in *The Countryman*, Joseph Addison Turner remarked of the Confederate Constitution, "It contains the saving element of English conservatism strained, as it were, through the hands of Washington and Hamilton, with a liberal infusion of the democracy of France administered by Jefferson, Madison, and Monroe. . . . [C]onservative, yet elastic, it restrains without oppressing, and protects, without infringing, the equal rights and liberties of an equal people" ("Confederate Constitution," *The Countryman*, December 15, 1862, 93).

2. "In That Cold Eye There Is No Relenting"

The epigraph comes from Edward William Sidney, *The Partisan Leader: A Tale of the Future* (Washington, D.C.: Duff Green, 1836), 219. The original 1836 text was published under the pseudonym Edward William Sidney. Subsequent reprints were published under the author's real name, Nathaniel Beverley Tucker, or, more commonly, Beverley Tucker. For consistency's sake, I use the latter. Unless otherwise noted all page citations are drawn from the 1862 Confederate printing: Beverley Tucker, *The Partisan Leader: A Novel, and an Apocalypse of the Origin and Struggles of the Southern Confederacy*, edited by Thomas A. Ware (Richmond, Va.: West and Johnson, 1862; reprint Chapel Hill, N.C.: Documenting the American South, 1999). Available at http://docsouth.unc.edu/imls/tucker/menu.html, accessed December 20, 2012. It is possible that the author's adoption of Sidney as his pseudonymous family name harkened back to Algernon Sidney, the Whig republican martyr executed in 1683 for his alleged complicity in a plot to assassinate King Charles II. Tucker himself was a Whig.

Earlier versions of this chapter were presented at the Southern Historical Association Annual Meeting in Atlanta (November 2005) and at The Historical Society Annual Meeting in Baltimore (June 2008), as well as at the Allegheny College Humanities Lecture Series (April 2007) and the 5th Biennial Allegheny College Intramural Faculty Conference (May 2008). Thanks are due to the panelists, commenters, and audience at those presentations.

1. That number was divided between Boston and Philadelphia (339 copies), Maryland and Virginia (446 copies), and Columbia, Augusta, and New Orleans (518 copies). See C. Hugh Holman's introduction to Nathaniel Beverley Tucker's *The Partisan Leader: A Tale of the Future* (Chapel Hill: University of North Carolina Press, 1971), xix.

2. Brugger, *Beverley Tucker*, 241; Holman, introduction to Tucker, *The Partisan Leader*.

3. John Beauchamp Jones, *Wild Southern Scenes: A Tale of Disunion! And Border War!* (Philadelphia: T. B. Peterson and Brothers, 1859); Misty Cates, "Jones, John Beauchamp (1810–1866)," in *The Dictionary of Missouri Biography*, edited by Lawrence O. Christensen et al. (Columbia: University of Missouri Press, 1999), 439–40. *Wild Southern Scenes* is not deemed significant enough to be mentioned in Jones's biographical entry. Jones is best known to history for the posthumous publication of his two-volume *A Rebel War Clerk's Diary at the Confederate States Capital* (Philadelphia: J. B. Lippincott, 1866). He edited a pro-Southern newspaper in Philadelphia,

the *Southern Monitor*, from 1857 to 1860, and had previously edited the *Baltimore Sunday Visitor* (1841) and the *Madisonian* (1842), the latter a voice for the Tyler administration. In 1856, his *Wild Western Scenes* (1841) reached its fortieth edition.

4. Edmund Ruffin, *Anticipations of the Future to Serve as Lessons for the Present Time, in the Form of Extracts of Letters from an English Resident in the United States, to the London Times, from 1864 to 1870* (Richmond, Va.: J. W. Randolph, 1860).

Robert E. Bonner briefly analyzes these three novels in *Mastering America*, 181–83. In Bonner's assessment, "In showing how proslavery Southerners might realize their destiny within historical time, they thus reminded readers what future generations might think of the present. . . . Slaveholders' broadening historical consciousness mattered most because of what it said about the present, which was implicitly set in conversation with both the past and the future" (182).

5. On this subject, see Babb, *Whiteness Visible*. For a white view of slave life in the South contemporaneous to the novels discussed in this chapter, see Edward A. Pollard, *Black Diamonds Gathered in the Darkey Homes of the South* (New York: Pudney and Russell, 1859).

6. Carl Van Doren, "Judge Beverley Tucker," in *The Cambridge History of English and American Literature*, vol. 15, book 2: "Colonial and Revolutionary Literature: Early National Literature: Part I," edited by A. W. Ward et al. (New York: G. P. Putnam's Sons, 1907–1921; New York: Bartleby.com, 2000). Available at http://www.bartleby.com/225/1608.html, accessed December 20, 2012.

7. Tucker, *The Partisan Leader*, 24.

8. Jones, *Wild Southern Scenes*, 17, 294.

9. Craven, *Edmund Ruffin, Southerner*, 189.

10. Hobson, *"Anticipations of the Future,"* 84–92; Hobson, *Tell about the South*, 27–44, 33 (quotation).

11. Edmund Ruffin, *The Diary of Edmund Ruffin, Volume I: Toward Independence, October, 1856–April, 1861*, edited by William K. Scarborough (Baton Rouge: Louisiana State University Press, 1972), 346.

12. Hobson, *Tell about the South*, 43.

13. Ibid., 33, 37.

14. Edmund Ruffin, *The Diary of Edmund Ruffin, Volume III: A Dream Shattered, June, 1863–June, 1865*, edited by William K. Scarborough (Baton Rouge: Louisiana State University Press, 1989), 949.

15. Jones, *A Rebel War Clerk's Diary*, vol. 2, 480. A text search of the version of this diary available via Project Gutenberg reveals that Jones mentioned *Wild Western Scenes* seven times, mostly in the context of a republication. He never, however, mentioned *Wild Southern Scenes*. http://www.gutenberg.org/files/31087/31087-h/31087-h.htm, accessed December 20, 2012.

16. Hobson, *Tell about the South*, 38. Except in passing, Hobson does not mention *Wild Southern Scenes*.

17. Ruffin, *The Diary of Edmund Ruffin, Volume III*, 593.

18. Ruffin, *The Diary of Edmund Ruffin, Volume I*, 407. Three days later, on February 29, Ruffin referred to the book by its correct title, "Wild Southern Scenes," and

acknowledged that the design of the author, "which is wretchedly carried out," was worth doing better. *Anticipations* was completed by May 1, and the *Charleston Tri-Weekly Mercury* began serialization (416). See also Hobson, *Tell about the South*, 38, which repeats Ruffin's initial use of the incorrect name of Jones's work. Neither Ruffin nor Hobson ever mention the author of the book by name.

19. Tucker, *The Partisan Leader*, 5, 6, 28.

20. Jones, *Wild Southern Scenes*, 20, 11, 375. Don Higginbotham notes that Washington himself referred to the nation's capital as the "Federal City" (*George Washington*, 78).

21. On this notion of the "overt act," see, for example, McPherson, "The Fruits of Preventive War": "Southern moderates tried in vain to persuade their hotheaded colleagues to give the Lincoln administration a chance to fulfill its promise of nonintervention toward slavery in the states. Wait for an 'overt act' against southern rights before taking the drastic step of secession with its risk of civil war, they implored. But fire-eaters insisted that the South could not afford to wait until the North loosed another John Brown or other weapons of mass destruction" (5).

22. Ruffin, *Anticipations of the Future*, 27, 57–58.

23. For a more literary explication of Tucker's use of family, see Hare, *Will the Circle Be Unbroken?* 107–26.

24. Tucker, *The Partisan Leader*, 95, 55–57.

25. Jones, *Wild Southern Scenes*, 25.

26. "Image," because, as we shall see, Southern ideas of the reality of that document were not born out by events or by the electorally expressed will of the American people.

27. Tucker, *The Partisan Leader*, 202–7.

28. Jones, *Wild Southern Scenes*, 23, 79.

29. Ruffin, *The Diary of Edmund Ruffin, Volume I*, 416.

30. Ruffin, *Anticipations of the Future*, 78, 79, 83, 219, 342.

31. In a letter written to John C. Calhoun in November 1844 supporting the annexation of Texas, Tucker bluntly noted, "I am a States Right Man. No more—No less." Beverley Tucker to John C. Calhoun, November 13, 1844, in *The Papers of John C. Calhoun, Volume XX: 1844*, edited by Clyde N. Wilson (Columbia: University of South Carolina Press, 1991), 287.

32. Tucker, *The Partisan Leader*, 127, 128.

33. In a letter written to John C. Calhoun in January 1846, Tucker disparaged "the presumption of men whose proper place is between the handles of the plough, but who affect to lead in great affairs." Beverley Tucker to John C. Calhoun, January 23, 1846, in *The Papers of John C. Calhoun, Volume XXII: 1845-1846*, edited by Clyde N. Wilson (Columbia: University of South Carolina Press, 1995), 502. One wonders if Mr. Hobson was just such a character.

34. Tucker, *The Partisan Leader*, 38, 40, 41.

35. Ibid., 219.

36. Jones, *Wild Southern Scenes*, 111–12.

37. See, for example, ibid., 134. At the very end of the novel they switch roles, with

the president assuming the role of "MARBLE," so that this daughter can resume her flesh and blood existence (500). Ruffin's *Anticipations of the Future*, perhaps given its epistolary nature, has no analog in strong female characters.

38. Tucker, *The Partisan Leader*, 109, 119–22. *Sidier dhu*, variously translated as "black soldiers" or "dark soldiers," refers to the "independent companies raised to keep peace in the Highlands; named from the tartans they wore." The term had been popularized in Sir Walter Scott's 1814 novel *Waverly*. See "Glossary," Sir Walter Scott, *ebooks@Adelaide* (Adelaide: The University of Adelaide Library, 2004). Available at http://etext.library.adelaide.edu.au/s/scott/walter/waverley/glossary1.html, accessed December 20, 2012. The Black Watch (or the Royal Highland Regiment) is the most famous of these companies, raised in 1725 and formed into a Regiment of the Line in 1739. See http://www.theblackwatch.co.uk/index/blackwatch-history, accessed December 20, 2012.

39. Tucker, *The Partisan Leader*, 112–13. Vernon Parrington, Carl Bridenbaugh, and Clyde N. Wilson all assume that Mr. B— was John C. Calhoun, but Hugh Holman, noting that Tucker was no friend of Calhoun's in 1836, suggests instead that "the temptation is strong to say that Mr. B— is really Mr. Beverley himself and that he is what Tucker would like to be as a powerful statesman" (Holman, introduction, xxii). See also Carl Bridenbaugh's introduction to the 1933 edition of Nathaniel Beverley Tucker's *The Partisan Leader*, edited by Carl Bridenbaugh (New York: Knopf, 1933), xxix; and Clyde N. Wilson, ed., *The Papers of John C. Calhoun, Volume XIII: 1835–1837* (Columbia: University of South Carolina Press, 1980), 257.

Wild Southern Scenes also has a mysterious Mr. B—, a respected (but reasonable) antislavery advocate who uses his reputation to protect Senator Langdon from the bloodthirsty abolitionist mob in Philadelphia. Jones, *Wild Southern Scenes*, 57–73. In this case Mr. B—'s initials are given as DPB (57). Mr. B— disappears from the narrative soon thereafter. Whether or not this character is an homage to Tucker's Mr. B— is, of course, purely speculative.

40. Tucker, *The Partisan Leader*, 113. Again, this is Mr. B— speaking to Douglas.

41. Jones, *Wild Southern Scenes*, 439, 466, 475–76.

42. Ibid., 420, 421 (quotation).

43. Ruffin, *Anticipations of the Future*, 237, 130 (quotation).

44. Ibid., 255, 246.

45. Tucker, *The Partisan Leader*, 2, 195, 95, 27, 90, 98–104, 87 (quotation). *Imperium in imperio* means an empire within an empire. For the Declaration of Independence, see http://www.archives.gov/exhibits/charters/declaration_transcript.html, accessed December 20, 2012. Jones says something very similar toward the end of *Wild Southern Scenes*. In his capacity as Lord Protector, General Ruffleton proclaims that "the Federal system was a failure—that the sovereignty of States and the National sovereignty constituted an absurdity—an *imperium in imperio*, which experience had proved a fallacy, and it was his mission to put a period to it" (424). So, both fictional tyrants, Van Buren and Ruffleton, share similar ambitions.

46. Tucker, *The Partisan Leader*, 98, 107, 211–12, 97. In particular, Van Buren wants to try enemies of the state *in absentia* in Washington, D.C., echoing Jefferson's

charge that George III "has combined with others to subject us to a jurisdiction foreign to our constitution, and unacknowledged by our laws," and that "He has made Judges dependent on his Will alone."

47. See Waldstreicher, *In the Midst of Perpetual Fetes;* Newman, *Parades and the Politics of the Street;* Len Travers, *Celebrating the Fourth: Independence Day and the Rites of Nationalism in the Early Republic* (Amherst: University of Massachusetts Press, 1997); and Purcell, *Sealed with Blood.*

48. Jones, *Wild Southern Scenes,* 288, 305, 365, 388.

49. Ibid., 296, 479. The names of Ruffleton's allies are worth comment. In addition to the Reverends Blood and Fire, we have Ruffleton's two aides, Majors Snare and Trapp; his agent, Virus; his puppet president, Smiley; and his functionary, Windvane, who attempts to conspire against his master on numerous occasions, even offering up Ruffleton's affianced, Flora Summers, to the guillotine in order to save himself. Add to that the corpulent Lord Slysir and you have a comedy of errors in the names of the minor players.

50. Ibid., 54, 59, 60.

51. Ruffin, *Anticipations of the Future,* 305, 128–31.

52. In his diary on June 30, 1863, Ruffin noted that "neither then nor since has the work been read except by very few persons, & has not been even noticed, or its existence known, by the great body of the reading southern public." Ruffin, *The Diary of Edmund Ruffin, Volume III,* 36. To be fair, he did note on October 21, 1860, that William Ruffin, son of Judge Thomas Ruffin of North Carolina, "gave to it [*Anticipations*] the credit of having removed his lingering devotion to the union, & hopes of preserving it—& that he now concurred in the necessity for secession" (*The Diary of Edmund Ruffin, Volume I,* 475).

53. At least one extensive review of *The Partisan Leader* was published, by Abel P. Upshur in *Southern Literary Messenger,* January 1837, 73–89. Upshur was a Virginian Whig who served in the administration of President John Tyler and was a regular correspondent of Beverley Tucker's. Upshur's anonymous review, which included lengthy quotations from the novel, was, as one might expect, quite positive. William W. Freehling lists Upshur as the author in *The Road to Disunion,* 607n.

54. Beverley Tucker, *A Key to the Disunion Conspiracy: The Partisan Leader* (New York: Rudd and Carleton, 1861); Beverley Tucker, *The Partisan Leader: A Novel, and an Apocalypse of the Origin and Struggles of the Southern Confederacy,* edited by Thomas A. Ware (Richmond, Va.: West and Johnson, 1862).

55. Nathaniel Beverley Tucker, *The Partisan Leader,* edited by Carl Bridenbaugh (New York: Knopf, 1933); Beverley Tucker, *A Key to the Disunion Conspiracy: The Partisan Leader* (Upper Saddle River, N.J.: The Gregg Press, 1968); and Nathaniel Beverley Tucker, *The Partisan Leader: A Tale of the Future,* edited by C. Hugh Holman (Chapel Hill: University of North Carolina Press, 1971). Variations in the name of the novel and the spelling of the author's name are faithfully reproduced.

56. Tucker, *A Key to the Disunion Conspiracy,* vi, v, vi, vii. Lecomptonism refers to the proslavery 1857 proposed constitution for Kansas, which became a touchstone for

antislavery forces in the North. See, for example, Robert Walter Johannsen, *Stephen A. Douglas* (Urbana: University of Illinois Press, 1975), 710.

57. Tucker, *The Partisan Leader* (Richmond, Va., 1862), iii, v. Ware quotes a letter from the lieutenant governor of Virginia, Robert Latane Montague, who in 1842 or 1843 was a student at William and Mary and enrolled in one of Professor Tucker's classes. Montague reported that he had heard Tucker "declare to his class that he wrote the book," and had subsequently discussed it with him in private, noting Tucker's opinion that "those who were then deriding him, and denouncing his book as a treasonable production would live to see the day when they would acknowledge that his appreciation of Yankee character was correct; and lament in tears and blood that his views were not sooner adopted by the South" (Ibid., iv–v).

58. Ibid., viii. In fact, Ware concluded his remarks by noting that he would trust "to the intelligence of the reader to apply the coincidences which mark its fulfillment as a political prophecy."

59. Ibid., v, vii. Ware was "sure that the '*Christian*' prefix was given by the author only because he had forgotten his *christian* name." Saunders Witt, then aged seventy-seven, appears in the 1870 Census for Patrick County, Virginia (Eunice B. Kirkman, "The Patrick County Census of 1870," http://files.usgwarchives.org/va/patrick/census/censmayo.txt, accessed December 20, 2012).

3. "The Pledge of a Nation That's Dead and Gone"

The epigraph is from Fuller, *Confederate Currency and Stamps,* 60. According to Fuller, this poem was "written on the back of the Confederate note" and later published by the New York *Metropolitan Record.* See also "Notes and Fragments," *Southwestern Historical Quarterly* 21, no. 1 (July 1917): 101–2, which tells a similar story.

1. Gates, *Agriculture and the Civil War*, 38–40.

2. Lerner, "Money, Prices and Wages."

3. Weigley, *A Great Civil War*, 222.

4. We can infer that these images were ubiquitous to at least a certain class of Southerners due to the nature of Southern education. See, for example, Durrill, "The Power of Ancient Words," 469–98. The images were also a part of the popular iconography of the time.

5. John Majewski argues that the most significant aspect of the iconography of Confederate Treasury notes was that they "featured representations of a modern slaveholding economy," with "larger-than-life" depictions of railroad locomotives and state capitols, for example. The former was "modern, powerful, and dynamic," while the latter was "a perfect symbol of how government authority and the need for collective action dwarfed the needs of individuals." That analysis may very well work in tandem with the one presented here. See *Modernizing a Slave Economy,* 140–41.

6. Ford, *Origins of Southern Radicalism*, 261, 275 on profitability; 65, 234, 267, 275 on the economic nature of planters.

7. Moneta was actually a Roman manifestation of Juno, but her temple eventually housed the Roman mint and the words for "mint" and "money" derive from her name.

8. Helleiner, *The Making of National Money*, 11.

9. The National Currency Act was superseded in 1864 by the National Banking Act, under whose authority the notes were issued by newly chartered national banks. For data, see "U.S. National Bank Notes, 1864–1935," EH.Net (2006), http://eh.net/databases/usnationalbanknotes, accessed December 20, 2012. Over the seventy-one-year history of these notes, some $17 billion dollars' worth were issued. The value of notes issued in 1865 ($146 million) was not reached again as an annual total until 1900, thus demonstrating the important role this form of currency had in financing the Union war effort.

10. Senator John Sherman, quoted in Helleiner, *The Making of National Money*, 105.

11. Spencer M. Clark to Secretary Chase, March 28, 1863, quoted in ibid., 106.

12. Ibid., 105.

13. Bureau of Engraving and Printing, "Selection of Portraits and Designs Appearing on Paper Currency," http://web.archive.org/web/20070928013452/http://www.moneyfactory.gov/document.cfm/18/118, accessed December 20, 2012. Archived from the original.

14. Increasingly, scholars have taken this subject matter seriously. See, for example, Potter, "Images of Majesty"; Helleiner, "National Currencies and National Identities"; Gilbert and Helleiner, eds., *Nation-States and Money;* Mwangi, "The Lion, the Native and the Coffee Plant"; Hymans, "The Changing Color of Money"; Hymans, "International Patterns in National Identity Content"; and Wallach, "Creating a Country through Currency and Stamps." For a different iconographic analysis, see Cerulo, *Identity Designs,* and Quigley, "Tobacco's Civil War."

15. "Beyond Face Value: Depictions of Slavery in Confederate Currency," The Civil War Center, Louisiana State University, http://exhibitions.blogs.lib.lsu.edu/?p=566/; "Confederate Currency: Color of Money—Depictions of Slavery in Confederate and Southern States Currency," Avery Research Center for African-American History and Culture, College of Charleston, http://www.colorsofmoney.com/exhibition.htm. In addition, the "American Currency Exhibit" at the Federal Reserve Bank of San Francisco shows one Confederate banknote in its "Showcase of Bills." That bill, T-29, depicts slaves picking cotton; see http://www.frbsf.org/currency/civilwar/show.html. Websites accessed December 20, 2012.

16. Six of fifty-one distinct designs on Confederate currency feature slaves, an incidence of 11.75 percent. In comparison, Ceres, the Greek goddess of agriculture and civilization, and not a figure closely tied to the Old South, appears in various guises on nine designs (17.65%).

17. Swanson, "Agents of Culture and Nationalism," 134. See also Douglas B. Ball, "Currency," in *The Encyclopedia of the Confederacy,* vol. 1, edited by Richard N. Current et al. (New York: Simon and Schuster, 1993), 433–38; and Douglas B. Ball, "The Confederate Currency Reform of 1862," in *America's Currency 1789–1866: Coinage of the Americas Conference at the American Numismatic Society, New York, October 31–*

November 2, 1985, edited by William E. Metcalf (New York: American Numismatic Society, 1985), 1–12. Ball makes no claims toward nationalistic motives in the currency reforms.

18. Harold Holzer, "Beyond Face Value: Slavery Iconography in Confederate Currency," http://exhibitions.blogs.lib.lsu.edu/?p=566&page=5, accessed December 20, 2012.

19. David Firestone, "Interpreting the Images of Slavery on the Confederacy's Money," *New York Times,* March 6, 2001. Available at http://www.nytimes.com/ 2001/03/06/arts/06SLAV.html, accessed December 20, 2012.

20. Modern U.S. currency is "legal tender" in that "you have made a valid and legal offer of payment of your debt when you tender United States currency to your creditor." Although no statute says that private businesses need accept cash, you have still made a legal attempt to settle a debt if you offer it to them. The 1965 Coinage Act (now U.S. Code, Title 31 § 392) mandates that "all coins and currencies of the United States, regardless of when coined or issued, shall be legal tender for all debts, public and private, public charges, taxes, duties and dues." Bureau of Engraving and Printing, "Legal Tender: A Definition," http://www.moneyfactory.gov/historicallegislation .html, accessed December 20, 2012.

21. Act of March 9, 1861, and Act of March 23, 1863. Fuller, *Confederate Currency and Stamps,* 58, 104.

22. Grover C. Criswell Jr., *Confederate and Southern State Currency: A Descriptive Listing, Including Rarity,* vol. 1 (Pass-A-Grille Beach, Fla.: Criswell's, 1957), 75; Slabaugh, *Confederate States Paper Money,* 60.

23. Fuller, *Confederate Currency and Stamps,* 32.

24. Lerner, "Money, Prices and Wages," 24.

25. Ramsdell, *Behind the Lines in the Southern Confederacy,* 19, 49, 75.

26. The T series numbers used to identify Confederate currency were assigned by Grover Criswell in his publications on the subject. These "type" designations remain in use today in the collectors' industry.

27. Jefferson Davis, Inaugural Address, February 18, 1861, *Journal of the Congress,* I, 64–66. All subsequent quotations in the next two paragraphs originate here.

28. George Washington was the first president of the Society of the Cincinnati, a fraternal organization of Revolutionary War veterans. He was often depicted as Cincinnatus himself, following the Roman statesman Lucius Quinctius Cincinnatus, who relinquished his rule of Rome after the crisis during which he had been appointed had passed, and entered in legend as the epitome of the selfless statesman.

29. The image of slaves planting cotton depicted on the T-4 bill was reused on the T-41 bill in the April 1862 issue. See Slabaugh, *Confederate States Paper Money,* 24, 49.

30. Slabaugh, *Confederate States Paper Money,* 53, 46. The Confederacy did not always advertise the origins of its images, so that, for example, the image we now know to be Lucy Holcombe Pickens on an 1863 $100 bill (T-49) was for decades assumed to be Varina Howell Davis, the Confederate first lady. Given that nineteenth-century collectors correctly identified the images of Lucy Pickens on $1 bills issued in 1862,

Slabaugh concludes that the Treasury intended the 1863 $100 note to depict a more general "Women of the South" image, denoted by the addition of a wreath encircling the portrait.

31. See, for example, Wallenstein, *From Slave South to New South*, and Williams, *Rich Man's War.*

32. See, for example, Wiley, *The Road to Appomattox*, 78–104; and Escott, *After Secession.* Some historians have gone so far as to lay blame for Confederate defeat at Davis's feet. See David Potter's contribution to Donald, ed., *Why the North Won the Civil War.*

33. Slabaugh, *Confederate States Paper Money*, passim.

34. Fuller, *Confederate Currency and Stamps*, 41.

35. Hoyer and Ludwig produced all of the May 1861 types but one. That exception, produced by Jules Manouvrier in New Orleans, is the only Confederate Treasury note without any images (T-12). The Department of the Treasury found it unsatisfactory, and while Manouvrier produced notes for the states, T-12 is his only national piece. The August and December 1861 issue, amounting to an eightfold increase in production over the first two issues, was divided between Hoyer and Ludwig, Keatinge and Ball, the Southern Banknote Company, and Blanton Duncan. By the 1864 issue, Keatinge and Ball was responsible for virtually all types. See Criswell, *Criswell's Currency Series, Vol. I*, passim.

36. Fuller, *Confederate Currency and Stamps*, 116. On the Southern Cross during wartime, see Bonner, *Colors and Blood.*

37. On the Great Seal of the Confederacy, see Faust, *The Creation of Confederate Nationalism*, 24–26.

38. Slabaugh, *Confederate States Paper Money*, 68.

4. "Thoughts That Breathe and Words That Burn"

The epigraph is from the opening line of the preface to Shepperson, ed., *War Songs of the South*, 2.

Versions of this chapter were delivered at the Illinois Program for Research in the Humanities Fifth Annual Conference at the University of Illinois at Urbana-Champaign (2003) and at the "Nationalism in the New World: The Americas and the Atlantic World" conference at Vanderbilt University (2003). The author thanks all attendees for their comments and suggestions. A portion of this chapter appears in "'And Bid Him Bear a Patriot's Part': National and Local Perspectives on Confederate Nationalism," in *Master Narratives: History, Storytelling, and the Postmodern South*, edited by Jason Phillips (Baton Rouge: Louisiana State University Press, forthcoming) (with Vernon Burton).

1. M. Louise Rogers, "Glad Tidings We Send Thee," *Southern Illustrated News*, October 18, 1862, 3.

2. *Southern Field and Fireside*, April 4, 1863, 110.

3. Editor's Table, *Southern Literary Messenger*, January 1864, 63.

4. While not often thought of as such, noise and silence are additional signifiers

attached to the words "white" and "black." If "white" contains implications of light and therefore of daytime, then it also must contain implications of the hustle and bustle of the day, so of noise. Similarly, if "black" is associated with darkness and therefore nighttime, it must also be associated with the relative silence of sleep. On this subject more generally, see Smith, *Listening to Nineteenth-Century America*.

5. Editor's Table, *Southern Literary Messenger*, January 1864, 64.

6. *Southern Literary Messenger*, May 1864, 314; January 1864, 63.

7. "Disenthrallment of Southern Literature," *De Bow's Review*, October–November 1861, 347–61; "Are We a Literary People?" *Southern Punch*, February 20, 1864, 2.

8. "Are We a Literary People?"

9. This was not the first time Timrod had articulated these concerns. Before the war, writing in *Russell's Magazine*, he had advanced many of the same themes he would address in the pages of the *Daily South Carolinian*. Henry Timrod, "Literature in the South," *Russell's Magazine*, August 1859, 385–95. Reprinted in Parks, ed., *The Essays of Henry Timrod*, 83–102.

10. Henry Timrod, "Southern Literature," *Columbia Daily South Carolinian*, January 14, 1864; reprinted in Hubbell, ed., *The Last Years of Henry Timrod*, 133–34.

11. For the theme of literary independence from the North, see, for example, "Disenthrallment of Southern Literature," *De Bow's Review*, October–November 1861, 347–61; M. Brooks, "The Intellectual Future of the South," *Southern Literary Messenger*, May 1862, 313–14; "Guessing," *The Countryman*, September 29, 1862, 12; "Are We a Literary People?" As Brooks put it, "We have too long allowed the North to be our literary censors," or as *The Countryman* more directly suggested, "Let us eschew the devil and his works."

12. Timrod, "Literature in the South," *Russell's Magazine;* reprinted in Parks, ed., *The Essays of Henry Timrod*, 87.

13. William Gilmore Simms to James Henry Hammond, December 24, 1847, in Mary C. Simms Oliphant et al., eds., *The Letters of William Gilmore Simms, Volume II: 1845–1849* (Columbia: University of South Carolina Press, 1953), 386. See also John Mayfield, "'The Soul of a Man!': William Gilmore Simms and the Myths of Southern Manhood," *Journal of the Early Republic* 15, no. 3 (Fall 1995): 477–500; and Joseph V. Ridgely, *William Gilmore Simms* (New York: Twayne, 1962).

14. O'Brien, "The Lineaments of Southern Romanticism," 50, 52.

15. On the development of an American literature and literary marketplace generally, see Loughran, *The Republic in Print;* McGill, *American Literature and the Culture of Reprinting;* Kaplan, *The Anarchy of Empire;* Giles, *Transatlantic Insurrections;* and Rowe, *Literary Culture and U.S. Imperialism*.

16. Giles, *Transatlantic Insurrections*, 2.

17. Timrod, "Nationality in Literature," *Columbia Daily South Carolinian*, January 19, 1864; reprinted in Hubbell, ed., *The Last Years of Henry Timrod*, 137–38. Apparently, by his own definition, Timrod was not guilty of producing great literature in writing "Ethnogenesis," *the* ode to the Confederacy, in early 1861. Timrod, "Ethnogenesis," in Parks and Parks, eds., *The Collected Poems of Henry Timrod*, 92–95. This poem, originally titled "Ode on the Occasion of the Meeting of the Southern Con-

gress," was first printed in the *Charleston Daily Courier,* February 23 and 25, 1861, and then in the *Living Age,* March 30, 1861; the *Charleston Tri-Weekly Mercury,* September 26, 1861; and the *Courier* again, January 31, 1862. It was also issued in at least two broadside formats. Parks and Parks, eds., *The Collected Poems of Henry Timrod,* 180.

18. Timrod, "Nationality in Literature," in Hubbell, ed., *The Last Years of Henry Timrod,* 138.

19. Timrod, "War and Literature," *Columbia Daily South Carolinian,* February 28, 1864; reprinted in Hubbell, ed., *The Last Years of Henry Timrod,* 142–43, 144.

20. Not quite everyone agreed with this conclusion. In May 1864, an article in the *Southern Literary Messenger* conceded the point that in a nation with "virtually no history, and . . . comparatively few of those great landmarks of thought and reflection in the shape of great events . . . for some time to come our most marked successes in literature will constitute simply an approximation to the numerous models before us." The key, according to the *Messenger,* was that Southern writers choose English models rather than Northern ones (May 1864, 314, 315).

21. Classic American literary critics have tended to agree with Alfriend and Timrod. Edmund Wilson noted the volume of wartime writings but largely dismissed their quality, commenting that "the period of the American Civil War was not one in which belles-lettres flourished" (*Patriotic Gore,* ix). Similarly, Daniel Aaron noted very accurately the overarching themes of wartime Confederate literature but dismissed the whole genre as leaving nothing of "any permanent literary value." He argued that none of the Southern wartime writers "managed to comprehend a society enmeshed in contradictions and smoldering in sectional, class, and racial hatreds." He dismissed this literature as "predominantly polemical and shrill, occasionally elegiac" (*The Unwritten War,* 228, 339, 228).

22. Fahs, *The Imagined Civil War,* 1–2. Fahs's source base seems skewed in favor of the North, perhaps because the Union had more resources to devote to literature as well as having a considerable head start in printing presses and so forth. Fahs notes that the 1860 Census recorded 986 printing offices in the Northern states and 151 in the Southern, a ratio of more than six to one. There was an even greater disparity in the volume of book binderies, 190 in the North to 17 in the South, a ratio of more than 11 to 1. Ibid., 21.

23. Ibid., 63.

24. Tyrtaeus, "The Voice of the South," *Charleston Tri-Weekly Mercury;* reprinted in Simms, ed., *The War Poetry of the South,* 33, and quoted in Fahs, *The Imagined Civil War,* 63.

25. Henry Timrod, "A Cry to Arms," in Parks and Parks, eds., *The Collected Poems of Henry Timrod,* 108; originally published in the *Charleston Tri-Weekly Mercury* and the *Charleston Daily Courier,* both on March 4, 1862. It should not surprise us that Charleston, South Carolina, was at the forefront of this movement to rhetorically create a united South.

26. The *Southern Illustrated News,* for example, published many poems of this ilk. See Charlie Wildwood, "The South," November 8, 1862, 3; Mary A. McCrimmon, "The

Land of the South," November 29, 1862, 6; Ianthe, "To Louise," December 6, 1862, 4; John R. Thompson, "A Word with the West," December 13, 1862, 4; John Esten Cooke, "The Song of the Rebel," January 24, 1863, 5; and Volunteer, "On to Richmond," January 31, 1863, 3.

27. Coleman Hutchinson correctly points to "our seemingly hypnotic fascination with printed versions of songs," arguing instead that we need to pay attention to the "culture of revisionism that has eluded traditional histories of the Civil War song and book." This analysis is guilty of that shortcoming. See Coleman Hutchinson, "Secret in Altered Lines," 255–75, 256 (quotation).

28. St. George Tucker, "The Southern Cross," dated February 22, 1861, printed in *Southern Literary Messenger*, March 1861, 189; reprinted in *Selma Reporter*, April 26, 1861, with the subtitle, "(Printed for the Magnolia Cadets)." The two versions have slight differences. In the last line of the second verse, "Freedom and Glory" are capitalized in the *Messenger* version and not in the *Reporter* version. The first word of the last verse is "but" in the *Messenger* and "and" in the *Reporter*. "To arms" in the third line of the last verse is followed by an exclamation mark in the *Messenger* and a comma in the *Reporter*. The only really substantive difference comes in the very last line of the poem. In the *Messenger* version, it is rendered as "the flag of the free *or* the pall of the brave," while in the *Reporter* version it is "the flag of the free *and* the pall of the brave." William G. Shepperson's edited *War Songs of the South* reprinted the *Messenger* version with respect to the last verse, preserving "but" and "or." St. George Tucker, "The Southern Cross, in Shepperson, ed., *War Songs of the South*, 35.

29. A similar preoccupation with Northern culpability comes through in another proposed Confederate national anthem, "God Save the South," published anonymously in *The Countryman* in September 1862. Although not nearly as eloquent as Tucker— in fact seemingly eschewing eloquence of any kind—this unnamed author was equally clear about who was to blame for the war: "War to the hilt, / Theirs be the guilt / Who fetter the freeman, / To ransom the slave. / Then still be undismayed, / Sheathe not the battle-blade, / Till the last foe is laid, / cold in the grave. "The Southern National Anthem," *The Countryman*, September 29, 1862, 5.

30. Tucker, "The Southern Cross."

31. Francis Scott Key, "The Star Spangled Banner," September 20, 1814, The University of Oklahoma Law Center, http://www.law.ou.edu/hist/ssb.html, accessed December 20, 2012.

32. Shepperson, "Preface," in Shepperson, ed., *War Songs of the South*, 2.

33. Julia Ward Howe, "Battle Hymn of the Republic," The University of Oklahoma Law Center, http://www.law.ou.edu/hist/bathymn.html, accessed December 20, 2012.

34. Daniel Decatur Emmett, "Dixie," September 1859, http://chnm.gmu.edu/lou doun tah/activities/pdf/DixieSongLyrics1.pdf, accessed December 20, 2012. Credit for the comparison between "Battle Hymn" and "Dixie" belongs to Vernon Burton. On the wartime lyrical revisionism of "Dixie," see Coleman Hutchinson, "Whistling 'Dixie' for the Union (Nation, Anthem, Revisions)," *American Literary History* 19, no. 3 (Fall 2007): 603–628. In particular, Hutchinson notes that the original lyrics of "Dixie" did

not necessarily find favor in the Confederacy, and that Brigadier General Albert Pike rewrote them in May 1861 or thereabouts as the more martial "War Song of Dixie," ibid., 615–16.

35. Sally Rochester Ford, *Raids and Romances; or, Morgan and His Men* (1863; reprint New York: Charles B. Richardson, 1866, from 1864 Mobile edition), 28. Sally Rochester Ford (1828–1910) was born in Kentucky and graduated from the female seminary in Georgetown, Kentucky, in 1849. In 1855, she married Samuel Howard Ford, a Baptist minister with whom she edited *The Christian Repository* and *The Home Circle.* She also became president of the Woman's Missionary Society of the South. Moving from Louisville to Memphis at the beginning of the Civil War, by 1864 her husband was pastor of the St. Francis Street Baptist Church in Mobile, Alabama. After the war, they returned to Memphis and thence to St. Louis after her husband retired in 1873. Ford's first novel, *Grace Truman,* was serialized in *The Christian Repository* in 1857, and sold some 30,000 copies in three years after it appeared in book form. She published a second novel, *Mary Bunyan,* in 1860. *Raids and Romances* was her third novel. See John Grant Wilson and John Fiske, eds., *Appleton's Cyclopedia of American Biography,* vol. 2 (New York: D. Appleton, 1888), 501; John W. Leonard, ed., *Who's Who in America: Biographical Dictionary of Notable Living Men and Women of the United States, 1901–1902* (Chicago: A. N. Marquis, 1901), 390; Lucian Lamar Knight, ed., *Biographical Dictionary of Southern Authors* (Atlanta: Martin and Hoyt Company, 1929; reprint Detroit: Gale, 1978), 151; Taryn Benbow-Pfalzgraf, ed., *American Women Writers: A Critical Reference Guide from Colonial Times to the Present,* vol. 3, 2nd ed. (Detroit: St. James Press, 2000), 61–62.

36. Ford, *Raids and Romances,* 34, 211.

37. Ibid., 12, 13, 23, 24, 57, 75.

38. Ibid., 81. Presumably the author meant Deutsch (German) rather than Dutch, a common usage at the time. See also pp. 121–123, 284, 317.

39. Ibid., 230–31.

40. Augusta Jane Evans, *Macaria; or, Altars of Sacrifice,* 2nd ed. (1863; Richmond, Va.: West and Johnston, 1864), 3. Augusta Jane Evans (1835–1909) was born to a wealthy family in Georgia that moved to San Antonio, Texas, when she was ten. In 1849, the family moved again to Mobile, Alabama, where her father, Matt Evans, began to work in the cotton industry. Between 1851 and 1854, Evans wrote her first novel, *Inez: A Tale of the Alamo,* which was published in 1855. Her second novel, *Beulah,* came in 1859, and her third, *Macaria,* in 1863. Her most celebrated novel, *St. Elmo,* was published in 1867. *Beulah, Macaria,* and *St. Elmo* have all been recently reprinted in critical editions, the first two from Louisiana State University Press in 1992, the last from the University of Alabama Press in the same year. In 1868, Evans married Colonel Lorenzo Madison Wilson, a bank director and railroad magnate, and over the next four decades she published another five novels. She was buried in a Confederate veteran's graveyard in Mobile. See *Dictionary of Literary Biography* (Gale Literary Databases, www.galenet.com, accessed October 1, 2003).

41. Evans, *Macaria,* 148–49.

42. M. J. (Mary Jane) Haw, *The Rivals: A Chickahominy Story* (Richmond, Va.: Ayres and Wade, 1864), 43, 48, 52, 53, 43–44, 54, 58.

43. James Dabney McCabe, *The Aid-de-Camp: A Romance of the War* (Richmond, Va.: Macfarlane and Fergusson, 1863), 28. According to the novel's preface, "The romance of 'THE AID-DE-CAMP,' was written during the fall of 1862, more for the purpose of beguiling a season of weariness than with the expectation of presenting it to the public. It was originally published in 'The Magnolia Weekly,' and the great success with which it met there has encouraged the Author to attempt a re-publication, this time in its present form" (3). James Dabney McCabe Jr. (1842–1883), was born in Virginia, the son of a minister in the Protestant Episcopal Church, and educated at the Virginia Military Institute. During the secession crisis, at the age of eighteen, he published a pamphlet entitled "Fanaticism and Its Results." *The Aide-de-Camp* was first serialized in the *Magnolia Weekly* (which McCabe later edited) and was issued in book form in 1863. He also wrote a number of plays that were performed in Richmond in 1862 and 1863, and by the latter year he had turned his hand to a series of military biographies, including ones of Thomas J. Jackson, Albert S. Johnston, and Robert E. Lee. After the war he became a prolific essayist and poet. See Wilson and Fiske, eds., *Appleton's Cyclopedia of American Biography,* vol. 4, 74; and Knight, ed., *Biographical Dictionary of Southern Authors,* 271.

44. McCabe, *The Aid-de-Camp,* 40, 42, 53–67 (quotation 53, 67). John Mayfield notes the similarities of this plot to John Pendleton Kennedy's *Horse-Shoe Robinson: A Tale of the Tory Ascendency* (1835). Private correspondence to the author.

45. McCabe, *The Aid-de-Camp,* 17.

46. Ibid., 20, 21, 22.

47. Ibid., 21, 23–24, 25.

48. For example, using the four novels for which modern, electronic versions exist, we find that the word "slave" appears only 5 times, "slavery" 6 times, "negro" 13 times, "nigger" twice (both from the mouth of a slave), "African" never, and "black" in the racial sense only once. That makes 27 individual references in some 437 printed pages of text. By contrast, the word "servant" appears at least 54 times. The ethnicity of the servant is rarely mentioned, but when it is, it is to make clear that the servant in question is not black—as in Colonel Maynard's "Irish servant" in *The Rivals* (50). The novels used for this survey are Haw, *The Rivals* (negro 6, servant 17, nigger 2); Evans, *Macaria* (slave 1, slavery 2, negro 5, servant 28); McCabe, *The Aide-de-Camp* (slave 2, slavery 4, negro 1, servant 4); and Napier Bartlett, *Clarimonde: A Tale of New Orleans Life, and of the Present War* (Richmond, Va.: M. A. Malsby, 1863) (slave 2, negro 1, black 1, servant 5). They are available at *Documenting the American South,* accessed December 20, 2012.

49. Haw, *The Rivals,* 5, 9, 12.

50. Bartlett, *Clarimonde,* 20.

51. Evans, *Macaria,* 19, 161, 162.

52. Haw, *The Rivals,* 12. The pointed use of the full "Thomas" rather than the diminutive "Tom" may have been intended by Haw to make a point about the respect

proper Southern women had toward their slaves, presumably in direct counterpoint to the casual familiarity of the abolitionist and agitator Harriet Beecher Stowe.

53. Ibid., 15.

54. Ibid., 50, 51, 52.

55. Ibid., 51.

56. Ibid., 52.

57. Ford, *Raids and Romances,* 12, 13.

5. To "Surpass All the Knighthood of Romance"

The epigraph is from Salutatory, *Southern Illustrated News,* September 6, 1862, 4.

A portion of this chapter was presented at the Douglas Southall Freeman and Southern Intellectual History Conference at the University of Richmond (2005). It has since been published as "Promoting the Confederacy: Virginia's *Southern Illustrated News,*" in *Virginians and the Civil War,* edited by Peter Wallenstein and Bertram Wyatt-Brown (Charlottesville: University of Virginia Press, 2004). The author wishes to thank the conference attendees and the collection's editors for their thoughtful comments and suggestions.

1. Higginbotham, *George Washington,* 8, 84, 85.

2. Purcell, *Sealed with Blood,* 1, 18.

3. Joseph Addison Turner, *The Countryman,* January 3, 1865, 1. In all fairness, Turner did not follow the Confederacy into death and was not even in uniform when he wrote these hyperbolic words. After the war's end, he did spend some time as a prisoner of the Union, before being released and returning to journalism.

4. Watie surrendered at Doaksville, in Indian Territory. See Josephy, *The Civil War in the American West,* 385. The last battle of the conflict was fought at Palmito Ranch, "on the east bank of the Rio Grande near Brownsville, down at the very tip of Texas," on May 12–13, 1865. It was a Confederate victory. See Foote, *The Civil War,* vol. 3, 1019. Foote's book "officially" ends at Appomattox, though he needs 103 pages to wrap up the rest of the war. The last Confederate "soldiers" to surrender were the surviving members of William Quantrill's bushwhackers, who gave themselves up just outside Louisville, Kentucky, on July 26, 1865, three and a half months after Appomattox. See Castel, *The Guerilla War,* 49.

5. "The Times," *Southern Illustrated News,* September 6, 1862, 5.

6. Ibid.

7. Gary W. Gallagher, "Nationalism: 'The Army of Northern Virginia Alone, as the Last Hope of the South, Will Win the Independence of the Confederacy,'" in Gallagher, *The Confederate War,* 85, 86–87.

8. Coincidentally, the motion picture *Gods and Generals* (Ted Turner Film Properties, 2002), directed by Ronald F. Maxwell and based on a novel by Jeffrey M. Shaara, represents—whether deliberately or not—a very 1860s vision of Stonewall Jackson's place in Confederate nationalism. This is even complete with pseudo-stigmata in a scene (DVD Chapter 51, "Crossing Over") in which Stephen Lang, as a dying Stonewall, raises his bandaged right hand to the heavens just before he utters his last word.

In the center of the bandaged hand is a circle of blood. Admittedly, Stonewall was shot in the right hand, but in the messianic context of his portrayal in the movie, it is difficult to see how else one could interpret the scene.

9. Connelly, *The Marble Man*, 18. There is a considerable historical literature on Robert E. Lee, his achievements, and his place in the Confederate pantheon. Among these works are Freeman, *R. E. Lee*, and *Lee's Lieutenants;* Connelly, *The Marble Man;* Nolan, *Lee Considered;* Thomas, *Robert E. Lee;* Roland, *Reflections on Lee;* Fellman, *The Making of Robert E. Lee;* Brian Holden Reid, *Robert E. Lee: Icon for a Nation* (London: Weidenfeld and Nicolson, 2005); and various works written and edited by Gary Gallagher, including *Lee the Soldier; The Confederate War; Lee and His Generals; Lee and His Army;* and *Causes Won, Lost, and Forgotten.* The Library of Congress catalog records 349 titles under the "Lee, Robert E." subject heading (http://catalog.loc.gov, accessed February 21, 2011).

The best of the works on Lee note the difficulties of separating out his contemporary, wartime reputation; the reputation created for him by late nineteenth- and early twentieth-century partisans of the Lost Cause; and his modern evaluation by historians. Lee the wartime general and Lee the postwar icon are clearly different people, serving different purposes and constituencies, and should be assessed as such.

10. Connelly, *The Marble Man*, 18–25. Two of these men have modern biographies: Robertson, *Stonewall Jackson,* and Hettle, *Inventing Stonewall Jackson;* and Symonds, *Joseph E. Johnston.* There are older works, one having been republished, for the other two: Roland, *Albert Sidney Johnston;* and Williams, *P. G. T. Beauregard.*

11. For example, on Stuart, see Thomas, *Bold Dragoon;* Yates, "The Concept of Nationalism in the Confederate Nation"; and Wert, *Cavalryman of the Lost Cause.* On Mosby, see Ashdown and Caudill, *The Mosby Myth.* On Ashby, see Anderson, *Blood Image.* On Forrest, see Browning, *Forrest,* and Ashdown and Caudill, *The Myth of Nathan Bedford Forrest.* On Smith, see Lagvanec, "Chevalier Bayard of the Confederacy."

12. See Orville Vernon Burton, *In My Father's House: Family and Community in Edgefield, South Carolina* (Chapel Hill: University of North Carolina Press, 1985); and "On the Confederate Homefront." On the connections between the local and the national in the Confederacy, see Burton and Binnington, "'And Bid Him Bear a Patriot's Part.'"

13. William Gilmore Simms, "Beauregard: A Song," *Southern Literary Messenger,* February–March 1862, 103. In French, Beauregard's name means something along the lines of "handsome (or beautiful) looking." As a play on words, "Beau-fusil" means beautiful rifle, "Beau-canon" means beautiful cannon, "Beau-sabreur" presumably means beautiful sabre or sword, though sabre is the same in French as in English, and a sword is an epée. "Beau soldat" means beautiful soldier.

14. Paul H. Hayne, "Beauregard: A Sonnet," *Magnolia Weekly,* November 12, 1864, 22. Although by November 1864 Beauregard was back in a field command in Virginia, he had spent a good part of the war in effective exile as commander of the port defenses of Charleston, South Carolina. Despite his record, he had a loyal following who thought he had been poorly served by Jefferson Davis. Haynes's poem seems to capture that sentiment.

15. "Forrest in Pursuit of the Foe," *Southern Punch,* November 8, 1864, 3.

16. "General Bragg—Ing," *The Countryman,* September 29, 1863, 98. "Amain" has several archaic uses, including "in great haste" and "to a high degree." The "Dutch horse" was Major General William Rosecrans, commanding officer of the Union Army of the Cumberland, defeated at Chickamauga and very shortly thereafter relieved of command.

17. "O, Braxton Bragg, My Jo!" *Southern Punch,* September 26, 1863, 3.

18. "A Farewell to Pope," *Southern Illustrated News,* September 20, 1862, 9.

19. M. Louise Rogers, "Glad Greetings We Send Thee," *Southern Illustrated News,* October 18, 1862, 3.

20. "Salutatory," *Southern Illustrated News,* September 6, 1862, 4.

21. George W. Bagby, "Editor's Table," *Southern Literary Messenger,* June 1863, 373.

22. "Resting on Their Laurels," *Southern Illustrated News,* September 6, 1862, 4.

23. George W. Bagby, "Editor's Table," *Southern Literary Messenger,* July–August 1862, 503.

24. McPherson, *Battle Cry of Freedom,* 465–66.

25. George W. Bagby, "Editor's Table," *Southern Literary Messenger,* July–August 1862, 503, 504.

26. J. A. Via, "The Death of Ashby," *Southern Literary Messenger,* May 1862, 315. The *Messenger's* masthead very clearly says May 1862, though Ashby did not die until June 6. As with many contemporary periodicals, the date on the masthead and the actual date of publication do not necessarily match up. On Ashby more generally, see Anderson, *Blood Image.*

27. John R. Thompson, "Ashby," *Southern Literary Messenger,* May 1862, 328.

28. John Harry Hartman, "Tribute," *Southern Illustrated News,* October 18, 1862, 7.

29. H. L. Flash, "Zollicoffer," *Southern Literary Messenger,* April 1862, 271.

30. "General Turner Ashby," *Southern Illustrated News,* October 18, 1862, 1; "General Robert Edmund Lee," *Southern Illustrated News,* January 17, 1863, 1. Most of the engravings presented in the *News* after its first few issues were completed by W. B. Campbell.

31. "Vicksburg, MS," *Southern Illustrated News,* November 8, 1862, 1; "The Society of Women," ibid., December 20, 1862, 1.

32. "General Thomas J. Jackson," *Southern Illustrated News,* September 6, 1862, 1.

33. Hard Cracker, "Foot-Cavalry Chronicle," *Southern Illustrated News,* October 18, 1862, 3; Hard Cracker, "Jackson's Foot-Cavalry," ibid., October 18, 1862, 8. See also "Stonewall Jackson's Way," ibid., December 13, 1862, 7; Virginia Norfolk, "Over the River," ibid., July 25, 1863, 18. The *News* reported Stonewall's last words as "Let us cross over the river, and rest under the shade of the trees." The quotation is from "Stonewall Jackson's Way."

34. "A Dirge for Jackson," *The Countryman,* May 19, 1863, 35.

35. H. L. Flash, "Jackson," *The Countryman,* May 26, 1863, 37; republished in *Southern Literary Messenger,* June 1863, 379.

36. George W. Bagby, "Editor's Table," *Southern Literary Messenger*, June 1863, 374.

37. "Close of Career of Four World Heroes," *The Countryman*, June 2, 1863, 41.

38. According to this report, among Jackson's last words were "Tell Maj. Hawkes to send forward provisions for the men." Ibid.

39. George W. Bagby, "Editor's Table," *Southern Literary Messenger*, June 1863, 374, 375. William Tell was a legendary Swiss national hero from the late thirteenth century. Robert the Bruce (1274–1329) was an early fourteenth-century king of Scotland (Robert I) and victor in 1314 at Bannockburn against the English. Tadeusz Andrzej Bonawentura Kociuszko (1746–1817; known in the United States as Thaddeus Kosciusko) was a Polish general who fought for the colonists in the American Revolution and then for Poland against the Russians and Prussians in a campaign that ultimately resulted in the final partition of Poland among Russia, Prussia, and Austria in 1795.

40. "No Such Thing as Death," *Southern Literary Messenger*, June 1863, 373.

41. George W. Bagby, "Editor's Table," *Southern Literary Messenger*, June 1863, 374.

42. "Recollections of Stonewall Jackson," *Southern Illustrated News*, August 29, 1863, 57.

43. Sheehan-Dean, *Why Confederates Fought*, 162.

44. On this see, for example, Gary W. Gallagher, "The Making of a Hero and the Persistence of a Legend: Stonewall Jackson during the Civil War and in Popular History," in Gallagher, *Lee and His Generals*, 101–17, esp. 111–14.

45. Robert K. Krick, "The Smoothbore Volley That Doomed the Confederacy," in Krick, ed., *The Smoothbore Volley*, 41.

46. "The Times," *Southern Illustrated News*, September 6, 1862, 5.

47. George W. Bagby, "Editor's Table," *Southern Literary Messenger*, July–August 1862, 504.

48. "General Robert Edmund Lee," *Southern Illustrated News*, January 17, 1863, 2.

49. "General Robert Edmund Lee," *Southern Illustrated News*, October 17, 1863, 1.

50. A series portraying the lives of these military exemplars was run in *Southern Illustrated News* between September 26 and October 24, 1863.

51. On Lee's transformation in the popular imagination during 1862, see, for example, Gallagher, "The Idol of His Soldiers and the Hope of His Country: Lee and the Confederate People," in Gallagher, *Lee and His Generals*, 3–20, esp. 8–11.

52. Paul H. Hayne, "Stuart," *Southern Illustrated News*, December 6, 1862, 7; John R. Thompson, "A Word with the West," ibid., December 13, 1862, 4.

53. John Esten Cooke, "The Song of the Rebel," *Southern Illustrated News*, January 24, 1863, 5.

54. A. J. Riquier, "Lee: A Sonnet," *Southern Literary Messenger*, November–December 1863, 747; reprinted from *Magnolia Weekly*.

55. Gallagher, *The Confederate War*, 8.

56. Ibid., 63.

57. "Gen. Robert E. Lee," *The Countryman*, October 20, 1862, 29.

58. George W. Bagby, "Editor's Table," *Southern Literary Messenger*, July–August 1862, 504; Bagby, "Editor's Table," ibid., June 1863, 374; "General Thomas J. Jackson," *Southern Illustrated News*, September 6, 1862, 1; "Recollections of Stonewall Jackson," ibid., August 29, 1863, 57; H. L. Flash, "Jackson," *The Countryman*, May 26, 1863, 37.

59. "The Great Struggle," *Southern Illustrated News*, September 1863, 82.

60. "Private in the Ranks," *Southern Punch*, August 22, 1863, 1.

61. "Our Southern Boys," *Southern Punch*, December 12, 1863, 6.

62. Lieut. Cluverius, "He Was Loving You Still," *Magnolia Weekly*, April 2, 1864.

63. Only a Private in Gray, "After the Battle," *Southern Illustrated News*, October 18, 1862, 7.

64. "I Give My Thoughts to Thee," *Magnolia Weekly*, November 12, 1864, 24.

65. C. Toler Wolfe, "A Dirge for the Dead Who Fell in Our Late Victories," *Southern Illustrated News*, September 13, 1862, 3.

66. Susan Archer Talley, "A Defiance," *Southern Illustrated News*, October 25, 1862, 8.

67. J. D. McCabe Jr., "Mississippians Never Surrender," *Southern Illustrated News*, December 27, 1862, 7. The title of the poem comes from the alleged "answer of the Confederate commander to the demand for the surrender of Vicksburg."

68. Alan T. Nolan, "The Anatomy of the Myth," in Gallagher and Nolan, eds., *The Myth of the Lost Cause*, 24–25.

69. According to Vinovskis, 104,000 Confederate soldiers deserted, of whom 21,000 (20.2%) were caught and returned. See Vinovskis, "Have Social Historians Lost the Civil War?"

70. Gates, *Agriculture and the Civil War*, 92–94.

71. "The Yankee Spirit of Rapine," *Southern Illustrated News*, October 11, 1862, 5. See also "The Burning of William and Mary College," ibid., October 11, 1862, 4.

72. "A Farewell to Pope," *Southern Illustrated News*, September 11, 1862, 3.

Conclusion

1. A literal translation of *Deo Vindice* would be "with god as our vindicator." *Vindicator* in Latin usually refers to a contemporary human agent, a protector or ally, mostly in legal contexts, rather than a Supreme Deity. Thanks are due to Jennifer C. Edwards and Judson Herrman for their help in translating Latin. Any errors herein, however, are solely the responsibility of the author.

2. A less embellished translation of this phrase might be "with God as our vindicator we imitate our ancestors."

3. For the preceding two paragraphs, see *Southern Historical Society Papers* 16 (Richmond: Virginia Historical Society, 1888): 419–21.

4. Joseph Addison Turner, "The Confederate Seal," *The Countryman*, May 19, 1863, 33.

5. *Deo Vindice, resurgam* may be more accurately translated as "with God as [my] protector, I will rise again."

6. Wilson, *Baptized in Blood*, 1.

7. Preamble, Permanent Constitution, *Journal of the Congress*, I, 909.

8. Daniel W. Stowell, "Stonewall Jackson and the Providence of the Death," in Miller et al., eds., *Religion and the American Civil War*, 187, 190, 192–93.

9. Levine, *Confederate Emancipation*. In an earlier iteration of this work, Levine argued that, contrary to the received wisdom on this issue, Cleburne's proposal and President Davis's eventual acceptance of it represents "a shrewd and cold-blooded appraisal of the slaveholders' actual situation and real options after the middle of 1863. Given the almost certain demise of slavery, one way or another, Cleburne, and later Davis, Benjamin, Lee and others, asked: what is the next-best state of affairs from the planters' point of view? They concluded: a minimum degree of personal liberty for black laborers whose real alternatives would be severely limited by the planters' monopoly of land and their control of the state apparatus." Bruce Levine, "'What Did We Go to War For?'" 249–50.

10. McCurry, *Confederate Reckoning*, 325–37, 332 (quotation).

11. Patrick Cleburne et al., "Letter to Joseph E. Johnston, General Commanding the Army of Tennessee," January 2, 1864, in *Official Records of the Union and Confederate Armies*, ser. I, vol. 52, part 2 (Washington, D.C.: Government Printing Office, 1900), 586–92. On page 589 Cleburne wrote, "If we are correct in this assumption it only remains to show how this great *national* sacrifice is, in all human probabilities, to change the current of success and sweep the invader from our country." And on page 590 he wrote, "The very magnitude of the sacrifice itself, such as no *nation* has ever voluntarily made before, would appal our enemies, destroy his spirit and his finances, and fill our hearts with a pride and singleness of purpose which would clothe us with new strength in battle" (emphases added).

12. Ibid., 589, 591, 592.

13. Joseph Addison Turner, "Negro Soldiers," *The Countryman*, January 17, 1865, 21.

14. John W. Overall, "The New Heresy," *Southern Punch*, September 19, 1864, 2. In the course of the article, Overall admits that secession was all about a fear of abolition and that the first cannon fired at Fort Sumter in April 1861 was a "States' Rights gun which thundered forth the doctrine that each State was a sovereignty and as such had a right to set up or pull down any institution within its limits." Many of his colleagues, both journalistic and political, were not as forthcoming.

15. See, for example, Baker, *What Reconstruction Meant*, 14–16, quoting James S. Pike, *The Prostrate State: South Carolina under Negro Government* (New York: D. Appleton, 1873).

Selected Bibliography

Primary Sources

Newspapers and Periodicals

Augusta Daily Chronicle and Sentinel
Charleston Daily Courier
Charleston Tri-Weekly Mercury
Columbia Daily South Carolinian
The Countryman (Tumwold, Ga.)
De Bow's Review (New Orleans)
Edgefield Advertiser
Hannibal Daily Messenger
Huntsville Southern Advocate
London Times
Magnolia Weekly (Richmond, Va.)
Milledgeville Southern Recorder

Milledgeville Southern Union
New Orleans Daily Picayune
New York Herald
Russell's Magazine (Charleston)
The Southern Field and Fireside
   (Augusta, Ga.)
The Southern Illustrated News
   (Richmond, Va.)
Southern Literary Messenger
   (Richmond, Va.)
Southern Punch (Richmond, Va.)

Literature

Bartlett, Napier. *Clarimonde: A Tale of New Orleans Life, and of the Present War.* Richmond, Va.: M. A. Malsby, 1863.

Evans, Augusta Jane. *Macaria; or, Altars of Sacrifice.* 2nd ed. Richmond, Va.: West and Johnston, 1864.

Ford, Sally Rochester. *Raids and Romances; or, Morgan and His Men.* 1863. Reprint New York: Charles B. Richardson, 1866.

Haw, M. J. (Mary Jane). *The Rivals: A Chickahominy Story.* Richmond, Va.: Ayres and Wade, 1864.

Jones, John Beauchamp. *Wild Southern Scenes: A Tale of Disunion! And Border War!* Philadelphia: T. B. Peterson and Brothers, 1859.

McCabe, James Dabney. *The Aid-de-Camp: A Romance of the War.* Richmond, Va.: Macfarlane and Fergusson, 1863.

O'Connor, Florence J. *Heroine of the Confederacy; or, Truth and Justice.* London, 1865.

Ruffin, Edmund. *Anticipations of the Future to Serve as Lessons for the Present Time, in the Form of Extracts of Letters from an English Resident in the United States, to the London Times, from 1864 to 1870.* Richmond, Va.: J. W. Randolph, 1860.

Sidney, Edward William. *The Partisan Leader: A Tale of the Future*. Washington, D.C.: Duff Green, 1836.

Additional Published Materials

Blada, V. [Adalbert Volck]. *Sketches from the Civil War in North America, 1861, '62, '63*. London, 1863. Reprint Tarrytown, N.Y.: William Abbatt, 1917.

Journal of the Congress of the Confederate States of America, 1861–1865. 7 vols. Washington, D.C.: Government Printing Office, 1904.

Parks, Edd Winfield, ed. *The Essays of Henry Timrod*. Athens: University of Georgia Press, 1942.

Parks, Edd Winfield, and Aileen Wells Parks, eds. *The Collected Poems of Henry Timrod*. Athens: University of Georgia Press, 1965.

Shepperson, William G., ed. *War Songs of the South*. Richmond, Va.: West and Johnson, 1862.

Simms, William Gilmore, ed. *The War Poetry of the South*. New York: Richardson and Co., 1866.

Southern Historical Society Papers. Richmond: Virginia Historical Society, 1888.

The War of the Rebellion: A Compilation of the Official Records of the Union and Confederate Armies. 70 vols. Washington, D.C.: Government Printing Office, 1880–1901.

Other Collections

American Memory. Washington, D.C.: Library of Congress, 2004. http://memory.loc .gov/ammem/index.html.

American Periodical Series: 1740–1900. Ann Arbor, Mich.: University Microfilms, 1946–1976 (microform). Also available through ProQuest Information and Learning Company, http://www.il.proquest.com/en-US/catalogs/databases/detail/aps .shtml.

Documenting the American South. Chapel Hill: University Library of the University of North Carolina at Chapel Hill, 2004. http://docsouth.unc.edu/index.html.

Making of America. Ithaca, N.Y.: Cornell University Library, 1999. http://ebooks.li brary.cornell.edu/m/moa/.

Wright American Fiction, 1851–1875. Bloomington: Indiana University Digital Library Program, 2004. http://www.letrs.indiana.edu/web/w/wright2/.

Secondary Sources

Aaron, Daniel. *The Unwritten War: American Writers and the Civil War*. New York: Knopf, 1973.

Alexander, John K. *The Selling of the Constitutional Convention: A History of News Coverage*. Madison, Wis.: Madison House, 1990.

Anderson, Benedict. *Imagined Communities: Reflections on the Origin and Spread of Nationalism*. 2nd ed. London: Verso, 1991.

Anderson, G. M. *The Work of Adalbert Johann Volck*. Baltimore: G. M. Anderson, 1970.

Anderson, Paul Christopher. *Blood Image: Turner Ashby in the Civil War and the Southern Mind*. Baton Rouge: Louisiana State University Press, 2002.

Andreano, Ralph L., ed. *The Economic Impact of the American Civil War*. Cambridge, Mass.: Harvard University Press, 1962.

Arieli, Yehoshua. *Individualism and Nationalism in American Ideology*. Baltimore: Penguin Books, 1966.

Armstrong, John A. *Nations before Nationalism*. Chapel Hill: University of North Carolina Press, 1982.

Ashdown, Paul, and Edward Caudill. *The Mosby Myth: A Confederate Hero in Life and Legend*. Wilmington, Del.: Scholarly Resources, 2002.

———. *The Myth of Nathan Bedford Forrest*. Wilmington, Del.: Scholarly Resources, 2004.

Asperheim, Stephen. "Double Characters: The Making of American Nationalism in Kentucky, 1792–1833." Ph.D. diss., University of Illinois at Urbana-Champaign, 2002.

Babb, Valerie. *Whiteness Visible: The Meaning of Whiteness in American Literature*. New York: New York University Press, 1998.

Baker, Bruce E. *What Reconstruction Meant: Historical Memory in the American South*. Charlottesville: University of Virginia Press, 2007.

Ball, Douglas B. *Financial Failure and Confederate Defeat*. Urbana: University of Illinois Press, 1991.

Ballard, Michael B. *A Long Shadow: Jefferson Davis and the Final Days of the Confederacy*. Jackson: University Press of Mississippi, 1986.

Basso, Hamilton. *Beauregard, the Great Creole*. New York: C. Scribner's and Sons, 1933.

Bateman, Fred, and Thomas Weiss. *A Deplorable Scarcity: The Failure of Industrialization in the Slave Economy*. Chapel Hill: University of North Carolina Press, 1981.

Beatty, Bess. *Alamance: The Holt Family and Industrialization in a North Carolina County, 1837–1900*. Baton Rouge: Louisiana State University Press, 1999.

Belohlavek, John M., and Lewis N. Wynne, eds. *Divided We Fall: Essays on Confederate Nation-Building*. Saint Leo, Fla.: Saint Leo College Press, 1991.

Belz, Herman. *Emancipation and Equal Rights: Politics and Constitutionalism in the Civil War Era*. New York: Norton, 1978.

Beringer, Richard E., et al. *Why the South Lost the Civil War*. Athens: University of Georgia Press, 1986.

Bernath, Michael T. *Confederate Minds: The Struggle for Intellectual Independence in the Civil War South*. Chapel Hill: University of North Carolina Press, 2010.

Bhabha, Homi. *Nation and Narration*. London: Routledge, 1990.

Billig, Michael. *Banal Nationalism*. Thousand Oaks, Calif.: SAGE, 1995.

Billings, Dwight B., Jr. *Planters and the Making of a "New South": Class, Politics, and Development in North Carolina, 1865–1900*. Chapel Hill: University of North Carolina Press, 1979.

Binnington, Ian. "Promoting the Confederacy: Virginia's *Southern Illustrated News*."

In *Virginia's Civil War,* edited by Peter Wallenstein and Bertram Wyatt-Brown, 114–22. Charlottesville: University of Virginia Press, 2005.

———. "Standing upon a Volcano: Cincinnati's Newspapers Debate Emancipation, 1860–1862." *American Nineteenth Century History* 10, no. 2 (June 2009): 163–86.

Blackett, R. J. M. *Divided Hearts: Britain and the American Civil War.* Baton Rouge: Louisiana State University Press, 2001.

Blight, David W. *Race and Reunion: The Civil War in American Memory.* Harvard University Press, 2001.

Blum, Edward J. *Reforging the White Republic: Race, Religion, and American Nationalism, 1865–1898.* Baton Rouge: Louisiana State University Press, 2005.

Bonner, Robert E. *Colors and Blood: Flag Passions of the Confederate South.* Princeton, N.J.: Princeton University Press, 2002.

———. "Flag Culture and the Consolidation of Confederate Nationalism." *Journal of Southern History* 68 (2002): 293–332.

———. *Mastering America: Southern Slaveholders and the Crisis of American Nationhood.* New York: Cambridge University Press, 2009.

———. "Roundheaded Cavaliers? The Context and Limits of a Confederate Racial Project." *Civil War History* 48 (2002): 34–59.

Brant, Irving. *James Madison and American Nationalism.* Princeton, N.J.: Van Nostrand, 1968.

Breuilly, John. *Nationalism and the State.* 2nd ed. Manchester: Manchester University Press, 1993.

Brown, Richard D. *Knowledge Is Power: The Diffusion of Information in Early America, 1700–1865.* New York: Oxford University Press, 1989.

Browning, Robert M., Jr. *Forrest: The Confederacy's Relentless Warrior.* Washington, D.C.: Brassey's, 2003.

Brubaker, Rogers. *Citizenship and Nationhood in France and Germany.* Cambridge, Mass.: Harvard University Press, 1992.

Brugger, Robert J., *Beverley Tucker: Heart over Head in the Old Dominion.* Baltimore: Johns Hopkins University Press, 1978.

Brundage, W. Fitzhugh, ed. *Where These Memories Grow: History, Memory, and Southern Identity.* Chapel Hill: University of North Carolina Press, 2000.

Burbick, Joan. *Healing the Republic: The Language of Health and the Culture of Nationalism in Nineteenth-Century America.* Cambridge: Cambridge University Press, 1994.

Burton, Orville Vernon. *The Age of Lincoln.* New York: Hill and Wang, 2007.

———. *In My House There Are Many Mansions: Family and Community in Edgefield, South Carolina.* Chapel Hill: University of North Carolina Press, 1985.

———. "Localism and Confederate Nationalism: The Transformation of Values from Community to Nation in Edgefield, South Carolina." Unpublished paper.

———. "On the Confederate Homefront: The Transformation of Values from Community to Nation in Edgefield, South Carolina." Paper presented at the Woodrow Wilson International Center for Scholars, July 19, 1989.

Burton, Orville Vernon, and Ian Binnington. "'And Bid Him Bear a Patriot's Part': National and Local Perspectives on Confederate Nationalism." In *Master Narratives: History, Storytelling, and the Postmodern South,* edited by Jason Phillips. Baton Rouge: Louisiana State University Press, forthcoming.

Calhoun, Craig. *Nationalism.* Minneapolis: University of Minnesota Press, 1997.

Carlton, David L., and Peter A. Coclanis. *The South, the Nation, and the World: Perspectives on Southern Economic Development.* Charlottesville: University of Virginia Press, 2003.

Carlton, J. H. Hayes. *The Historical Evolution of Modern Nationalism.* 1931. Reprint New York: Russell and Russell, 1968.

Carp, Benjamin L. "Nations of American Rebels: Understanding Nationalism in Revolutionary North America and the Civil War South." *Civil War History* 48 (2002): 5–33.

Carpenter, Jesse T. *The South as a Conscious Minority: A Study in Political Thought.* New York: New York University Press, 1930.

Casdorph, Paul D. *Lee and Jackson: Confederate Chieftains.* New York: Laurel, 1992.

Cash, W. J. *The Mind of the South.* New York: Knopf, 1941.

Casper, Scott E., Joanne D. Chaison, and Jeffrey D. Groves. *Perspectives on American Book History: Artifacts and Commentary.* Amherst: University of Massachusetts Press, 2002.

Castel, Albert. *The Guerilla War, 1861–1865.* Gettysburg, Penn.: Historical Times, 1974.

Cerulo, Karen A. *Identity Designs: The Sights and Sounds of a Nation.* New Brunswick, N.J.: Rutgers University Press, 1995.

Chatterjee, Partha. *The Nation and Its Fragments: Colonial and Postcolonial Histories.* Princeton, N.J.: Princeton University Press, 1993.

Coclanis, Peter A. *The Shadow of a Dream: Economic Life and Death in the South Carolina Low Country, 1670–1920.* New York: Oxford University Press, 1989.

Commager, Henry Steele. *Jefferson, Nationalism, and the Enlightenment.* New York: G. Braziller, 1975.

Confino, Alon. *The Nation as a Local Metaphor: Württemberg, Imperial Germany, and National Memory, 1871–1918.* Chapel Hill: University of North Carolina Press, 1997.

Connelly, Thomas L. *God and General Longstreet: The Lost Cause and the Southern Mind.* Baton Rouge: Louisiana State University Press, 1982.

———. *The Marble Man: Robert E. Lee and His Image in American Society.* New York: Knopf, 1977.

Connor, Walker. *Ethnonationalism: The Quest for Understanding.* Princeton, N.J.: Princeton University Press, 1994.

Cornelius, Janet Duitsman. *When I Can Read My Title Clear: Literacy, Slavery, and Religion in the Antebellum South.* Columbia: University of South Carolina Press, 1991.

Crandall, Marjorie Lyle, and Richard B. Harwell. *Confederate Imprints.* 2 vols. Boston: Boston Athenæum, 1955.

Craven, Avery. *Edmund Ruffin, Southerner: A Study in Secession.* New York: D. Appleton, 1932.

Criswell, Grover C., Jr. *Criswell's Currency Series, Vol. I: Confederate and Southern State Currency.* 2nd rev. ed. Citra, Fla.: Grover C. Criswell, Jr., 1976.

Criswell, Grover, and Herb Romerstein. *The Official Guide to Confederate Money and Civil War Tokens.* New York: HC Publications, 1971.

Crook, D. P. *The North, the South, and the Powers, 1861–1865.* New York: Wiley, 1974.

Cullen, Jim. *The Civil War in Popular Culture: A Reusable Past.* Washington, D.C.: Smithsonian Institution Press, 1995.

Curtin, Philip D. "The Black Experience of Colonialism and Imperialism." *Daedalus* 103, no. 2 (Spring 1976): 17–29.

Dangerfield, George. *The Awakening of American Nationalism, 1815–1828.* New York: Harper and Row, 1965.

Davidson, Cathy N., ed. *Reading in America: Literature and Social History.* Baltimore: Johns Hopkins University Press, 1989.

Davis, William C. *"A Government of Our Own": The Making of the Confederacy.* New York: Free Press, 1994.

———. *Jefferson Davis: The Man and His Hour.* New York: HarperCollins, 1991.

Deutsch, Karl. *Nationalism and Social Communication: An Inquiry into the Foundations of Nationality.* 2nd ed. Cambridge, Mass.: MIT University Press, 1966.

DeRosa, Marshall L. *The Confederate Constitution of 1861: An Inquiry into American Constitutionalism.* Columbia: University of Missouri Press, 1991.

Dew, Charles B. *Apostles of Disunion: Southern Secession Commissioners and the Causes of the Civil War.* Charlottesville: University of Virginia Press, 2001.

———. *Ironmaker to the Confederacy: Joseph R. Anderson and the Tredegar Iron Works.* New Haven, Conn.: Yale University Press, 1966.

Diffley, Kathleen. *Where My Heart Is Turning Ever: Civil War Stories and Constitutional Reform, 1861–1876.* Athens: University of Georgia Press, 1992.

Dirck, Brian R. "Communities of Sentiment: Jefferson Davis's Constitutionalism." *Journal of Mississippi History* 58 (1996): 135–162.

———. *Lincoln & Davis: Imagining America, 1809–1865.* Lawrence: University Press of Kansas, 2001.

———. "Posterity's Blush: Civil Liberties, Property Rights, and Property Confiscation in the Confederacy." *Civil War History* 48 (2002): 237–256.

Donald, David, ed. *Why the North Won the Civil War.* New York: Collier Macmillan, 1960.

Doyle, Don Harrison, ed. *Secession as an International Phenomenon: From America's Civil War to Contemporary Separatist Movements.* Athens: University of Georgia Press, 2010.

Doyle, Don Harrison, and Marco Antonio Villela Pamplona, eds. *Nationalism in the New World.* Athens: University of Georgia Press, 2006.

Dumond, Dwight Lowell, ed. *Southern Editorials on Secession.* New York: The Century Company, 1931.

Durrill, Wayne K. "The Power of Ancient Words: Classical Teaching and Social Change at South Carolina College, 1804–1860." *Journal of Southern History* 65 (1999): 469–498.

———. *War of Another Kind: A Southern Community in the Great Rebellion*. New York: Oxford University Press, 1990.

Eastman, Carolyn. *A Nation of Speechifiers: Making an American Public after the Revolution*. Chicago: The University of Chicago Press, 2010.

Eaton, Clement. *Jefferson Davis*. New York: Free Press, 1977.

Egnal, Marc. *Divergent Paths: How Culture and Institutions Have Shaped North American Growth*. New York: Oxford University Press, 1996.

Ellis, B. G. *The Moving Appeal: Mr. McClanahan, Mrs. Dill, and the Civil War's Great Newspaper Run*. Macon, Ga.: Mercer University Press, 2003.

Erikson, Thomas Hylland. *Ethnicity and Nationalism: Anthropological Perspectives*. Boulder, Colo.: Pluto Press, 1993.

Escott, Paul D. *After Secession: Jefferson Davis and the Failure of Confederate Nationalism*. Baton Rouge: Louisiana State University Press, 1978.

Evans, Curtis J. *The Conquest of Labor: Daniel Pratt and Southern Industrialization*. Baton Rouge: Louisiana State University Press, 2001.

Fahs, Alice. "Commentary: The Civil War as a Popular Literary Event." In *Perspectives on American Book History*, edited by Scott E. Casper, Joanne D. Chaison, and Jeffrey D. Groves, 212–22. Amherst: University of Massachusetts Press, 2002.

———. *The Imagined Civil War: Popular Literature of the North and South, 1861–1865*. Chapel Hill: University of North Carolina Press, 2001.

Farwell, Byron. *Stonewall: A Biography of General Thomas J. Jackson*. New York: Norton, 1992.

Faust, Drew Gilpin. "Altars of Sacrifice: Confederate Women and the Narratives of War." *Journal of American History* 76 (1990): 1200–1228.

———. *The Creation of Confederate Nationalism: Ideology and Identity in the Civil War South*. Baton Rouge: Louisiana State University Press, 1988.

———. *Mothers of Invention: Women of the Slaveholding South in the American Civil War*. Chapel Hill: University of North Carolina Press, 1996.

———. "Race, Gender, and Confederate Nationalism: William D. Washington's Burial of Latané." *Southern Review* 25 (1989): 297–307.

Fehrenbacher, Don E. *Constitutions and Constitutionalism in the Slaveholding South*. Athens: University of Georgia Press, 1989.

———. *Sectional Crisis and Southern Constitutionalism*. Baton Rouge: Louisiana State University Press, 1995.

Fellman, Michael. *The Making of Robert E. Lee*. New York: Random House, 2000.

Fitts, Albert N. "The Confederate Convention: The Constitutional Debate." *Alabama Review* 2 (1949): 189–210.

Fleche, Andre M. *The Revolution of 1861: The American Civil War in the Age of Nationalist Conflict*. Chapel Hill: University of North Carolina Press, 2012.

Fogel, Robert W. *Without Consent or Contract: The Rise and Fall of American Slavery*. New York: Norton, 1989.

Fogel, Robert W., and Stanley L. Engerman. *Time on the Cross: The Economics of American Negro Slavery*. Boston: Little, Brown, 1974.

Foote, Shelby. *The Civil War: A Narrative*. 3 vols. New York: Vintage Books, 1974.

Ford, Lacy K., Jr. *Origins of Southern Radicalism: The South Carolina Upcountry, 1800–1860*. New York: Oxford University Press, 1988.

Foster, Gaines M. *Ghosts of the Confederacy: Defeat, the Lost Cause, and the Emergence of the New South, 1865 to 1913*. New York: Oxford University Press, 1987.

Franklin, John Hope. *The Emancipation Proclamation*. New York: Doubleday, 1963.

Freehling, William W. *Prelude to Civil War: The Nullification Controversy in South Carolina, 1816–1836*. New York: Harper and Row, 1966.

———. *The Reintegration of American History: Slavery and the Civil War*. New York: Oxford University Press, 1994.

———. *The Road to Disunion: Secessionists at Bay, 1776–1854*. New York: Oxford University Press, 1990.

———. *The South vs. the South: How Anti-Confederate Southerners Shaped the Course of the Civil War*. New York: Oxford University Press, 2001.

Freeman, Douglas Southall. *Lee's Lieutenants*. 3 vols. New York: Scribner's Sons, 1942–1944.

———. *R. E. Lee: A Biography*. 4 vols. New York: C. Scribner's and Sons, 1934–1935.

Friedman, Lawrence Jacob. *Inventors of the Promised Land*. New York: Knopf, 1975.

Fuller, Claud E. *Confederate Currency and Stamps, 1861–1865*. Nashville, Tenn.: The Parthenon Press, 1949.

Fuller, Randall. *From Battlefields Rising: How the Civil War Transformed American Literature*. Oxford: Oxford University Press, 2011.

Gallagher, Gary W. *Causes Won, Lost, and Forgotten: How Hollywood & Popular Art Shape What We Know about the Civil War*. Chapel Hill: University of North Carolina Press, 2008.

———. *The Confederate War*. Cambridge, Mass.: Harvard University Press, 1997.

———. *Lee and His Army in Confederate History*. Chapel Hill: University of North Carolina Press, 2001.

———. *Lee and His Generals in War and Memory*. Baton Rouge: Louisiana State University Press, 1998.

———. *Lee the Soldier*. Lincoln: University of Nebraska Press, 1995.

———. *The Union War*. Cambridge, Mass.: Harvard University Press, 2011.

Gallagher, Gary W., and Alan T. Nolan, eds. *The Myth of the Lost Cause and Civil War History*. Bloomington: Indiana University Press, 2000.

Gardner, James A. "Southern Character, Confederate Nationalism, and the Interpretation of State Constitutions: A Case Study in Constitutional Argument." *Texas Law Review* 76 (1998): 1219–92.

Gates, Paul W. *Agriculture and the Civil War*. New York: Knopf, 1965.

Gellner, Ernest. *Nationalism*. London: Weidenfeld and Nicolson, 1997.

———. *Nations and Nationalism*. Ithaca, N.Y.: Cornell University Press, 1983.

Gerteis, Louis G. *From Contraband to Freedman: Federal Policy toward Southern Blacks, 1861–1865*. Westport, Conn.: Greenwood Press, 1973.

Gibson, Ernest Lewis. "The Southern Yeomanry and the Myth of Southern Nationalism." M.A. thesis, California State University, Dominguez Hills, 1996.

Gilbert, Emily, and Eric Helleiner, eds. *Nation-States and Money: The Past, Present and Future of National Currencies*. London: Routledge, 1999.

Giles, Paul. *Transatlantic Insurrections: British Culture and the Formation of American Literature, 1730–1860*. Philadelphia: University of Pennsylvania Press, 2001.

Gilmore, William J. *Reading Becomes a Necessity of Life: Material and Cultural Life in Rural New England, 1780–1835*. Knoxville: University of Tennessee Press, 1989.

Grant, Susan-Mary. *North over South: Northern Nationalism and American Identity in the Antebellum Era*. Lawrence: University Press of Kansas, 2000.

Grant, Susan-Mary, and Brian Holden Reid, eds. *The American Civil War: Explorations and Reconsiderations*. London: Pearson Education, 2000.

Greenberg, Kenneth S. *Masters and Statesmen: The Political Culture of American Slavery*. Baltimore: Johns Hopkins University Press, 1985.

Greenfeld, Liah. *Nationalism: Five Roads to Modernity*. Cambridge, Mass.: Harvard University Press, 1992.

Hare, John L. *Will the Circle Be Unbroken? Family and Sectionalism in the Virginia Novels of Kennedy, Caruthers, and Tucker, 1830–1845*. New York: Routledge, 2002.

Harwell, Richard B. *More Confederate Imprints*. 2 vols. Richmond: Virginia State Library, 1957.

Helleiner, Eric. *The Making of National Money: Territorial Currencies in Historical Perspective*. Ithaca, N.Y.: Cornell University Press, 2003.

———. "National Currencies and National Identities." *American Behavioral Scientist* 41, no. 10 (August 1998): 1409–37.

Hess, Earl J. *Liberty, Virtue, and Progress: Northerners and Their War for the Union*. New York: New York University Press, 1988.

Hettle, Wallace. *Inventing Stonewall Jackson: A Civil War Hero in History and Memory*. Baton Rouge: Louisiana State University Press, 2011.

Higginbotham, Don. *George Washington: Uniting a Nation*. Lanham, Md.: Rowman and Littlefield, 2002.

Hobsbawm, Eric. *Nations and Nationalism since 1780: Programme, Myth, Reality*. 2nd ed. Cambridge: Cambridge University Press, 1990.

Hobson, Fred. "*Anticipations of the Future;* or, The Wish-Fulfillment of Edmund Ruffin." *Southern Literary Journal* 10, no. 1 (Fall 1977): 84–91.

———. *Tell about the South: The Southern Rage to Explain*. Baton Rouge: Louisiana State University Press, 1983.

Horwitz, Tony. *Confederates in the Attic: Dispatches from the Unfinished Civil War*. New York: Pantheon, 1998.

Hroch, Miroslav. *Social Preconditions of National Revival in Europe: A Comparative Analysis of the Social Composition of Patriotic Groups among the Smaller European Nations*. Cambridge: Cambridge University Press, 1985.

Hubbell, Jay B., ed. *The Last Years of Henry Timrod, 1864–1867*. Durham, N.C.: Duke University Press, 1941.

Humphrey, Edward Frank. *Nationalism and Religion in America, 1774–1789*. New York: Russell and Russell, 1965.

Hutchinson, Coleman. *Apples and Ashes: Literature, Nationalism, and the Confederate States of America*. Athens: University of Georgia Press, 2012.

———. "Secret in Altered Lines: The Civil War Song in Manuscript, Print, and Performance Publics." In *Cultural Narratives: Textuality and Performance in American Culture before 1900*, edited by Sandra M. Gustafson and Caroline F. Stoat, 255–275. Notre Dame, Ind.: Notre Dame University Press, 2010.

Hutchinson, John, and Anthony D. Smith, eds. *Nationalism*. Oxford: Oxford University Press, 1994.

Hymans, Jacques E. C. "The Changing Color of Money: European Currency Iconography and Collective Identity." *European Journal of International Relations* 10, no. 1 (2004): 5–31.

———. "International Patterns in National Identity Content: The Case of Japanese Banknote Iconography." *Journal of East Asian Studies* 5 (2005): 315–46.

Jimerson, Randall C. *The Private Civil War: Popular Thought during the Sectional Conflict*. Baton Rouge: Louisiana State University Press, 1988.

Jones, Howard. *Blue & Gray Diplomacy: A History of Union and Confederate Foreign Relations*. Chapel Hill: University of North Carolina Press, 2010.

Josephy, Alvin M., Jr. *The Civil War in the American West*. New York: Knopf, 1991.

Kammen, Michael G. *Mystic Chords of Memory: The Transformation of Tradition in American Culture*. New York: Knopf, 1991.

Kaplan, Amy. *The Anarchy of Empire in the Making of U.S. Culture*. Cambridge, Mass.: Harvard University Press, 2002.

Kedourie, Elie. *Nationalism*. 4th ed. Cambridge, Mass.: Harvard University Press, 1993.

Knupfer, Peter. *The Union as It Is: Constitutional Unionism and Sectional Compromise, 1787–1861*. Chapel Hill: University of North Carolina Press, 1991.

Kohn, Hans. *American Nationalism: An Interpretative Essay*. New York: Macmillan, 1957.

———. *The Idea of Nationalism: A Study in Its Origins and Background*. New York: Macmillan, 1945.

Krick, Robert K., ed. *The Smoothbore Volley That Doomed the Confederacy: The Death of Stonewall Jackson and Other Chapters on the Army of Northern Virginia*. Baton Rouge: Louisiana State University Press, 2002.

Kristeva, Julia. *Nations without Nationalism*. New York: Columbia University Press, 1993.

Lagvanec, Cyril M. "Chevalier Bayard of the Confederacy: The Life and Career of Edmund Kirby Smith." Ph.D. diss., Texas A&M University, 1999.

Lawson, Melinda. *Patriot Fires: Forging a New American Nationalism in the Civil War North*. Lawrence: University Press of Kansas, 2002.

Lee, Charles R., Jr. *The Confederate Constitutions*. Chapel Hill: University of North Carolina Press, 1963.

Lehuu, Isabelle. *Carnival on the Page: Popular Print Media in Antebellum America*. Chapel Hill: University of North Carolina Press, 2000.

Leonard, Thomas C. *News for All: America's Coming-of-Age with the Press*. New York: Oxford University Press, 1995.

Lerner, Eugene M. "Money, Prices and Wages in the Confederacy, 1861–1865." *Journal of Political Economy* 63, no. 1 (February 1955): 20–40.

Leslie, William T. "The Confederate Constitution." *Michigan Quarterly Review* 2 (1963): 153–65.

Levine, Bruce. *Confederate Emancipation: Southern Plans to Free and Arm Slaves during the Civil War.* New York: Oxford University Press, 2006.

———. *Half Slave and Half Free: The Roots of Civil War.* New York: Hill and Wang, 1992.

———. "'What Did We Go to War For?' Confederate Emancipation and Its Meaning." In *The American Civil War: Explorations and Reconsiderations,* edited by Susan-Mary Grant and Brian Holden Reid, 239–64. London: Pearson Education, 2000.

Loughran, Trish. *The Republic in Print: Print Culture in the Age of U.S. Nation Building, 1770–1870.* New York: Columbia University Press, 2007.

Luraghi, Raimondo. *The Rise and Fall of the Plantation South.* New York: New Viewpoints, 1978.

McCardell, John. *The Idea of a Southern Nation: Southern Nationalist and Southern Nationalism, 1830–1860.* New York: Norton, 1979.

McClintock, Russell. *Lincoln and the Decision for War: The Northern Response to Secession.* Chapel Hill: University of North Carolina Press, 2008.

McCurry, Stephanie. *Confederate Reckoning: Power and Politics in the Civil War South.* Cambridge, Mass.: Harvard University Press, 2010.

McGill, Meredith L. *American Literature and the Culture of Reprinting, 1834–1853.* Philadelphia: University of Pennsylvania Press, 2003.

Machor, James L. "Historical Hermeneutics and Antebellum Fiction: Gender, Response Theory, and Interpretive Contexts." In *Readers in History: Nineteenth-Century American Literature and the Contexts of Response,* edited by James L. Machor, 54–84. Baltimore: Johns Hopkins University Press, 1993.

McPherson, James M. *Battle Cry of Freedom: The Civil War Era.* Oxford: Oxford University Press, 1988.

———. *For Cause and Comrades: Why Men Fought in the Civil War.* New York: Oxford University Press, 1997.

———. "The Fruits of Preventive War." *AHA Perspectives,* May 2003, 5–6.

———. "No Peace without Victory, 1861–1865." *American Historical Review* 109 (2004): 1–18.

———. *The Struggle for Equality: Abolitionists and the Negro in the Civil War and Reconstruction.* Princeton, N.J.: Princeton University Press, 1964.

———. *What They Fought For, 1861–1865.* Baton Rouge: Louisiana State University Press, 1994.

McWhiney, Grady, and Perry D. Jamieson. *Attack and Die: Civil War Military Tactics and the Southern Heritage.* Tuscaloosa: University of Alabama Press, 1982.

Majewski, John. *Modernizing a Slave Economy: The Economic Vision of the Confederate Nation.* Chapel Hill: University of North Carolina Press, 2009.

Martinez, J. Michael, et al., eds. *Confederate Symbols in the Contemporary South.* Gainesville: University Press of Florida, 2000.

Mayfield, John. *Counterfeit Gentlemen: Manhood and Humor in the Old South.* Gainesville: University Press of Florida, 2009.

Merritt, Richard L. *Symbols of American Community, 1735–1775.* New Haven, Conn.: Yale University Press, 1966.

Miller, Randall M., et al., eds. *Religion and the American Civil War.* New York: Oxford University Press, 1998.

Millican, Edward. *One United People: The Federalist Papers and the National Idea.* Lexington: University Press of Kentucky, 1990.

Morgan, James F. *Graybacks and Gold: Confederate Monetary Policy.* Pensacola, Fla.: Perdido Bay Press, 1985.

Murrin, John M. "A Roof without Walls: The Dilemma of American National Identity." In *Beyond Confederation: Origins of the Constitution and American National Identity,* edited by Richard Beeman, Stephen Botein, and Edward C. Carter II, 333–48. Chapel Hill: University of North Carolina Press, 1987.

Mwangi, Wambui. "The Lion, the Native and the Coffee Plant: Political Imagery and the Ambiguous Art of Currency Design in Colonial Kenya." *Geopolitics* 7, no. 1 (Summer 2002): 31–62.

Myers, Phillip E. *Caution and Cooperation: The American Civil War in British-American Relations.* Kent, Ohio: Kent State University Press, 2008.

Nagel, Paul C. *This Sacred Trust: American Nationality, 1798–1898.* New York: Oxford University Press, 1971.

Neely, Mark E., Harold Holzer, and Gabor S. Boritt. *The Confederate Image: Prints of the Lost Cause.* Chapel Hill: University of North Carolina Press, 1987.

Newman, Simon Peter. *Parades and the Politics of the Street: Festive Culture in the Early American Republic.* Philadelphia: University of Pennsylvania Press, 1997.

Nieman, Donald. "Republicanism, the Confederate Constitution, and the American Constitutional Tradition." In *An Uncertain Tradition: Constitutionalism and the History of the South,* edited by Kermit L. Hall and James W. Ely, Jr., 201–24. Athens: University of Georgia Press, 1989.

Nixon, H. C., and John T. Nixon. "The Confederate Constitution Today." *Georgia Review* 9 (1955): 369–76.

Nolan, Alan T. *Lee Considered: General Robert E. Lee and Civil War History.* Chapel Hill: University of North Carolina Press, 1991.

O'Brien, Michael. *Conjectures of Order: Intellectual Life and the American South, 1810–1860.* Chapel Hill: University of North Carolina Press, 2004.

———. "The Lineaments of Southern Romanticism." In *Rethinking the South: Essays in Intellectual History,* edited by Michael O'Brien, 38–56. Baltimore: Johns Hopkins University Press, 1988.

Owens, Harry P., and James J. Cooke. *The Old South in the Crucible of War: Essays.* Jackson: University Press of Mississippi, 1983.

Özkirimli, Umut. *Theories of Nationalism: A Critical Introduction.* 2nd ed. New York: Palgrave Macmillan, 2010.

Parish, Peter J. *The North and the Nation in the Era of the Civil War.* Edited by Adam I. P. Smith and Susan-Mary Grant. New York: Fordham University Press, 2003.

Parrish, T. Michael, and Robert M. Willingham, Jr. *Confederate Imprints: A Bibliography of Southern Publications from Secession to Surrender*. Austin, Tex.: Jenkins; Katonah, N.Y.: Gary A. Foster, 1987.

Persky, Joseph J. *The Burden of Dependency: Colonial Themes in Southern Economic Thought*. Baltimore: Johns Hopkins University Press, 1992.

Pessen, Edward. "How Different from Each Other Were the Antebellum North and South?" *American Historical Review* 85 (1980): 1119–49.

Phillips, Jason. *Diehard Rebels: The Confederate Culture of Invincibility*. Athens: University of Georgia Press, 2007.

Potter, Clifton W., Jr. "Images of Majesty: Money as Propaganda in Elizabethan England." In *Money: Lure, Lore, and Literature*, edited by John Louis DiGaetani, 69–76. Westport, Conn.: Greenwood Press, 1994.

Potter, David M. "The Historians' Use of Nationalism and Vice Versa." In *The South and the Sectional Conflict*, edited by David M. Potter, 34–84. Baton Rouge: Louisiana State University Press, 1968.

Purcell, Sarah J. *Sealed with Blood: War, Sacrifice, and Memory in Revolutionary America*. Philadelphia: University of Pennsylvania Press, 2002.

Puri, Jyoti. *Encountering Nationalism*. Malden, Mass.: Blackwell, 2004.

Quigley, Paul. *Shifting Grounds: Nationalism and the American South, 1848–1965*. New York: Oxford University Press, 2012.

———. "Tobacco's Civil War: Images of the Sectional Conflict on Tobacco Package Labels." *Southern Cultures* 12, no. 2 (Summer 2006): 53–57.

Rable, George C. *Civil Wars: Women and the Crisis of Southern Nationalism*. Urbana: University of Illinois Press, 1989.

———. *The Confederate Republic: A Revolution against Politics*. Chapel Hill: University of North Carolina Press, 1994.

———. *God's Almost Chosen Peoples: A Religious History of the American Civil War*. Chapel Hill: University of North Carolina Press, 2010.

Ramsdell, Charles W. *Behind the Lines in the Southern Confederacy*. Baton Rouge: Louisiana State University Press, 1944. Reprint Westport, Conn.: Greenwood Press, 1964.

Ratner, Lorman A., and Dwight L. Teeter, Jr. *Fanatics and Fire-eaters: Newspapers and the Coming of the Civil War*. Urbana: University of Illinois Press, 2003.

Reid, Brian Holden. *The Origins of the American Civil War*. New York: Longman, 1996.

Reinfeld, Fred. *The Story of Civil War Money*. New York: Sterling, 1959.

Ricouer, Paul. *Time and Narrative*. 3 vols. Translated by Kathleen McLaughlin and David Pellauer. Chicago: University of Chicago Press, 1984–1988.

Robertson, James I. *Stonewall Jackson: The Man, the Soldier, the Legend*. New York: Macmillan, 1997.

Robinson, William M., Jr. "A New Deal in Constitutions." *Journal of Southern History* 4 (1938): 449–61.

Roland, Charles P. *Albert Sidney Johnston, Soldier of Three Republics*. Austin: University of Texas Press, 1964. Reprint Lexington: University Press of Kentucky, 2001.

————. *Reflections on Lee: A Historian's Assessment*. Mechanicsburg, Penn.: Stackpole Books, 1995.

Rowe, John Carlos. *Literary Culture and U.S. Imperialism from the Revolution to World War II*. New York: Oxford University Press, 2000.

Royster, Charles. "Founding a Nation in Blood: Military Conflict and American Nationality." In *Arms and Independence: The Military Character of the American Revolution*, edited by Ronald Hoffman and Peter J. Albert, 25–49. Charlottesville: University Press of Virginia, 1984.

Rubin, Anne Sarah. *A Shattered Nation: The Rise and Fall of the Confederacy, 1861–1868*. Chapel Hill: University of North Carolina Press, 2005.

Rubin, Louis D., Jr., ed. *The History of Southern Literature*. Baton Rouge: Louisiana State University Press, 1985.

Samuels, Shirley. *Facing America: Iconography and the Civil War*. New York: Oxford University Press, 2004.

Schwab, John C. *The Confederate States of America, 1861–1865: A Financial and Industrial History of the South during the Civil War*. New York: C. Scribner's Sons, 1901.

Schweikart, Larry. *Banking in the American South from the Age of Jackson to Reconstruction*. Baton Rouge: Louisiana State University Press, 1987.

Searle-White, Joshua. *The Psychology of Nationalism*. New York: Palgrave, 2001.

Seton-Watson, Hugh. *Nations and States: An Inquiry into the Origins of Nations and the Politics of Nationalism*. Boulder, Colo.: Westview Press, 1977.

Shalhope, Robert E. *The Roots of Democracy: American Thought and Culture, 1760–1800*. Boston: Twayne, 1990.

Sheehan-Dean, Aaron. *Why Confederates Fought: Family and Nation in Civil War Virginia*. Chapel Hill: University of North Carolina Press, 2007.

Silber, Nina. *The Romance of Reunion: Northerners and the South, 1865–1900*. Chapel Hill: University of North Carolina Press, 1993.

Slabaugh, Arlie R. *Confederate States Paper Money*. 11th ed. Iola, Wis.: Krause, 2008.

Smith, Anthony D. *The Ethnic Origins of Nations*. New York: Blackwell, 1986.

————. *Theories of Nationalism*. 2nd ed. New York: Holmes and Meier, 1983.

Smith, Mark M. *Listening to Nineteenth-Century America*. Chapel Hill: University of North Carolina Press, 2001.

————. *Mastered by the Clock: Time, Slavery, and Freedom in the American South*. Chapel Hill: University of North Carolina Press, 1997.

Snay, Mitchell. *Fenians, Freedmen, and Southern Whites: Race and Nationality in the Era of Reconstruction*. Baton Rouge: Louisiana State University Press, 2007.

Spencer, Benjamin Townley. *The Quest for Nationality: An American Literary Campaign*. Syracuse: Syracuse University Press, 1957.

Starobin, Robert. *Industrial Slavery in the Old South*. New York: Oxford University Press, 1970.

Still, William N., Jr. "Facilities for the Construction of War Vessels in the Confederacy." *Journal of Southern History* 31 (1965): 285–304.

Swanson, Guy R. "Agents of Culture and Nationalism: The Confederate Treasury and

Confederate Currency." In *The Banker's Art: Studies in Paper Money*, edited by Virginia Hewitt, 132–39. London: British Museum Publications, 1995.

Symonds, Craig L. *Joseph E. Johnston: A Civil War Biography*. New York: Norton, 1992.

Taylor, William R. *Cavalier and Yankee: The Old South and American National Character*. New York: George Braziller, 1961.

Thomas, Emory M. *Bold Dragoon: The Life of J. E. B. Stuart*. New York: Harper and Row, 1986.

———. *The Confederacy as a Revolutionary Experience*. New York: Prentice-Hall, 1971.

———. *The Confederate Nation: 1861–1865*. New York: Harper and Row, 1979.

———. *The Dogs of War: 1861*. New York: Oxford University Press, 2011.

———. *Robert E. Lee: A Biography*. New York: Norton, 1995.

Todd, Richard C. *Confederate Finance*. Athens: University of Georgia Press, 1954.

Trefousse, Hans L. *The Radical Republicans: Lincoln's Vanguard for Racial Justice*. New York: Knopf, 1969.

Van Alstyne, Richard Warner. *Genesis of American Nationalism*. Waltham, Mass.: Blaisdell, 1970.

Van Den Berghe, Pierre. "Race and Ethnicity: A Sociobiological Perspective." *Ethnic and Race Studies* 1 (1978): 401–11.

Vandiver, Frank E. "Jefferson Davis—Leader without Legend." *Journal of Southern History* 43 (1977): 3–18.

———. *Ploughshares into Swords: Josiah Gorgas and Confederate Ordnance*. Austin: University of Texas Press, 1952.

Vinovskis, Maris A. "Have Social Historians Lost the Civil War? Some Preliminary Demographic Speculations." *Journal of American History* 70 (1989–1990): 37–41.

Wakelyn, Jon L., ed. *Southern Pamphlets on Secession, November 1860–April 1861*. Chapel Hill: University of North Carolina Press, 1996.

Waldstreicher, David. *In the Midst of Perpetual Fetes: The Making of American Nationalism, 1776–1820*. Chapel Hill: University of North Carolina Press, 1997.

Wallach, Yair. "Creating a Country through Currency and Stamps: State Symbols and Nation-Building in British-Ruled Palestine." *Nations and Nationalism* 17, no. 1 (2011): 129–47.

Wallenstein, Peter. *From Slave South to New South: Public Policy in Nineteenth-Century Georgia*. Chapel Hill: University of North Caroline Press, 1987.

———. "Rich Man's War, Poor Man's Fight: Civil War and the Transformation of Public Finance in Georgia." *Journal of Southern History* 50 (1984): 15–42.

Weigley, Russell. *A Great Civil War: A Military and Political History, 1861–1865*. Bloomington: Indiana University Press, 2000.

Wells, Cheryl A. *Civil War Time: Temporality & Identity in America, 1861–1865*. Athens: University of Georgia Press, 2005.

Wert, Jeffry D. *Cavalryman of the Lost Cause: A Biography of J. E. B. Stuart*. New York: Simon and Schuster, 2008.

Wiebe, Robert H. "Imagined Communities, Nationalist Experiences." *Journal of the Historical Society* 1 (2000): 33–63.

———. *Who We Are: A History of Popular Nationalism.* Princeton, N.J.: Princeton University Press, 2002.

Wiener, Jonathan M. *Social Origins of the New South: Alabama, 1860–1885.* Baton Rouge: Louisiana State University Press, 1978.

Wiley, Bell Irvin. *Confederate Women.* Westport, Conn.: Greenwood Press, 1975.

———. *The Life of Johnny Reb: The Common Soldier of the Confederacy.* Indianapolis: Bobbs-Merrill, 1943.

———. *The Plain People of the Confederacy.* Baton Rouge: Louisiana State University Press, 1943.

———. *The Road to Appomattox.* Memphis, Tenn.: Memphis State College Press, 1956.

Williams, David. *Rich Man's War: Class, Caste, and Confederate Defeat in the Lower Chattahoochee Valley.* Athens: University of Georgia Press, 1998.

Williams, T. Harry. *P. G. T. Beauregard: Napoleon in Gray.* Baton Rouge: Louisiana State University Press, 1955.

Wilson, Charles Reagan. *Baptized in Blood: The Religion of the Lost Cause, 1865–1920.* Athens: University of Georgia Press, 1980.

Wilson, Edmund. *Patriotic Gore: Studies in the Literature of the American Civil War.* New York: Oxford University Press, 1962.

Wilson, Major L. *Space, Time, and Freedom: The Quest for Nationality and the Irrepressible Conflict, 1815–1861.* Westport, Conn.: Greenwood Press, 1974.

Withington, Ann Fairfax. *Toward a More Perfect Union: Virtue and the Formation of American Republics.* New York: Oxford University Press, 1991.

Wright, Gavin. *The Political Economy of the Cotton South: Households, Markets, and Wealth in the Nineteenth Century.* New York: Norton, 1978.

Wyatt-Brown, Bertram. *Southern Honor: Ethics and Behavior in the Old South.* New York: Oxford University Press, 1982.

Yates, Bernice-Marie. "The Concept of Nationalism in the Confederate Nation as Symbolized through a Knight-Errant Interpretation of Major General James Ewell Brown Stuart and the Cavalry of Northern Virginia." Ph.D. diss., Union Institute, 1993.

Young, Robert W. *Senator James Murray Mason: Defender of the Old South.* Knoxville: University of Tennessee Press, 1998.

Zboray, Ronald J. *A Fictive People: Antebellum Economic Development and the American Reading Public.* New York: Oxford University Press, 1993.

Zelinsky, Wilbur. *Nation into State: The Shifting Symbolic Foundations of American Nationalism.* Chapel Hill: University of North Carolina Press, 1988.

Index

A Nation Divided: Studies in the Civil War Era

Neither Ballots nor Bullets: Women Abolitionists and the Civil War
Wendy Hamand Venet

Black Confederates and Afro-Yankees in Civil War Virginia
Ervin L. Jordan Jr.

Longstreet's Aide: The Civil War Letters of Major Thomas J. Goree
Thomas W. Cutrer

Lee's Young Artillerist: William R. J. Pegram
Peter S. Carmichael

Yankee Correspondence: Civil War Letters between New England Soldiers and the Homefront
Nina Silber and Mary Beth Sievens, editors

Southern Rights: Political Prisoners and the Myth of Confederate Constitutionalism
Mark E. Neely Jr.

Apostles of Disunion: Southern Secession Commissioners and the Causes of the Civil War
Charles B. Dew

Exile in Richmond: The Confederate Journal of Henri Garidel
Michael Bedout Chesson and Leslie Jean Roberts, editors

Ashe County's Civil War: Community and Society in the Appalachian South
Martin Crawford

The War Hits Home: The Civil War in Southeastern Virginia
Brian Steel Wills

Lincoln's Tragic Admiral: The Life of Samuel Francis Du Pont
Kevin J. Weddle

A Separate Civil War: Communities in Conflict in the Mountain South
Jonathan Dean Sarris

Civil War Petersburg: Confederate City in the Crucible of War
A. Wilson Greene

Take Care of the Living: Reconstructing Confederate Veteran Families in Virginia
Jeffrey W. McClurken

The Big House after Slavery: Virginia Plantation Families and Their Postbellum Experiment
Amy Feely Morsman

The Enemy Within: Fears of Corruption in the Civil War North
Michael Thomas Smith

Civil War Talks: Further Reminiscences of George S. Bernard and His Fellow Veterans
Hampton Newsome, John Horn, and John G. Selby, editors

Worth a Dozen Men: Women and Nursing in the Civil War South
Libra R. Hilde

Reconstructing the Campus: Higher Education and the American Civil War
Michael David Cohen

Frederick Douglass: A Life in Documents
L. Diane Barnes, editor

Confederate Visions: Nationalism, Symbolism, and the Imagined South in the Civil War
Ian Binnington